PENGUIN

Far from the

Iris Jones Simantel grew up in Dagenham and South Oxhey, but now resides in Devon where she enjoys writing as a pastime. Her memoir about her childhood beat several thousand other entries to win the Saga Life Stories Competition.

Far from the East End

*The Moving Story of an Evacuee's Survival
and Search for Home*

IRIS JONES SIMANTEL

PENGUIN BOOKS

PENGUIN BOOKS

Published by the Penguin Group
Penguin Books Ltd, 80 Strand, London WC2R ORL, England
Penguin Group (USA) Inc., 375 Hudson Street, New York, New York 10014, USA
Penguin Group (Canada), 90 Eglinton Avenue East, Suite 700, Toronto, Ontario, Canada M4P 2Y3
(a division of Pearson Penguin Canada Inc.)
Penguin Ireland, 25 St Stephen's Green, Dublin 2, Ireland (a division of Penguin Books Ltd)
Penguin Group (Australia), 250 Camberwell Road,
Camberwell, Victoria 3124, Australia (a division of Pearson Australia Group Pty Ltd)
Penguin Books India Pvt Ltd, 11 Community Centre,
Panchsheel Park, New Delhi – 110 017, India
Penguin Group (NZ), 67 Apollo Drive, Rosedale, Auckland 0632, New Zealand
(a division of Pearson New Zealand Ltd)
Penguin Books (South Africa) (Pty) Ltd, Block D, Rosebank Office Park,
181 Jan Smuts Avenue, Parktown North, Gauteng 2193, South Africa

Penguin Books Ltd, Registered Offices: 80 Strand, London WC2R ORL, England

www.penguin.com

First published 2012
001

Copyright © Iris Jones Simantel, 2012
All rights reserved

The moral right of the author has been asserted

Set in 11.75/13.75 pt Garamond MT Std
Typeset by Jouve (UK), Milton Keynes
Printed in England by Clays Ltd, St Ives plc

Except in the United States of America, this book is sold subject
to the condition that it shall not, by way of trade or otherwise, be lent,
re-sold, hired out, or otherwise circulated without the publisher's
prior consent in any form of binding or cover other than that in
which it is published and without a similar condition including this
condition being imposed on the subsequent purchaser

ISBN: 978-0-718-19894-7

www.greenpenguin.co.uk

MIX
Paper from
responsible sources
FSC
www.fsc.org   FSC™ C018179

Penguin Books is committed to a sustainable
future for our business, our readers and our planet.
This book is made from Forest Stewardship
Council™ certified paper.

ALWAYS LEARNING   **PEARSON**

In loving memory of my dear parents, Kit and Ted Jones,
who did the best they could

To my brother Peter, who will understand
and
To my brothers, Robert and Christopher, who perhaps will not

To my lovely 'other parents', Nell and Dilwyn Cooper of
Maerdy, South Wales, who provided me with a safe
and caring home during the Second World War
and
To all my fellow evacuees whose lives were disrupted, altered
and traumatized by the events of the Second World War,
and especially
To one of them, Ralph Laurence Brooks, who became my
life partner

To my children, Wayne and Robin, and my
beautiful granddaughters, Erin, Devon and Chelsea, who have
brought joy to my life

and
To the memory of my dear childhood friend,
Sheila McDonald Cinnamond,
who left this world too soon

Contents

CONTENTS

Acknowledgements

To everyone at the Writers' Colony at Dairy Hollow in Eureka Springs, Arkansas, for providing the wonderful setting and the resources that helped me to learn and hone my writing skills. To author Rosemary Daniell who, through her Zona Rosa writing workshops and her personal encouragement, gave me the courage to continue and complete this book. A very special thank-you goes to my friend and fellow evacuee Roger Stanley, for his tireless encouragement and editorial assistance. To Kate Lucariello, friend and editor, for being the first brave soul to wade through the first draft of what she then called my 'million-word manuscript'. To the members of my Zona Rosa writing group, Marianne Le Grande, Jenny Wagget, Charlotte Buchanan, Helga Dietzel, Harrie Farrow, Marci Hayes, Megan Kirk, Tom Morin and Patti Hanson, I give my heartfelt gratitude for all their feedback, positive criticism, and encouragement. Last, but by no means least, to my brilliant writing partner and friend, Woody Barlow, who always told it like it was. Thank you all for sharing my amazing journey.

Preface

Old London's East End was a maze of filthy, overcrowded tenements. Its streets and myriad seamy back alleys were strewn with rotting garbage while the stench and sight of raw sewage in the gutters assaulted the senses.

Its sombre huddled buildings wore the mourning-black soot from a million chimneys that had, for decades, belched clouds of smoke. The busy River Thames, England's main artery to the world, flowed through it all, bringing trade, rats, disease and more stinking rubbish to its banks and docks, as well as thousands of immigrants from the Far and Middle East.

These slums had supposedly been cleaned up during Queen Victoria's reign but they were still like an open cesspit, with fetid odours and disease-ridden air, a silent killer that stalked the streets. This hellhole was home to London's poorest, but its people were proud and brave. It had also become home to the scum of the earth.

Death was a frequent visitor to almost every family. They died from disease, starvation, murder or injury; the hopeless were often found floating in the murky waters of the river. Crime was rampant, especially around the docklands; the streets were not safe to walk at night. Little value was placed on the lives of London's poor, yet those who survived, by their wits and sheer determination, became, and still are, famous for their humour, creativity and ability to make do. Consider the complexity of Cockney rhyming slang: it is a language unto itself, created as a secret code between the entrepreneurs of London's back streets. You could buy or sell anything in London and might have been killed for it.

Nevertheless, there existed another side to the darkness of this ghetto, the side that turned its international babel into a comical common language. Its misery became laughter; its infamy, fame; and its unrecorded stories evolved into song and literature. That side of London's underbelly was to be found in its street markets, with their sharp-witted barrow boys; its pubs, with their poets and songsters; its music halls, with their comedians, musicians and actors. Here lay the creativity and the fine art of survival that were the foundations of the East Ender's indomitable spirit.

This was the London of my family history. Into this history, I was born. This is my proud heritage.

Iris Jones Simantel

Born a Cockney Girl

'Only those born within the sound of Bow Bells are
properly called Cockneys.'
The Victorian Dictionary

It all began on 5 July 1938, and it's 'God's honest truth', according to my mother, that my first life-journey almost terminated in a toilet bowl. Thinking she needed to move her bowels, she sat straining on the porcelain throne until caught there by a vigilant nurse, who threw up a verbal roadblock: 'Stop pushing, Mother.' I can only imagine what a shitty view of the world I might have had were it not for that nurse and her timely intervention.

I managed a more appropriate debut in the delivery room at the East End Maternity Hospital in Poplar, East London. Located within the sound of Bow Bells (St Mary-le-Bow Church), it bestowed upon me the dubious label 'Cockney', which carried many less-than-desirable connotations.

The fact is, I should never have been a Cockney. My family had moved from the old East End before my conception and now lived in Dagenham, Essex, eight miles away from the sound of Bow bloody Bells, hence eight miles outside Cockney territory. However, with Dad working out of town, Mum feared being alone when she received the warning signals that I was en route. Also, there would be no one to care for Peter, my four-year-old brother. She decided to stay with her parents, who lived on Blackwall Pier in Poplar, close to the maternity hospital and, of course, well within the sound of Bow Bells. She still found herself alone when she felt the first contractions. Afraid, not knowing when someone might come home, she set out alone, small shabby suitcase in hand, to catch a bus to the hospital.

As she stood waiting at the bus stop, her sister's fiancé, Walter, happened along the road in his car. He stopped in front of Mum and lowered the window. 'Where are you off to, Kitty?'

'Oh, 'ello, Walt, I'm going to the 'ospital,' replied Mum, in her strong Cockney accent. 'I think me time's come.'

'Why are you going alone? Where's Ted? Does anyone know you're going?'

'I don't think so, Walt,' she said. 'Ted's workin' away, Mum went down Chrisp Street with Peter to do a bit of shoppin', and me dad's at work, so I thought I'd just catch the bus so I wouldn't 'ave to bother no one.'

'Did you leave a note to say where you were going?'

'Oooh, no, I s'pose I should've but I didn't think of it.'

'Well, come on, climb in and I'll take you.'

'Are you sure? I don't wanna put you out.'

Walter convinced her it would be no trouble at all, and she loaded her sizeable self into the car.

After he had deposited her at the hospital's entrance, Walter rushed back to the house, found her parents – his own future in-laws – and informed them their daughter was about to deliver their second grandchild.

'Silly cow. I thought she'd gone out to buy some fags,' my grandmother responded, rolling her eyes and tutting in disbelief.

After a quick visit to the hospital to see Mum and me, Granddad went off to send Dad a telegram. A few days later Mum received a letter from him, the only letter he ever wrote to her; she kept it all her life, passing it on to me shortly before her death. The envelope bore a penny-ha'penny stamp, and the letter, written in pencil, reads in part, 'Well, I couldn't have done anything if I was there could I?'

So, that was how it happened, and how I became a Cockney instead of the Essex Girl I should have been. Years later, I learned that an 'Essex Girl' had lower-class origins and a reputation for being fast and loose. One might say I'd been 'saved by the Bells'.

When Mum was discharged from the maternity hospital, she, Peter and I stayed on with Nan and Granddad at Blackwall Pier until Dad came home. Nan and Granddad lived in the station master's house at Blackwall railway station, where Granddad worked as station master. Situated on Brunswick Wharf, the house and station were part of the historic East India Docks on the River Thames. Brunswick Wharf was where Captain John Smith set sail on his voyage to America to establish the first British settlement in Virginia. It was also where the Indian princess Pocahontas first set foot in England with her British husband, Captain John Rolfe. You could say Pocahontas and I had something in common in that we both made our London debut at the same address.

The Victorian Dictionary fails to mention that, to England's so-called upper classes, the term 'Cockney' suggested indolence, dishonesty, illiteracy, lack of manners and absence of personal hygiene. The label, and our telltale accents, defined our station in life and trapped us in an often cruel world. Not always proud of my Cockney heritage, I'd tell people, 'Yes, I was born a Cockney, but I've risen above it.' I learned early in life to use humour as a defence against the shame of being poor and on the lowest level of the British class system – our 'station in life'.

An aunt once told me, 'You can spend all the money in the world on appearance, but when you open your mouth, people know who you are.' Her words inspired me to try to better myself, but my own parents were discouraging, reminding me often to remember my place. I tried to explain that I wanted a better life, but they referred to me as 'a proper little madam', chiding, 'Who do you think you are?'

I will never forget an incident that occurred one evening when I was twelve or thirteen. As we sat by the fire, Mum darning socks and Dad reading the newspaper, Dad began one of his tirades about some social injustice, how it kept us enslaved to the rich, and how hopeless our lives were. On and on he ranted, with Mum telling him to calm down, and me frightened by his fury.

I had always accepted my father's ideas and opinions in the past; to me his word had been gospel, but this time, his comments jarred. Already fed up with my lot in life, I had begun to develop a defiant attitude and a few opinions of my own, one of which I now dared to voice.

'Well, I don't care what you say, Dad. I've decided I'm as good as anyone.'

His face paled. 'No – you – are – not, Iris,' he spat. 'You have to remember your place. You're not as good as everyone else and you'd better not forget it, my girl.'

Shocked, I didn't ask or wait for an explanation. Strangled by my own rage, I stormed out of the room. I felt as though he had slapped my face. Perhaps it was his way of preparing me for the realities of life, but that moment haunted me for years. His words replayed in my mind to erode my confidence and self-image, and for a long time I hated who and what I was.

The negative connotations surrounding Cockneys or East Enders were, I must confess, true to some extent. Well, in our family they were. Foul language was frowned on, but passing wind, or 'blowing off', as we called it, and belching, were a form of at-home entertainment and, sometimes, a source of dubious pride. Dad could produce the most amazing farts: he could reach high notes that sounded as though he had a squeaker in his pocket. Mum told us she was scared to blow off because of what it might do to her haemorrhoids. When she did succumb, usually in the loo, the sound would reverberate throughout the house. We would chorus, 'The lion roars,' and when she emerged, she'd be laughing so hard that tears rolled down her cheeks. 'Ooh, stop it, you lot,' she'd choke out, dabbing her eyes.

Lesser farts were always followed by someone saying, 'Penny on the drum.' No one knew what that meant, but we always said it. Silent-but-deadlies would be met with a sniff and 'Whose shit?' and the reply, 'Yours if you wannit.' But if someone said, 'Pooh, who blew off?' Mum always responded with, 'Take big sniffs. It'll soon be gone.' I must reiterate that this was strictly at-home entertainment. We may have been crude but even we poor Cockneys knew not to blow off in public.

As for belching, again Dad ruled. A plain, ordinary burp would be out of the question. He'd go from a simple 'Wally Wally' or 'Bibbly Bob', to a burped 'Ali Baba', to which we'd respond, 'And the forty thieves'; he could even burp whole sentences, like 'I don't want to', or 'Where's me tea?' My brothers and I were proud of his performances, and over the years we all tried to emulate his talent, but with far less success.

Yes, it was a crude form of entertainment and always made us laugh – we had little else to laugh at or about. It was also harmless, except, potentially, to Mum's haemorrhoids.

In spite of the hardships and often felt discrimination, I eventually learned to embrace and take pride in my East London beginnings and my colourful Cockney heritage. I was glad I had not been born in Dagenham: I would have hated people to think of me as fast and loose.

2

Carey Road: My First
Remembered Home

Mum and Dad had had their name on the government-housing list for five or six years when they were allocated a two-bedroom house, 10 Carey Road in Dagenham. I was less than a year old and my brother four.

The house was on the Becontree Estate, which was then the largest public housing estate in the world. The London County Council (LCC) had built it to reward the families of soldiers who had served in the First World War. It provided affordable rental housing for more than a hundred thousand poor working-class people.

All of the estate houses had gas and electricity, inside toilets, fitted baths and front and back gardens. In return for this new luxury, tenants had to live by government rules and standards. The council had strict guidelines on home and garden mainten-ance, residents' behaviour, and the keeping of pets. Unannounced inspections of properties occurred periodically, and rent was collected each week.

Our new home, with its pebbledash exterior and red-tiled roof, shared a front porch with the next-door neighbour. It had a tiled floor, which was kept shiny with Red Cardinal polish and what Mum called 'elbow grease'. Women were proud of their doorsteps; some even whitened the concrete surround with something called 'whitening stone'. They might have had little food on the table but it was a matter of pride to have sparkling windows and a smart doorstep.

Using wet newspaper, women cleaned windows inside and out each week. Both Mum and Nan claimed that chemicals in the newsprint kept the flies away. Little proof of their theory existed in our house, especially in the loo, where cut-up newspaper served another purpose – as toilet paper.

Our 'two-up, two-down' house consisted of entry hall, front room, kitchen and toilet on the ground floor. A narrow wooden staircase led upstairs to two bedrooms and a bathroom with tub and hand basin. Gas and electric meters hung on the wall behind the front door, and under the stairs, a low door opened to the 'coalhole'. The coal, too valuable to store outside, was always shot from sacks straight into the coalhole inside the house.

To the front of the house there was a small patch of garden, enclosed by a privet hedge and a wooden gate, complete with iron latch. The back garden was large. Outside the back door, a trellis arch with climbing roses led to a lumpy lawn with flowerbeds down each side. Mum, and Mum alone, took care of the flowerbeds after the day she came in shouting, 'Where's all me flippin' flowers gone?'

'Oh, was they flowers? I thought they was weeds,' mumbled Dad, who hated gardening.

She never let him near them after that, and I always wondered if that had been his plan from the beginning.

At the bottom of the garden, there was an area meant for planting vegetables, but the only thing Dad ever 'planted' was the air-raid shelter. He had to dig a deep hole for it. Every house was expected to have a shelter during the Second World War.

I shiver when I think of our bleak kitchen, or the scullery as we called it, with its bare concrete floor and exposed brick walls. Dad painted them with dark green enamel paint, but it did nothing to cheer the room. The kitchen fittings consisted of a shallow stone sink, a brass cold-water tap and a wooden draining-board. In one corner stood a cast-iron cooker, which Mum scrubbed with a wire brush and polished with black lead to stop it rusting.

Resembling a witch's cauldron and called the 'copper', a

second cast-iron monster dominated another corner. Used primarily for laundry, a gas-ring heated it from below. Boiling clothes and sheets compensated for lack of soap and reduced the need for hand scrubbing.

Mum also used the copper for cooking her infamous steamed suet puddings, which were large dumplings made from flour, water and beef suet. When the big floppy lump of dough was ready, Mum placed it in a basin, covered it with greaseproof paper, wrapped the whole thing in an old cloth, tied it with string and suspended it over the boiling water to cook in the steam. She said she could make bigger puddings in the copper than she could in a saucepan. I wished she never made them at all, especially after I'd seen her strip the blood-streaked membranes from a hunk of raw suet before grating and blending it into the dough.

'Yuck,' I'd say.

'Don't watch,' she'd snap back.

Mum made several kinds of suet pudding. First, there were her savoury bacon puddings, which sometimes had a little left-over chopped cabbage added. Bacon, that's a laugh: I don't remember there ever being any real bacon in them. Mum used minced bacon fat to flavour them. Although I was usually hungry, I always gagged on those.

Next, and a little nicer, were the plain suet puddings, eaten with either a dribble of treacle or a dab of jam on top. My favourite, though, was Spotted Dick, made on the rare occasion that she had some raisins or sultanas. Sultanas, juicier than raisins, made the best pudding: it was yummy eaten hot or cold. In those days, suet puddings were a staple. They might have had little nutritional value, but they were filling.

I often went to bed with hunger pains cramping my stomach. I'd curl up in bed and try to sleep, but after a while, I'd call out to Mum, 'Can I just 'ave a bit of bread and jam, Mum, please,

Mum?' I don't remember ever getting it. Exhausted, I'd eventually cry myself to sleep.

We ate our scant meals at a small, scrubbed-wood table in the kitchen. That little table had many purposes. Mum used it to do the ironing, with flatirons heated on the stove. Dad used it as his workbench for all manner of odd jobs. He repaired our shoes there and even tried to make clothes for us during the war and for some time after it had ended.

On laundry days, steam from the hot water in our ice-cold kitchen caused rivers of condensation to run down the walls and windows. At times, the steam would be as thick and heavy as a London fog – you could barely see across the room.

Mum had to rinse the washing piece by piece in the sink, in ice-cold water, then wring it out herself because we didn't own a mangle. Her poor hands would be red and raw, more so in the winter after she'd hung the laundry outside. How I hated rain on washday. Rainy days meant that wet laundry was draped everywhere inside the house, adding to the already bone-chilling damp. Worse yet was when the wash froze outside on the clothesline and had to thaw inside the house. Thick ice would often coat the insides of the windows, icicles hung from the toilet cistern, and we could see our own breath. I don't remember ever being warm in those days. At night, even when Mum piled overcoats on top of me, I still shivered and my bones ached.

The kitchen copper had yet another important use: it heated bath water. It had a wooden hand pump on one side, similar to those I'd seen used in pubs for dispensing draught beer; it pumped the heated water from downstairs into the bathtub upstairs. Considered a modern labour-saving convenience, it took a lot of muscle to achieve this amazing feat. I'm sure Mum was grateful that it only had to be done once each week.

On Saturday nights, we took turns using the same water for our weekly bath. Pity the person whose turn came last – I think it was me, or was it poor old Mum? By that time, the almost cold water had accrued a nasty layer of scum. The rest of the week, if we washed at all, it was at the kitchen sink. Sometimes we'd simply go through the motions, using cold tap water for what Mum called 'a lick and a promise', or a 'spit-wash', performed with nothing but a generous donation of Mum's saliva on a handkerchief. No wonder we had tide marks around our necks, and grimy, stinky feet.

The front room of this tiny house had a linoleum-covered floor and contained a sofa, two chairs and a wireless; but best of all was the upright pianola. Dad had received it as payment for some work he'd done. Mum was not pleased: it had put no food on the table.

Listening to our pianola introduced me to classical music. Many piano rolls of that genre had come with it, as well as sing-along rolls complete with printed words. As young as I was, I loved the pianola and thought my heart would break when Dad sold it. He never told me why he did and, of course, I knew better than to ask: it must have been because he needed money. Why else would he sell something we all loved?

Dad had played the piano by ear since he was a small boy. It was one of his many talents. He often played at the Cherry Tree pub on Wood Lane, in Dagenham, where he earned free drinks from the publican and a few extra shillings from the customers. Jealous of the attention he received from the women there, Mum hated going to the pub. It's ironic that one of her favourite stories was of the night 'Yer dad played the piano till his fingers was bleedin'.' Although she was proud of him, she resented everyone fawning over him; she called him 'Big Head', in reference to his often-inflated ego.

Not allowed inside the pub, we children had to wait outside on the steps. Sometimes we'd have a bag of crisps or a glass of lemonade handed to us as we waited for Mum and Dad. We'd listen for the clang of the closing bell, and for the loud voice of the bartender: 'Last call. Time, gentlemen, please.' Ten o'clock was the last moment at which anyone could order drinks. With that, and the end of the music and singing, we knew we'd soon be going home.

Dad played the piano once on *Workers' Playtime*, a radio programme broadcast from various factory canteens during the war. By the time he'd finished telling the story, you would have thought he'd played in the Royal Albert Hall.

'Oh, blimey, that's just what he needed, somethin' else to crow about. We'll never 'ear the end of it,' said Mum.

Mum and Dad's bedroom, upstairs at the front of the house, had blue linoleum on the floor to match the puffy embroidered silk eiderdown they'd received as a wedding gift. They also had a handsome bedroom suite, consisting of bed, wardrobe and dressing-table. Dad built the furniture before they were married. He said he'd made it from tea chests, 'acquired' from the docks.

The dark-stained wooden furniture had intense graining, and at night the wardrobe scared me. The bold grain on its door looked like grotesque monster-faces; I hated it, but it did have a funny side. Dad had built the wardrobe in two parts, the top being separable from the bottom. Mum, who liked rearranging the furniture, would somehow remove the wardrobe top from the bottom; then she'd get inside, pull the door closed and walk it to its new location. It was not unusual to come into the house to find the wardrobe walking about upstairs with Mum's muffled voice coming from inside.

'Someone 'elp me. I'm stuck in the wardrobe.'

'One of these days, Kitty, you're gonna fall down them stairs and break yer flippin' neck movin' that bloody wardrobe around,' Dad warned her. It never stopped her, though.

On Mum's dressing-table stood a pink frosted-glass dresser set, and on the tray a jar of Pond's Cold Cream, a lipstick and powder compact, a bottle of Amami hair-waving lotion, a brush and comb set and a few bits of jewellery. I remember one necklace in particular: it was made of clam shells, strung on a silk cord.

Nosing through her top drawer one day, I found a large photograph of a man I knew as Uncle Bill. I often wondered about that and in later years teased her about it. She would become indignant. 'Don't be wicked, Iris,' she'd say. 'Uncle Bill and Auntie Rose have been our friends for donkey's years.'

'Well, then, why don't you have a picture of Auntie Rose, and why was Uncle Bill's photo hidden under your knickers?'

'Kids,' she'd say, shaking her head. 'Stop asking stupid questions.'

Peter and I shared the small back bedroom. It had bare floorboards and overlooked the back garden. On one side of the room I slept in a white-painted iron cot, and on the opposite side, Peter had a single bed. I didn't get a big-girl's bed until after the war, when you could buy one as it was classified 'utility'.

My cot stood next to a tall, painted cupboard inside which, my big brother insisted, lived all manner of scary monsters. I hated that cupboard, it scared me to death, but I hated my brother more.

Under my bed there was a kingdom of beautiful fairies, my friends and companions. Under Peter's bed, or so he told me, lived his kingdom of fairy monsters. I'd be drifting off to sleep when he'd whisper across the room, 'I'm sending my monsters over to kill all your fairies. Then they're gonna stab you with their spears. Here they come – watch out, they're nearly there.' On and on he'd go. I'd cry at the threat to my imaginary friends, and had nightmares following his unkind storytelling. Wasn't it bad enough that I had to sleep next to whatever lived in the cupboard?

Perhaps the idea of fairies came from a mural Dad painted on our bedroom wall of a country scene with fairy-tale characters and a fairy castle. The sun always shone there, and bluebirds flew in a perfect sky. I don't know how well it was painted, but Dad was a man of many talents. It might not have been a masterpiece, but it gave me countless hours of pleasure and escape.

My usual playground was the world of my imagination. I don't remember having toys but a neighbour's daughter once gave me an old china doll. I didn't have her for long, though: my brother and his mate murdered her. Playing Zulus one day, they speared poor Dolly to death with sharp sticks. I called them 'big fat German pigs', the worst thing I could think of.

To tell the truth, Dolly's demise didn't upset me too much. Cold and hard, she had no clothes of her own. I had to wrap her in one of my old dresses so she looked like an orphan. Oh, yes, and she had no proper hair. It was painted on and had almost disappeared. One of the big kids taunted me: 'Look at 'er doll – it's got ringworm!' she miaowed, and that turned me right off.

Some early memories of Carey Road, including those of my brother Peter, are blurred, possibly because the Second World War began when I was just a year old, and Peter was rarely with us: he was evacuated off and on from 1939.

3

My War: the Early Days

Until my arrival on the scene in 1938, Peter had the starring role in our family. For four years, he held centre stage as an only child and the first grandchild. When he lost his throne to a baby sister, whom his daddy called 'Her Ladyship', his displacement must have felt more like replacement. I'm sure the events of the following year served to exacerbate those feelings, when he was five and I was one.

Peter and I were both born into peacetime Britain, but it was not long before Europe erupted into the full-scale war that changed our lives for ever. In September 1939, Britain declared war on Germany. With that, and in anticipation of invasion, the evacuation from London of more than a million children began. Countless thousands more would follow, including women and the infirm.

Posters appeared in public places, and every household received letters from the government, all implying it would be irresponsible of parents not to send their children to safety. One poster showed the ghost-like image of Hitler leaning over a weeping mother's shoulder, whispering into her ear, 'Don't send your children away, Mother', suggesting that to keep them at home would be signing their death warrant. How could a parent resist such propaganda? Mum registered Peter early for evacuation: he was of school age and among the first wave of evacuees to leave London. Because of my age, Mum had the option of going away with both of us but she decided she could not, or would not, abandon Dad and her own parents. I can imagine the desolation Peter felt, when the mummy and daddy he now had to share with a baby sister, were sending him away. He did not know at that point, of course, that he would be gone for almost six of his most formative years. From things he has said over the years, I know he felt unwanted, and that he has harboured resentment throughout his life. How could a five-year-old understand that they'd sent him away out of love and concern for his safety? Why wouldn't he think another child had replaced him?

Four years later, with the war still raging, I too experienced the same emotional torture.

Evacuation was a gallant effort to protect Britain's next generation, the children . . . or was it? In later years I often wondered if we were sent away to free up more of the workforce. Many married women joined the war effort, our own mother included. They worked in factories and on farms, filling jobs left vacant by their men who were at war. Could they have done so with young children at home?

Far too many young lives were shattered, not by bombs but in other ways. How many of those children carried the scars throughout their lives? I know that Peter and I have, he more so than I.

My earliest war memory is of the eerie sound of air-raid sirens, which usually came at night. When I heard that mournful sound, I knew I'd be snatched from my bed by my mother and rushed from the house, down the garden and into the shelter. There, in the flickering candlelight, I'd lie on my bunk, staring at the spiders and cobwebs on the ceiling, waiting for the familiar drone of warplanes.

As well as the thumping of my heart, I listened to the sound of anti-aircraft guns from the nearby park and the whistle of bombs as they plunged to earth, followed by the explosions. The ground shook, and soil sifted down on us through cracks in the corrugated iron overhead. With my stomach in knots, hands over my ears, my eyes tight shut and teeth clenched, I had but one hope: that the bombs would miss us. When the explosions sounded close, I'd hide my head under the blankets and wish that my mother would hold me in her arms.

The Anderson shelter, known as the 'dugout', was half buried in the ground. The curved roof usually had a covering of earth, planted with grass or vegetables to disguise its presence; ours, of course, grew only weeds. In addition, a three-deep wall of sandbags protected the steps leading down to the entrance. The truth was, had a bomb hit anywhere near, the shelter would have provided little or no protection. I suppose they gave a sense of security, though, even when we heard stories of families killed inside their shelters while nearby, their homes stood undamaged.

There were many nights, perhaps weeks or months during the Blitz, when we didn't wait for the sirens. We would take a few necessities and bed down in the shelter for the night, especially if Dad was away on fire-watch duty. (He hadn't been called up for the army: instead, his skills were needed at the Woolwich Arsenal.) I remember wearing, over my clothes, an all-in-one garment called a siren-suit. Made from an old blanket, it zipped up the front, keeping me warm and ready to go. Many years later, I made the connection between sirens and siren-suits.

Air raids also occurred during the daytime. Fighter planes came ahead of the bombers, to clear the way and keep the anti-aircraft guns busy. We sometimes watched dogfights in the distant sky. German planes often flew so low we could see the pilots and the planes' dreaded Iron Cross and swastika insignia. We witnessed several enemy planes go down, smoke pouring from the back, and once saw a pilot bail out. Watching the descending parachute, we kids cheered. I remember wishing I could see him up close, wondering what those evil Germans looked like, sure they were nothing like us.

During one of Peter's home visits, between his evacuations and before mine, he and I stood outside, on top of the air-raid shelter. A plane came flying low towards us. Thinking it to be one of ours, we began jumping up and down and waving our arms.

'Germans!' Peter suddenly screamed, and shoved me down the shelter steps, behind the sandbags. I started to cry, but froze as the deafening sound zoomed overhead. I was shaking from head to foot, and my heart was in my throat, almost choking me, as I clung to him. We stayed locked in each other's arms until the danger had passed; then, on wobbly legs, we ventured from our hiding place.

'Blimey, that was close,' Peter muttered, in a strange voice I'd never heard before. 'Did you see the machine gun stickin' out?'

I had not and, of course, I will never know if we were in actual danger of being shot. Lucky for me, my big brother happened to be home; and lucky for us, he had learned to identify aircraft and recognized, just in time, the enemy plane for what it was.

I don't know where Mum was at the time but Peter told me not to tell her what had happened.

'Why?' I asked.

'We coulda been shot, twerp,' he said. 'If Mum finds out we'll get in big trouble, and she'll think we're stupid and she'll say it would have served us right if we'd been killed.'

During the Blitz, intense bombing occurred both day and night. I read that on one night alone almost a thousand enemy aircraft came over in wave after wave. That particular raid lasted until four thirty the following morning, and would have continued had the weather not prevented it. Besides the devastation to London and other cities, more than three thousand people lost their lives on that one fateful night.

We stayed in the shelters until morning, awaiting the sound

of the all-clear. Then we'd emerge from the darkness, eyes adjusting to the bright light of day, to see what damage the night attacks had wrought and to have a much-needed cup of tea.

In the midst of all the insanity, I recall a funny incident that occurred just after the all-clear had sounded one morning. As Mum opened the shelter's plywood door, we could hear someone screaming nearby. 'Oh, my Gawd, someone's been 'it,' she muttered, as she stuck her head cautiously outside, then scrambled up the steps to see what had happened. I didn't follow her but ventured far enough to peer over the top of the sandbags.

An elderly woman, who lived just a few houses away, was running around her garden in her flannel nightgown, screaming for help. Seeing no signs of imminent danger, Mum went to her. She learned that the poor woman had fallen asleep in the shelter the previous night, leaving a candle burning on a shelf above her head. During the night, until it burned itself out, the candle had dripped wax onto her hair, forming a skullcap of now-hardened wax. Upon waking, she noticed that her head felt strange. She put up her hands to investigate, found the waxen lump and thought the top of her head had been blown off.

It took several neighbours and, according to Mum, a dose of medicinal whisky to calm her down and convince her that she was not going to die.

'Medicinal, my eye,' said Dad, after hearing the story. 'She'd probably 'ad too much medicine last night or she wouldn't 'ave bloody slept through it.'

Each day, as soon as I had dressed and finished my toast, I'd rush out into the street to join the other children. We kids couldn't wait to get outside and begin our search for shrapnel. I kept my pieces hidden in a box under my bed. Mum didn't want me to have it. She told me more than once, 'I don't want anything in this 'ouse from them Germans.'

I also recall hundreds, if not thousands, of shiny streamers hanging from the trees, bushes and roofs. The long strips of aluminium foil, called 'chaff' or 'window', were dropped from planes to confuse the radar. They looked almost festive.

As we lived close to several heavily targeted areas, including Dagenham Docks and the Ford Motor Works, which I believe was now making military vehicles, other sights and sounds pervaded our daily lives. Barrage balloons filled the sky to hinder aircraft and radio communications; they reminded me of enormous tethered silver elephants. Parsloes Park, just two streets away, where children had once played, now housed a large installation of anti-aircraft guns. We often heard their familiar ack-ack-ack – sometimes it went on all night.

I loved playing outside. When Mum called me to come in each evening, I'd hide under the privet hedge, where it always stank of cat's pee. Inured to war, we played in the streets from morning until night. Mum shoved me out of the door in the morning under strict orders: 'Don't sit on the kerb cos dirty old men spit there. Don't play around the drain holes cos you'll get scarlet fever. Don't speak to no strangers and don't touch nothing what looks like a tin-can cos it might be a bomb and it could blow yer 'ead off.'

We played in the ruins of bombed-out houses following air raids. We'd climb through the rubble, rummaging around to see what treasures we could find. I remember one of the older boys finding a set of false teeth. He took them home to give to his granny. I'm sure she must have been delighted.

When we heard of a military convoy coming through, we would dash up to the main road to watch the Army trucks and tanks, big guns and marching soldiers go by. We'd cheer and wave at them. The soldiers would grin and wave back at us. In the excitement, we forgot or were unaware that those smiling men were on their way to the battlefront.

In addition to war-related activities, we played all kinds of other street games. We put stink bombs, made from lighted bits of celluloid film, through old people's letterboxes. We strung lines across the street from lamp post to lamp post in the hopes of knocking the helmet off a policeman as he went by on his bike. It never occurred to us that we might cause injury to anyone. We played hopscotch, kick the can, stick games, spin the top, hide and seek and other simple games that required little except our own endless imaginations and energy. I played house with Sylvia Schofield, and built bonfires and baked spuds with Peter Cooper, Dudley Tan, Douglas Harris and Brian Beadle in Peter's back garden. I remember surprising everyone, including myself, when I punched Peter's nose, even though I was half his size, for nicking my spud and making fun of me.

Cruel as children can be, we also found entertainment in making fun of Ollie Simpson, an obese teenager who lived around the corner on Maxey Road. Poor Ollie could hardly walk. You could hear him huffing and puffing well before he came into sight, his big fat face red and sweaty.

One of our more distasteful activities involved wandering the streets looking in the gutters for cigarette ends, 'dog ends', as we called them. We'd take them home to our mums and dads, who took them apart and rolled the tobacco into cigarettes, using new ciggie-papers, of course. It's hard to believe they would do such a thing, but in wartime people do many things they normally wouldn't consider.

On quiet days, we would sometimes go for long walks. We'd knock on people's doors and ask them if we could use their toilet. We did it for fun, not really needing to go, just wanting to see inside their houses. There was an exception, however, when one day I had an urgent need to do number two.

We must have been about a mile from home at the time, with no public toilet anywhere near. Unable to convince any homeowner of the urgency or legitimacy of my need, and unable to hold it any longer, I found myself with a nasty mess in my drawers. Mum was furious: 'You dirty girl! You should be ashamed of yourself. It serves you right for goin' off on yer own.' But no one ever stopped us wandering off all day; I suppose they had other things on their minds.

When bombs were not falling, we children thought ourselves invincible. However, under attack, we curled up, like frightened animals, in our underground burrows.

To this day, when I encounter the familiar smell that hangs in the air after a candle has been extinguished, I am, for just a moment, transported back to my bunk in that dank, earth-covered shelter.

4

My War Continues, and Other Battles

Each evening, before the air-raid sirens went off, we'd huddle around the wireless, awaiting news of the day, straining to hear through the ever-present static. Excitement filled the air when King George VI or Winston Churchill gave speeches. Mum and Dad never missed their broadcasts: they were the voices of hope and encouragement, the King's that of parent-protector, the Prime Minister's that of strength, vengeance and determination. They acknowledged the people's sacrifices, and offered sympathy and gratitude for their suffering and personal losses. It felt as though they spoke to each of us personally. We'd cheer at news of victories overseas, become quiet and sad when we heard of death and defeat on the battlefield and at home. Although young, I already understood the horror of war and the danger we faced each day.

With Dad working at an arsenal, Peter evacuated far away, air-raid sirens sounding, bombs falling ever closer, friends and relatives losing homes and lives, it's no wonder Mum was having difficulties. The Blitz was taking its toll on her, and I remember hearing something about a 'nervous breakdown'. At the time, I suspect I was experiencing a kind of benign neglect: when I was sent to stay with relatives for a couple of days, the first thing they did was put me in the bath. I remember a sick feeling of shame at having the dirt on my feet pointed out to me, and the harsh washing it took to get my greasy uncombed hair clean. I don't remember owning a toothbrush, but maybe no one did, I just don't know.

At home, there were occasions when I would hide behind the

sofa and cry, not knowing why. Perhaps I hoped someone would notice, but no one ever did.

Often, when I went out with Mum to the shops or to visit her best friend Rhoda Clemens, I'd have to ask her repeatedly to hold my hand. 'Tighter, Mum,' I'd insist. I also asked her constantly if she loved me.

'Don't be daft, of course I do,' she'd say.

'How much do you love me, Mum?'

'Ten pounds o' sugar,' was always her reply, which never seemed enough to me.

I'd think, maybe next time she'll say ten tons of sugar, not that I knew what a ton was, just that it must be a lot. I wanted her to hold me close in her arms, or at least to hold my hand tight, just to let me feel something of and from her, but perhaps she had nothing left to give.

In later years, I learned that Mum suffered from terrible nightmares during that time. According to Dad, she had recurring dreams of falling, spiralling downwards into a bottomless pit. She'd dream of being buried alive, and would wake up screaming. He said he had to hold on to her for hours at a time to reassure her that she was safe, that she was not dying. Sometimes Dad wasn't able to get home: the bombings often caused severe damage to roads and transport, making it impossible to travel even short distances. On such occasions, I would hear or find Mum crying, which frightened me; I would go off by myself and, in some dark corner, I'd cry too. I believe her fears for my father caused most of her tears. Mum had never been strong emotionally, especially where Dad was concerned. I wanted to be able to comfort her, as I needed comforting, but she seemed to have an invisible wall around her. She had become a shadowy figure, living somewhere on the edge of my life. I missed her. I missed my father. They were both there, yet somehow not for me.

In desperation over Mum's health – she had now stopped eating – Dad consulted a doctor, who told him he had to start making her drink Guinness every day, if he could get it. He explained its nutritional value, and said it could save her life.

Guinness was almost impossible to buy locally, and Dad could never have paid black-market prices. As a last resort, he went to his brothers, who still lived in the old East End. He knew they had 'connections' and might be able to help him. He was right. They came by a few cases that had 'fallen off the back of a lorry', and continued to do so on an as-needed basis. Dad swore that Guinness saved Mum's life, and I'm sure it did.

After a while, her health improved. She started eating again, and ventured out a little more often. On one of those occasions, however, my good intentions almost sent her scurrying home in embarrassment. As we rode on the top deck of a bus one day, the driver made a stop next to, and at eye-level with, an enormous billboard bearing a larger-than-life advertisement for Guinness. Excited, I stood and announced to our fellow passengers, 'Look! That's my mum's Guinness.' Everyone laughed, except Mum, of course: she looked as though she'd like nothing more than to kill me.

The government had conscripted Dad as a sand-blaster at the Woolwich Arsenal. Working there, in a major enemy-targeted facility and under attack night after night, Dad thought he had seen and experienced it all. Obviously, he had not.

One morning, after a particularly intense air raid, he stumbled in through the door. He had been trying to get home all night and now, blackened by soot, he looked terrible. He sat, his head in his hands, shaking as he spoke. He told us how he had looked out over the River Thames and at London's skyline: the entire city had appeared to be on fire. The sky and river looked like a churning red inferno. Barrage balloons glowed red, reflecting the colour of the raging fires below. He broke down then, his shoulders convulsed by sobs, and confessed to having wept earlier at the sight of the devastation.

'I know what Hell looks like now,' he said. 'I've just been there.'

That night the enemy had undertaken an all-out effort to destroy London's docks and the warehouses that crowded the banks of the river. It was also an attempt to break the spirit of the British people. With so much flammable cargo stored in the warehouses, just one bomb or incendiary caused an incalculable chain effect, but they dropped hundreds, if not thousands, that night. Molten metal, oil, alcohol and other liquids spewed into the Thames, creating a flowing river of flames; not even the river rats escaped.

Dad's work at the arsenal was to sandblast huge bomb casings, both inside and out; it was a dangerous and gruelling job. He told of workmates dropping dead beside him from exhaustion. Others were killed when they lost control of the high-powered sandblasting hoses, which turned into thrashing killing machines.

He told of the hardship of working for hours inside huge bomb casings, of the furnace-like heat and physical pain he endured. Dad sustained permanent damage to his eyes from numerous metal fragments. His body contained so much metal dust that he left permanent rust stains, in the shape of his body, from sweating on the bed sheets. By the end of the war, he weighed less than a hundred pounds, and boils covered his arms and legs. I often wondered how people like him survived. It could only have been through sheer will-power.

Men like my father received no medals or recognition for their war efforts; neither did they expect them. However, Dad did receive a commendation for the part he claimed to have played in helping to identify and capture a spy found to be working at the arsenal. Perhaps it made him feel more a part of the actual fight. Although he received no medals, he seemed proud to pass on to me the dog-tags he wore while working at the arsenal. Identical to those worn by the military, Dad wore his on his own battleground.

In spite of, or perhaps because of, the misery, Londoners always seemed able to ferret out the funny side of life. One of my favourite stories is about another of Dad's experiences, and so typical of wartime Cockney London.

The air-raid sirens were blaring as he made his way home one evening, after being on fire-watch with his brothers in Poplar. Everyone in the area ran for cover into an Underground station. Once they were safely on the platform, someone took charge, as was usual, to make sure those with special needs received assistance. That night, a vicar hoisted himself onto a bench. When he had everyone's attention, he addressed the crowd in what Dad called a very 'posh' voice.

'Are there any pregnant women here?' he shouted, through cupped hands. After a moment's silence, the voice of a Cockney wag came from the back: 'Give us a chance, mate, we've only bin 'ere five minutes.' Dad said everyone had a good laugh, including the red-faced vicar.

It seemed that each day brought new and surprising happenings, some good, most bad. One such incident remains etched on my mind. As I played in the street one afternoon, I looked up to see two dirty, dishevelled strangers walking towards me. At first, I thought they were gypsies, and it wasn't until they turned and entered our house that I realized they were my nanny and granddad.

Heat and flames from incendiaries had set fire to and melted the lead roof of their home at Blackwall. With molten lead dripping all around them, they had barely escaped. After watching all their worldly possessions destroyed, and still in shock, they had walked eight miles to get to us. They could find no transport after another fiery night of bombing.

Until Nan and Granddad found new accommodation, they lived at our house. I don't know how long they stayed since soon after their arrival Mum and Dad had me evacuated.

Before I went away, however, Mr and Mrs Jackson, our neighbours at number eight, went to live with relatives in Scotland. They said they would not return until after the war.

'If it ain't over, we ain't comin' back,' Mrs Jackson told Mum.

To my delight, they left their pet parrot in our care. A large macaw, his language proved even more colourful than he was.

'Ooh, I wonder who taught him that one. I hope no one thinks we use that kind of language in this 'ouse,' Mum said, and usually, we did not. He'd sit in his cage, on top of the kitchen copper, and jabber away all day. I knew better than to put my fingers into his cage. He could be vicious, especially if he thought his food supply was threatened.

While Nan and Granddad were with us, Nan, always a big tease, foolishly decided to bait the parrot – at his dinnertime. She loved to get him riled up and swearing. On that particular occasion, she must have gone too far. Suddenly he lunged, and took the end off her finger. Mum stood there with that I-told-you-so look on her face. Nan, with blood dripping all over the kitchen floor, tried to look nonchalant, but that was the end of her parrot-teasing days.

When I was about four, Mum and Dad became friendly with Mr and Mrs Easy, the neighbours across the road. The four of them would get together to play cards at the Easys' house. They had one son, a little younger than me, named Victor, and we would amuse ourselves while our parents played cards. Occasionally, during the daytime, we were left in Mr Easy's care while our mothers went to the shops. That was when the problems began: Mr Easy started exposing himself to me. It happened every time I was alone with him. That was why I hated going to their house.

Grossly obese, the man had ugly rolls of fat that hung over the top of his trousers. He could hardly walk, and waddled when he did. He seemed to have difficulty breathing, always had a red face, perspired profusely and smelt like a dirty toilet. When no one was around, he would take out that white ugly 'thing'.

'Come on, love, come and rub it. It feels nice, you'll like it,' he'd whisper, as he shook it at me.

'No. No, thanks, I don't want to,' I'd say, and I would pretend to be interested in something else. I remember thinking it looked like one of those big shellfish called whelks that Mum and Dad got from the winkle man on Sundays; it smelt like it too. Out of its shell, a whelk reminded me of a slimy garden slug, only white and much bigger. It made me feel sick.

'Come on, don't be scared. Victor likes it. He plays with it all the time and makes it do funny things,' he'd whisper to me. He would rub himself, start breathing more heavily, and he'd be sweating like a pig. I was glad he was too fat to get up off the sofa fast: I would have had to run and someone might have found out. I'm positive I never touched him; I was far too frightened. It also confused me. I remembered what Mum had told me about strangers, but Uncle Bill, as I called him, was not a stranger. So why was I scared of him? Was I supposed to do what he told me? Was I being disobedient?

He also touched me several times 'down below', the first time being when Victor and I were leaning out over the windowsill, watching a military band march by. He came up behind me and pushed his fat sweaty hand inside my underpants, hissing into my ear, 'It's okay, Victor likes it.'

Should I let him? Would I like it? No, I just couldn't. I pushed my way past him and ran outside. Somehow, I knew something bad was happening, but I didn't know if it was him or me being bad. I hated him, but was too frightened to tell anyone the truth.

I begged Mum and Dad not to make me go there, but they refused to leave me alone in our house.

'No,' they'd say. 'Something bad might happen to you.'

How could I tell them something bad was already happening to me?

Eventually, I did tell them what had happened, but not until many years later. The word 'paedophile' was not in their vocabulary. They were shocked, and seemed to find it hard to believe that their friend would have done such a thing. Did they think I imagined it? Did they think I had made it up?

I have never enjoyed playing cards and wonder if those memories had anything to do with it.

5

The *Flying Scotsman*, Jaundice and the Loch Ness Monster

I was almost five when Mum told me we were going to Scotland, and that we'd be travelling overnight on the famous *Flying Scotsman* train. We were going to help her sister, Iris, who had just had her first baby.

The soot-encrusted railway station, air thick with the smell of smoke, bustled with travellers rushing back and forth. Porters called, 'Mind your backs, please,' as they pushed or pulled creaking carts piled high with luggage and other goods. Conductors blew whistles and shouted, 'All aboard, please,' as the great locomotives spewed steam and smoke in readiness for their journeys. As I watched one of the engines lunge into motion, it reminded me of a fire-breathing dragon with its tail snaking and swishing behind it.

Somewhere overhead loudspeakers made scratchy announcements of train arrivals and departures, but with all the noise and commotion, I couldn't understand what the voices said. Fortunately, Mum heard our train and platform number called out. She grabbed my hand – 'That's us' – and dragged me behind her as she steered a path through the crowds towards the *Flying Scotsman*.

And there it stood, a giant, surrounded by travellers jostling for access to any one of its hundred gaping doors. We joined the crowd, and in its crush I felt myself propelled forward and up, onto the train. Mum had let go of my hand and for a moment I panicked, but there she was, just inches away. I clutched her coat.

Finding vacant seats on the train was not easy. Having priority, hundreds of soldiers had boarded ahead of civilians. As we passed from carriage to carriage in search of space, I noticed some of the men laughing and joking, while others stared out through finger-cleared peepholes made on the steam-fogged windows.

'They're going off to fight in the war, Iris,' Mum told me.

'Have they got guns, Mum?' I asked.

'Yes, and I hope they get to use 'em,' she said.

I didn't see any guns but some soldiers had crutches or walking sticks, and some wore bandages. 'What about them, Mum?' I asked. 'Are they going as well?'

'No, I think they've already been. It looks like they've been wounded, poor blokes. They're probably on their way home for a rest.'

Several men said hello as we pushed by, then shifted themselves and their belongings, making room for us to sit. A few soldiers sat in the corridors on their kitbags; one had a mouth organ, which he began to play.

'Aw, that's nice,' commented Mum, as she hoisted me onto the seat. Then, letting out a sigh of relief, she plopped down beside me. 'Ooh, my dogs are barking,' she said, to no one in particular. She always said that when her feet hurt.

Nearby, a soldier burst out laughing. 'Well, ain't that music to me ears,' he said. 'I can tell where you're from, missus. I ain't 'eard that expression for a long time.' Mum blushed.

For days I'd been excited about going away with Mum so I hadn't told her I wasn't feeling well, fearing she'd make me stay at home. I'd also prayed there would be no bad air raids to ruin everything, and my prayers had been answered.

Now, here we were at last, on board the train, waiting to embark on this adventure. Then, with a mighty roar, my imaginary dragon leaped forward; soon we'd be flying through the night.

Everyone settled back in their seats and seemed to exhale

a collective sigh. We were on our way, leaving behind the clamour of London and, hopefully, the fear.

Sandwiched between Mum and a tall skinny soldier, I tried hard to stay awake, not wanting to miss anything. At first I'd been comfortable, but soon the air in the carriage became hot and stuffy. The heat from bodies and the sour smell of sweat began to suffocate me; I could hardly breathe. With head aching, eyes not wanting to stay open and afraid I might vomit, I curled up on the lumpy seat. Laying my head on Mum's lap and feeling the rough wool of her skirt against my cheek, I drifted off to the rhythmic clickety-clack clickety-clack of metal wheels on railway lines.

Later, jarred back to consciousness by someone shaking my arm, I struggled to open my eyes. The half-bandaged face of a ginger-haired soldier looked down at me. His voice sounded far away, but I could feel the warmth of his breath as he spoke.

'Blimey, missus, she looks 'alf dead. Are you sure she's all right?' I tried to lift my head.

'See? I told you – she's just tired from all the excitement. She'll be fine after she's 'ad a little kip,' Mum said, patting my arm. Then, once again, my world disappeared into a dark fuzzy spin and I have no memory of the rest of our journey.

The next thing I remember I was waking up at Auntie Iris's house, unsure if we were, in fact, in Scotland.

'Are we there, Mum?' I asked.

'Yes,' she replied. 'Now try to go back to sleep.'

Lying there in that cool, strange bed, I wondered why everyone was standing over me, staring. Unaccustomed to such attention, I knew something was wrong.

'I've got to go to the lav, Mum,' I said, trying to get up, and finding I couldn't stand.

'Here,' she said, pushing her arms under me. 'I'll carry you if you can't walk.' She picked me up, carried me to the bathroom, pulled down my knickers and perched me on the frigid toilet seat.

After I'd finished doing my duty, Mum wiped my bottom.

'Crikey, what's that?' she said. She had noticed that my 'whoopsie', as she called it, was white. 'Come and look at this, Iris,' she called.

Auntie Iris and Uncle Walter both joined Mum and me in the tiny bathroom. The four of us peered down the toilet at the ominous white lump.

'It don't look right, Kitty. There's something definitely wrong with her,' Uncle Walter said.

'I ain't never seen anything like it, Walt, except maybe some dog muck,' Mum replied.

'Oh, Lord,' piped up Auntie Iris. 'Let's look it up in the medical book instead of just standing around staring at it.'

Dizzy, I tottered back to bed and curled up under the covers. There, I drifted in and out of sleep and strange dreams where I hadn't the strength to run from the dogs that chased me.

After checking symptoms in a medical encyclopedia and finding that my skin now had a yellowish hue, they decided that Mum should take me to see a doctor in Glasgow. I don't remember how we got to the surgery but the memory of clanging tram bells, which jarred my aching head, is somehow connected to the journey. That, and having to carry a bag to vomit into, and the smell of it making me heave even more.

Clinging to Mum's hand as we walked, I gazed up at the tall, dark buildings until Mum stopped in front of one. She pushed through its enormous revolving doors and we found ourselves in a museum-like lobby; our footsteps echoed as we crossed its marble floor. We rode in the lift up to the fourth floor where Mum struggled to open the doors, and then we stepped out into an icy corridor with marble walls.

'Brrr, it's colder in 'ere than it was outside,' Mum said. Then she asked, 'Are you all right, Iree?' I wasn't, but what could I say?

After reading several gold-lettered signs, Mum pushed open a door and we tiptoed inside. 'I think this is the right one,' she whispered.

We jumped when a man, who turned out to be the doctor, appeared from an inner room. He wore a long white coat, and had little gold-rimmed glasses perched on the end of his nose. A bushy moustache covered his mouth, and below that, a beard hid the rest of his face and neck. Except for the white coat, he didn't look like any doctor I had seen before.

'Come in, come in. I've been expecting you,' he said. 'Your brother-in-law, Mr Mannings, I believe, phoned to say you were bringing the wee girlie. Now let's have a look at her.'

He peered at me for what seemed an eternity. I stared down at the squiggles in the carpet and jiggled from foot to foot. Mum jerked my arm. 'Stop fidgeting, Iris,' she muttered. 'Stand still and let the doctor look at you.'

At last, stroking his beard and nodding, the doctor spoke again in his strong Scottish accent: 'This poor wee lass has yellow jaundice, Mother. She's verra, verra contagious. I hope she hasnae been in contact with any other children.' He bent down, picked me up and sat me on the edge of his examination table. 'Now, lie down, lassie, and don't you be afeared.' I was afraid, but I also wanted to giggle at the way he rolled his *r*s.

Lying on the frigid, leather-covered table, I couldn't stop shivering. To make matters worse, he pulled up my dress and pulled down my knickers. Then, from a drawer, he produced some kind of writing instrument and proceeded to draw a large purple square on the right side of my abdomen. Pointing at the square, he gave Mum instructions: 'You'll be putting hot mustard plasters, three times a day, on this area, Mother. It will not be pleasant for the child but it'll draw out all o' the poison.' My imagination went to work and all I could picture was my belly filled with poison. How was it going to get out? What did he mean, 'draw it out'? Would it come out through the purple square, or my belly button? I looked to Mum for some kind of reassurance, but she was clearly as confused as I felt.

'She'll be kept to her bed for a goodly while. She'll only be getting up for toileting and she'll no go near any children. Do I make m'self clear, Mother?' enquired the doctor, peering at Mum through those little glasses on the end of his beak-like nose.

'Oh, yes, I think so, sir, thanks ever so much, sir,' said Mum. The doctor gave her some further instructions as she helped me off the table and rearranged my clothing.

It wasn't until years later that I learned 'yellow jaundice' was a symptom of hepatitis, and that the purple square, drawn on the right side of my abdomen, was over the affected liver area.

Except for an occasional tut, Mum remained quiet when we left the doctor's office. I looked up at her. Her lips were tucked in, as though she wanted to keep her words inside. Was she angry with me? Had I spoiled everything? The only thing I could be certain of at that moment was that they'd never allow me to see the new baby now; my poison might kill it, and then they'd probably kill me.

Confined to a bedroom at Auntie's house, I felt lonely and sorry for myself. Outside my quiet room, I could hear chatter and the baby's cries, laughter and the clink of dishes coming from the kitchen. I wanted to be a part of the movement and sound out there; I wanted to know what was going on. Weak and lethargic, I contented myself with an endless supply of picture books, eating lots of jelly, the only thing I could keep down, and sleep. At first, they only permitted me out of bed to go to the toilet and even then someone had to help me, and make sure the baby was nowhere near. Someone always followed me with a bottle of smelly disinfectant too; it made me feel awful, as though they thought I was dirty. Uncle Walter terrified me: he told me off if I so much as poked my head out from the bedroom. He was small in stature but his presence was enormous.

I don't recall how long the illness or isolation period lasted but I'm sure it seemed longer than it was. As my health improved, short visits outside were allowed. As my strength began to return, outdoor excursions grew longer. When pronounced well or, at least, non-contagious, I joined what had been the invisible world outside my bedroom. At last I saw the new baby. Uncle Walter stopped glaring at me, but he still scared me. I watched him one day. He didn't seem to walk like everyone else, he seemed to be propelled: he always did things quickly. I asked Mum about it.

'He's ever so clever, Iris. His mind is so quick it makes him move fast. At least, I think that's it.'

'Oh,' I said. 'You must have a slow mind then, eh, Mum?'

'Cheeky monkey,' she said.

Mum seemed happy while we were in Scotland. She nattered for hours with her sister and they took turns to tend the baby. She seemed a different person there, younger somehow, and I loved hearing her laughter.

As an early birthday present, Auntie Iris made me a new dress with matching underpants. Proud of my beautiful outfit, too proud perhaps, I insisted on showing the underpants to everyone. Mum was mortified. Before going out anywhere, she would point her finger in my face and proceed with the warnings. 'Don't you dare show anyone them knickers, Iree, or you won't be goin' out again, do you 'ear me?'

'Yes, Mum, I promise. I won't show me knickers to anyone.'

'All right then, and don't you forget it, my girl, or I'll take them new knickers down and smack yer bum in front of everyone.' I knew she wouldn't, though: she'd be more embarrassed than I would if she did that.

On one of Scotland's rare sunny days, we all went on a day's outing to Loch Lomond. I'd never seen such a lovely place. It was like something out of a picture book, or a dream. Surrounded by rhododendron-covered hills, or 'braes', as I learned they were called in Scotland, the lake and sky were the bluest blue imaginable.

I took off my shoes and socks, paddled in the lake's icy water, and collected shiny pebbles and tiny shells.

'Why are there seashells here?' I asked.

'They're not seashells, silly, they're loch-shells,' Auntie Iris replied. Loch-shells or seashells, they were the same shape as snail-shells, but smaller and prettier. Whatever they called them, I thought they were beautiful.

The previous night, Uncle Walter had cautioned me to watch out for the Loch Ness Monster while we were at the lake. 'It looks like a dragon,' he'd said. 'Not too many people have seen it but you never know when it might decide to come up for a bit of fresh air.'

I watched for the mysterious creature all the time we were there, but it didn't make an appearance that day. 'I wish I could have seen the monster, Mum,' I said, as she dried my feet.

'Think yerself lucky, Iris. If he'd seen yer feet under the water, he might have sneaked up and bit yer bum,' she replied. I shuddered. If she had told me that before I'd paddled, I would never have gone anywhere near the water, let alone into it.

Some years later, the truth surfaced. As I thought back over my narrow escape from the Loch Ness Monster, it suddenly occurred to me that my uncle had fooled me: what would the Loch Ness Monster have been doing in Loch Lomond?

On that magical day, among the tall pines in the woods surrounding the lake, I saw and fed some of Scotland's red squirrels.

They were beautiful, with their fat bushy tails flashing auburn in the sun. Thrilled to have them come close enough to eat from my hands, I happily shared my picnic lunch with them. A city child, the only wildlife I'd ever seen before were sparrows, mice and rats, and most of them I didn't see up close unless they were dead.

As far as I could see, Scotland had only one fault: it rained almost every day. I don't know how people managed to dry their washing: it was worse than England. However, we did learn one trick from my clever aunt. After she'd washed a woollen jumper, she laid it flat between newspapers and placed it under the carpet, and there it stayed until it was dry.

With no carpets in our house, we couldn't use her special trick. Our jumpers remained unwashed until summer. Mum had to be sure of a few warm days so that we wouldn't freeze to death waiting for them to dry. In those days, we had no extras to wear while the dirty clothes were laundered.

In spite of the weather, it was wonderful to be in Scotland with our favourite relatives, in a house that had carpets on the floors, where we were always warm and cosy, and could sleep undisturbed by air raids. I would have been happy to stay there for ever, and I believe Mum would have too, if it hadn't been for Dad.

Auntie Iris had gone through a difficult time giving birth to my new cousin, Laurence, and, according to Mum, her recovery was taking a little longer than usual. We stayed with her until she could manage on her own, but eventually the time came for us to leave. My fifth birthday, just weeks away, meant only one thing: we had to get back for me to start school.

Our dreaded departure day arrived. Dabbing tears and runny noses, we said our goodbyes at the railway station; Auntie Iris, Uncle Walter and baby Laurence had come to see us off. Reluctant to leave loved ones, the peace and warmth, we climbed aboard the train to begin our long journey home. Leaning out of the carriage window, Mum waved a soggy handkerchief and surrendered to the reality of London and the air raids we'd been able to forget for just a little while.

6

Starting School

My fifth birthday passed with little fanfare but the milestone brought unwelcome change to my life. It was time for my official schooling to begin, and when the day arrived, I put up a big fuss. I did not want to go.

'Don't be a baby, Iris. You've got to go, so go on before I get really cross.'

'Please don't make me, Mum, please,' I begged. 'What if there's an air raid?' She didn't reply; she had zipped her mouth closed. I thought she might kiss me but her lips had disappeared. Ignoring my pleas, she shoved me out of the door and closed it. Bang.

I stood on the step, staring back at the faded green paint on the door. I thought she might be standing on the other side, crying like me. Half expecting her to change her mind, my ears strained to hear the turning of the knob. I waited for the door to open, to let me back in, but it did not.

I didn't want to leave her there, alone, but I knew it would do no good to knock on the door again. Her face had told me what I had not wanted to hear. I was to go to school, like it or not. So began my long journey away from her to my first encounter with the great big world. With tears and snot streaming down my face, I headed down the road. Glancing back at our house before turning the corner, I stood for a moment and choked back a sob. Wiping my face on the back of an already sodden cardigan sleeve, I wondered if she would be there when I got home.

Clinging to my gas mask, I wondered what would happen if there was an air raid while I was at school. When I entered the school playground and saw the enormous concrete air-raid shelter, I stopped worrying. It took up half of the playground and had sandbags piled high around the entrance. What about Mum, though? Where would she be? Would she remember to go into our shelter if I wasn't there?

When I saw all the other children laughing and screaming in the playground, I felt a bit better. They had left their mums at home so it must be okay.

A tall grey-haired woman strode onto the playground and, swinging her entire arm, rang a wooden-handled bell. I guessed she was one of the teachers. As the bell fell silent at her side, the children ceased all activity, but only for a moment. Sound and motion resumed as they ran to her and began forming lines.

There were three other children who, like me, appeared unsure of what to do. They must have been new too. We stood there, shifting from foot to foot, until the bell-ringer called to us: 'Come quickly, we're all waiting for you.' The four of us tagged on to the end of the snaking line of children and followed them into the building. I whispered to the girl in front of me, 'I hate school. I wish the Germans would drop a bomb on it.'

'I do as well,' she said, as tears began streaming down her face.

When we were released that afternoon, I ran all the way home. Out of breath, a stitch in my side, I was relieved to see that our house was still there. I let myself in at the front door, and there, standing in the kitchen doorway, wiping her hands on her apron, stood Mum. 'Well, how'd you like school, Iree?' she asked.

'I dunno yet,' I said. I wanted to throw my arms around her and hold on to her but, of course, I didn't, and I knew she would not embrace me.

'See? It wasn't as bad as you thought, was it? Wanna cup of tea?' she said.

'Yes, please, Mum,' I replied, and we sat there in the cold kitchen, neither of us saying a word, just sipping our tea together.

The following day I went off to school without protest. What good would it do?

By the end of the first week, the routine seemed natural. Cold-water face-wash, hair combed, cup of tea, slice of toast and out of the door. I still hated leaving Mum, but I was beginning to like school.

I did wonder why some children's mums walked them to school, and why they met them at the gate at going-home time. I looked for Mum a couple of times, especially on rainy days when other parents held up umbrellas, waiting to meet their children. Mum didn't have an umbrella, so I took solace from telling myself there was no point in her coming if she didn't have one, was there?

I don't remember much about what we called 'infants' school', perhaps because of the disruption caused by the new, more intense air raids. The few things I recall are of sitting on benches around long worktables. There was always something fun to do, which made it easier to forget about war and mothers left alone at home.

The classroom was full of wonderful smells. I loved the smell of books and paint, and of the modelling clay called Plasticine. Best of all was the scent of lavender each time our teacher came close. She was old but she didn't smell old, like my nan did.

In that first classroom, I met my life-long friend Sheila McDonald. It was Sheila who, many years later, reminded me of when I'd fashioned a pair of spectacles out of bright green Plasticine. I had just arranged the 'specs' on my face when the air-raid siren sounded. Our teacher gathered us together, herded us from the classroom, out of the building and into the shelter. Once safely inside, I discovered that, in the urgency of the moment, I had forgotten to remove my Plasticine glasses. They were now a shapeless mass and had become hopelessly mashed into my hair.

The other children thought it was very funny and, although it wasn't funny to me, I laughed too.

'You and the other children won't think it funny if we can't get this out of your hair, young lady. You'll look most peculiar going home with it green,' said the teacher, who then promised to remove it before the end of the school day, and kept her word.

During that period, I also went to Sunday school at a nearby Baptist Church. Mum and Dad didn't practise any particular religion in those days. I'm sure I was sent off to get me out of the house on Sunday afternoons so that they could have a little 'nap'.

When I arrived home I'd find the front door locked; it was the only day they ever locked it. I'd have to wait for ages for someone to open the door and often came close to wetting myself. I'd stand there crossing my legs, clutching my crotch with one hand and banging on the door knocker with the other. What are they doing in there? I wondered.

I was too scared to use the church toilets. They were down a long flight of stairs in the basement. If God and Jesus were upstairs in the church, I thought, then surely the devil was down there. No, I'd rather take my chances on making it home than risk Hell.

For good attendance, the Baptist Sunday school on Wood Lane presented me with a Bible. It always had petals pressed between its pages; it made a wonderful flower-press. I think that's all I ever used it for. Well, maybe not quite.

During my first five years, besides yellow jaundice, the only other illness I remember having was German measles. Had those measles come in the bombs dropped by German bombers? I wondered. Perhaps even at that age, I had premonition of germ warfare.

'Do we send English measles over there?' I asked Mum.

'Ooh, I'm sure we must do,' she replied.

At night, I often cried due to terrible pains in my legs. I also lost my appetite and was losing weight. Mum took me to the doctor several times but he never determined what was wrong with me. He prescribed dietary supplements, extract of malt and orange juice, obtained from the children's clinic. Those symptoms went on for a long time, even after the war. We never discovered what caused them, perhaps simply the lack of proper nutrition.

Many children showed signs of malnutrition by then. As a result, large numbers ended up with rickets. Soon after the war, health clinics were equipped with sunlamps and children sat under them for the beneficial ultra-violet rays. Unfortunately, it was too late for some. The most common defect evidenced, besides decayed teeth, was bowed legs and hunched backs. I was lucky to escape it.

Shortly after I started school, Mum went to work in a parachute factory, and I believe it was at about that time that we began to hear rumours that Germany planned to use unmanned rockets in its air attacks on Britain. With those new fears, plus a stray bomb that killed one of Mum's friends, and intense, frequent air raids, it was decided that I should be evacuated for the rest of the war.

7

My Evacuation

The most frightening journey of my life began on a grey, overcast morning in July 1943, shortly after my fifth birthday. The events of that day remain imprinted on my mind.

Overwhelmed, and numb with confusion, I found myself, with hundreds of other children, marching in pairs along London's bomb-damaged streets. The scenes of devastation worsened as we neared the centre.

A dusty pall hung over everything and evidence of heavy bombings and fires lay scattered in piles all around. The acrid, damp smell of burned-out buildings, some still smouldering, filled the air; its density made breathing difficult.

Sections of charred walls, like accusing fingers, pointed at the open sky, awaiting the next downpour of terror. Those broken walls with wallpaper fluttering in the breeze had once been family homes. Their smashed windows, like blinded eyes, stared out at us; shattered by explosion, they waved tattered shreds of curtains at our passing parade. I wondered where the families were now, or if they were dead.

A mangy, perhaps burned, cat emerged from a tangle of rusty bedsprings lying in the gutter. Limping and miaowing, it followed us for a while. I wanted to stop and pet it, but as I was one of the youngest, already having difficulty keeping up with the others, I couldn't afford to lag. My legs ached and I wondered if we'd ever arrive where we were going.

We were led at last into one of London's cavernous railway stations and a sense of relief rippled through our ranks: perhaps now we could rest for a while.

Around my neck, flapping at the end of a piece of string, I wore a brown paper label bearing my name and identity number. I stood there, clutching a few of my belongings in a small home-made case, and a newspaper-wrapped parcel containing jam sandwiches. My red and blue Mickey Mouse gas mask, in its cardboard container, hung from my shoulder.

The previous day, kneeling on our stone-cold kitchen floor, Dad, with tears in his eyes, had fashioned the little case from odd bits of plywood. We had no real luggage, but he had done his best, using the only available materials. He made the handle from a piece of leather, which he'd cut from his own belt. Sniffing, he wiped a drip off the end of his nose with the back of his hand.

'I can't have her carryin' her belongin's in a paper bag, can I?' he said. Mum made no response, just sat silently, watching.

I have no recollection of saying goodbye to my family or of anyone coming to see me off at the railway station; we must have left from school. I believe the actual day and details of our departure were secret: I didn't know I was leaving until the day before.

'I would've died of shame if you'd gone off in dirty knickers,' was all Mum had said.

I remember being afraid, as faceless strangers herded us, like lambs, towards waiting train carriages. Dwarfed by dozens of noisy, scruffy children, many of them sobbing and screaming for their mothers, I was too frightened to cry. Who were all these children and why were some of them so dirty? Although it wasn't Saturday, I had had a bath the night before *and* had my hair washed.

I learned later that most of the children came from London's poorest slums, even poorer than we were. Many had already lost their families and homes, and had suffered worse hunger, fear and neglect. My thoughts were all questions. What are we doing here and where are we going? The noise was deafening, my throat ached, I wanted to drop everything and run. Instead, turning my small wooden case on end, I sat and waited.

I had been placed in the care of a twelve-year-old girl, named Eileen Harvey. She lived around the corner from us on Maxey Road, near to where a bomb had left a crater in the street. Now my only connection with the world I knew and understood, Eileen became my lifeline. I clung to her as prodding fingers ushered us forward.

Before boarding the train, I stopped for a moment and looked up at the great black steam engine. It belched thick stinking smoke from one funnel, and steam hissed from another as it waited to take its occupants on their journey. It reminded me of a horse at the starting gate of a race, pawing at the ground. Suddenly, through the fog of bewilderment and smoke, I thought of my granddad. Didn't he work at a railway station? Might this be the one? Could he be here somewhere, looking for me? I stood on tiptoe, straining to see over the crowds. Maybe, just maybe, this was one of his trains. Then, signalling its readiness, the shrill engine whistle pierced my thoughts. I mounted the last step and entered the carriage. Behind me, the sound of compartment doors slamming destroyed my brief moment of hope.

After much jostling and elbowing, Eileen found us two seats together. She shoved our belongings onto the overhead luggage rack, then pushed me onto the seat. Gripping her hand and keeping as close to her as I could, I leaned my head back against the dirty red-velvet seat cover. Then, feeling the surge of the chugging steam engine, my eyes closed and I escaped into sleep.

I remember nothing more of the journey until Eileen shook me awake as the train, now almost empty, pulled into a small dark station. I have no recollection of stops along the way to drop off children, or of changing trains, as surely we must have.

We pressed our noses to the window, straining to see where we were. With no lights visible outside, it was impossible to distinguish anything except our own reflections staring back at us.

At last, with the squeal of brakes, we clanked to a complete stop. Children who had risen fell back into their seats. For a moment, there was an eerie silence. I sat there, looking from face to face, bewildered and searching for clues. Now what?

A woman came striding through the long train carriage shouting orders. 'Gather your things, children. Quickly now, single file, follow me.'

We scrambled to obey, dragging baggage and our weary bodies off the train. I walked behind Eileen, hanging on to the belt of her coat so there would be no chance of her leaving me behind.

'For God's sake, stop pullin' on me. I ain't goin' nowhere without you,' she snapped.

Once off the train, we huddled together on the platform until the woman regrouped us into pairs. She marched this last group of tired, bedraggled children out of the station into the darkness.

After struggling with our belongings up a long steep hill, with aching arms and legs and bellies begging for food, we entered a dimly lit church hall. Inside, a stern-looking man and a woman, wearing a funny black hat with a long feather sticking straight up, made us stand in a line around the edge. The man, with his big moustache, resembled a walrus wearing a suit and tie.

'Someone will be coming to take you home shortly,' he told us, which confused me. Why would we be going home again, so soon after coming all this way?

People from the village began to arrive. They looked as apprehensive as I felt. Each of them walked up and down the line of children and began choosing whom they would take into their homes. None of them looked eager to make a selection. I was terrified that no one would want me.

'Don't go without me, Eileen. Please don't leave me here by meself,' I begged.

'Shuddup,' she said. 'Stop whinin'.'

After what seemed an eternity, a woman wearing a black-fringed shawl stopped in front of me. She beckoned to the man in charge. 'Can I just be taking the little one?' she asked. I hung on to Eileen with both hands and began wailing. The kindly woman patted my head. She turned to the walrus-man and laughed. 'Well, now, it looks like I'll be taking the two of them, then, and I hope that's all right,' she said.

'Right, madam,' he replied. He wrote something in a book, handed her some papers and off we went, just like that. We were going to live with strangers who talked as though they were singing. It was difficult to understand what they were saying, but whatever it was, it sounded friendly.

8

Maerdy

We had arrived in the coal-mining village of Maerdy, a small, bleak place, surrounded by lush green mountains in the Rhondda Valley of South Wales. The village consisted of row upon row of small houses, staggered up the hills on either side of a deep valley. Maerdy was like a giant scab: it covered a deep wound, inflicted by coal barons upon the once-tender valley floor. From its heart loomed the black skeletal towers of mineshafts, surrounded by the lesions of filthy slag.

The colliery owners had built hundreds of these terraced houses for their employees, and since the late 1800s, almost every man and boy in the village had worked 'down below', including the men of the family I was to live with for the next two years.

Dorothy Davies, the woman who had picked Eileen and me out of the line of evacuees, was the younger unmarried sister of Nell Cooper, our designated foster-mother. Dorothy had promised to help care for us, since Nell already had two young children.

Our new family consisted of Nell and Dilwyn Cooper, whom we were to call Auntie Nell and Uncle Dil, and their two daughters, Ann and Christine. Another child, Sylvia, had recently died of pneumonia. Nell's sister, 'Auntie' Dorothy, their mother, 'Gran', and Arthur, their teenaged brother, lived a few houses away.

Eileen and I shared one of three small bedrooms. We slept together in an old iron bedstead and I giggled at the *sproing-sproing* sound the springs made every time we moved. The billeting officers offered canvas camp beds for us but Auntie Nell told them, 'Thank you very much but that won't be necessary.'

At the bottom of our bed there was an old-fashioned steamer trunk. I had nightmares after Eileen lied to me about its contents. 'There's a dead body inside,' she'd whisper. Petrified, but not wanting to get her into trouble, I told no one.

Eileen continued to tease and terrorize me. She did not like sharing a bed with me. I had clung to her in the beginning, but had come to fear and hate her. She ran away after about a month and the authorities allowed her to return to her Dagenham home.

Auntie Nell broke the supposed bad news to me. 'Eileen has gone,' she said, 'and, I'm sorry to say, she won't be coming back.' A worry line creased her forehead and she appeared nervous as she awaited my response.

'Hooray. Good riddance to bad rubbish,' I said, as I clapped my hands. Auntie Nell smiled with relief.

With that prayer answered, I thought my troubles were over until a new problem arose: I now had head lice. Had I caught them on the train from those dirty slum children? Had they come with me all the way from London? Guilt and shame washed over me. Now these nice people would hate me, I thought.

'Children everywhere get the head lice. You can't be takin' all the blame, silly girl,' Auntie Nell told me.

However, her assurance did little to allay another lurking fear. I remembered something Mum had told me, about what used to happen when she was a schoolgirl. Children found to be 'lousy', or to have what they called a 'dirty head', had to have their hair shaved off, a prospect that terrified me. 'Please don't shave me head,' I begged. 'Please don't cut all me hair off, Auntie.'

'Well, now, there's silly you are. Why would we be doing a thing like that to such a pretty head?' was her gentle response. 'Auntie Dorothy will be coming to put medicine on your hair every night. It won't smell very nice, but no one's going to shave it off. So stop your worrying, lovely girl.'

Auntie Dorothy came to the house each evening. She spread newspapers over the kitchen table and patiently combed turpentine through my hair, watching for lice and searching for nits at the roots of my hair and in the comb. She'd crack the nits between her fingernails, to make sure they were dead. Auntie Nell had to leave the room. She couldn't stand hearing the nits crack. I didn't blame her: it was gruesome.

Everyone in the house had to have regular head inspections to make sure lice had not taken up residence, and, oh, what a happy day it was when Auntie Dorothy announced that my head was clear of the dreaded vermin. I danced around the kitchen.

'Hooray. I'm not lousy any more. I've got a clean head. Me head's not dirty any more,' I shouted. Auntie Dorothy was quick to correct me.

'You never had a dirty head, girlie, just some uninvited visitors.'

I will always be grateful for the patience and kindness extended by those dear, gentle people throughout that ordeal. Instead of making me feel dirty, as Mum's descriptions had conjured in my mind, they had comforted me with assurances that things like that happened every day and that I should not be ashamed.

In the two years I spent with the Coopers, I received nothing but kind treatment. Unless my memory deceives me, they did their best to treat me as one of their own. Yet, as I think about that part of my history, I remember a terrible feeling of aloneness. It stayed with me day and night for the duration of my evacuation. It was a hollow feeling, the same gnawing emptiness that comes with physical hunger, a feeling of not belonging accompanied by an overwhelming sadness.

No, I had not received the kind of loving I needed at home,

from my natural family, but this well of despair and loneliness struck deeper and served to drive me into a shell of self-preservation. It was a world of make-believe that would protect me from the cruelties and fears of a world at war. It also protected me from my own emotions.

The village children did not accept evacuees into their circles. They considered us foreigners, intruders and undesirable company. They stayed away from us, except when they were calling us nasty names.

I wandered up the mountainside and spent most of the time playing alone. There I would create my own world of make-believe, complete with fantasy companions. Taking stones from the ancient rock walls that surrounded the old farms and fields, I'd build the outline of 'my house', and there I became part of a happy family. We laughed and played, and always had plenty to eat. I spent countless hours there and, in my own way, made happy times for myself.

Once more, as in my bedroom at home, fairies were my constant companions, only now they did not live under my bed. They floated on fallen leaves down a rocky mountain stream to watch over me and grant my wishes, which were always the same: for the war to end, to feel safe again but, most of all, to feel wanted.

I grew to love the mountains and the sheep that roamed over them. I'd lie awake at night, listening to their mournful bleating, wondering if they, too, were crying for their mothers.

I loved the wildflowers, made chains from daisies, and picked berries for the aunties or Gran to make into pies. I had no fears on the mountains except of the dreaded bogs that they taught me to recognize by the swamp grass and reeds that grew around them. They told me that if you fell into one it would suck you under and that no one would ever know what had happened to you. The images evoked by their warnings kept me ever-vigilant.

One sunny day as I wandered up the mountain path, I saw what appeared to be a sheep in distress. It was lying on its side, on the grass verge by the road. Seeing it wriggling, I guessed it was trying to get up but too ill or badly injured to do so. I knew I should run for help but first I wanted to see it up close. This would be my chance to get a good look. Maybe I'd even be able to pet him or her.

I tiptoed up to the poor animal and knelt beside it. As I reached out to stroke its thick woolly coat, I discovered, to my horror, that the movement was not that of an injured animal at all but of the millions of maggots devouring it. I heaved a couple of times, then ran to wash my hands in the stream. It took a long time to wash the memory of that disgusting sight from my mind.

My carefree alone-time ended. With summer holidays over, it was time for me to start at Maerdy Infants School, just a short walk from where we lived. The school, a dingy Victorian building with a small playground in front, enclosed by iron railings and tall iron gates, reminded me of a prison. I was prepared to hate it, and I did.

My biggest surprise was finding that we wrote on slates instead of paper. Slates were wonderful. If you made a mistake, you could erase it with a spit-dampened finger. I also learned to sing songs in Welsh. I hadn't a clue what the words meant but I felt clever singing in a different language.

On most mornings, I had the responsibility of getting myself ready for school, but on one occasion, I didn't do a very good job. Trudging up the steep hill to school, I became aware of an unusual chill around my bottom. At that moment, the wind picked up my skirt to reveal to God and the world that I had forgotten to put my knickers on. Sure that all of Maerdy would be laughing at me, I ran home crying. Auntie Nell allowed me to stay with her, and she promised to check my knickers every day after that, and assured me that by tomorrow no one would remember what had happened.

At about that time, I suffered another painful and embarrassing experience. I had picked at a cold sore on my lip, causing it to spread around my mouth. When I arrived at school, the sour-faced teacher took one look at me and appeared to explode. Using her long cane, she prodded at me, shooing me from the classroom and out of the building.

'Get away with you, child,' she ordered. 'You cannot be here with impetigo. You are infectious and must not come back until you are clean.'

The door slammed behind me.

As I ran home, I thought of the lepers I'd learned about in Sunday school. I felt dirty, as they must have. Would I have to walk around ringing a bell and calling out, 'Unclean, unclean'?

Auntie Nell took me to the doctor, who assured her that I didn't have impetigo. He then uttered words that I knew came straight from Heaven.

'Keep the girl home from school until her face is healed, Mrs Cooper, until all the scabs are completely gone,' he said. Thank you, God, I thought.

Each day, holding a handkerchief over my mouth, I ran to the end of the street. There, at the edge of the village, satisfied no one would see my scabby face; I stuffed the handkerchief into my pocket and went back to playing on my mountainside, alone.

9

Wales, a Different Life

Life in Wales was different from what I had known in London. Memories of war-sounds – air-raid sirens, gunfire and explosions, the constant clanging of fire engine and ambulance bells – began to fade.

Here the sounds were different: they were softer and somehow kinder. Shift-change whistles from the mines, sheep bleating on hillsides, pigs grunting and squealing in the farmyard nearby, school bells, singing and laughter echoed throughout the Rhondda Valley; they were the sounds of peace.

The smells were different in the valley too. Gone was the stench of burning buildings, of cordite and sulphur, ruptured gas lines, damp underground shelters, urine-filled buckets and unwashed bodies. Here, mountain breezes tempered the curling trails of smoke-smells that billowed from hundreds of rooftop chimneys. The odours of silage and farmyard bonfires wafted away to the mountaintops and beyond; and when the hillsides were purple with heather, I thought I would drown in the warmth of its earthy scent.

Other delicious fragrances tantalized my nostrils' and imagination. Cottage kitchens and the village bakery sent out the comforting aromas of baking; they floated low over the village, like a soft, warm blanket.

I have vivid memories of standing outside the Coopers' house, drinking in the smell of comfort and safety, coupled with the knowledge that I would not go to bed hungry.

Each morning, a young boy of twelve or thirteen delivered bread. He carried the day's orders in an enormous square basket, which hung over his arm and was almost as big as he was. He always wore a large checked floppy cap, and as he made his rounds, he whistled non-stop.

'He'll be blowin' his teeth out one of these days,' said Gran, and I wondered if that was how she'd lost hers.

That fresh crusty bread, still warm when delivered, made my mouth water, and my stomach craved its crunchy newness. However, we never ate bread on the day it was baked. 'You'll be gettin' worms if you eat bread straight out of the ovens, boyo,' Gran warned. And, of course, we believed her. She was very old and we were sure she knew everything.

A creaking horse-drawn farm cart delivered milk each day. In London, milk came in glass bottles, but here, the farmer poured it from the dairy's metal urns directly into china jugs that we left outside on the doorstep at night. No one worried about theft or vandalism back then. Before sunrise, the dairyman filled each container with fresh creamy milk. By the time Auntie Nell brought the jugs inside, it had separated and formed a thick layer of rich yellow cream on top. She often scooped the cream off and later poured it over hot apple pie or whimberry tart. There was nothing quite like it.

The nearby bakery threw its burned loaves over the back wall into an alley that ran behind our terrace, separating the dwellings from the farm and the mountain path beyond. I often clambered up and sat on top of the old stone wall, nibbling on a discarded loaf after scraping away the blackest part. I didn't worry about eating burned fresh-baked bread. Surely the ovens would have burned the worms too, I reasoned.

Once I brought home one of the not-too-burned loaves. I thought it shameful to waste bread when I knew people were starving in Europe. Back home in England, we received reminders almost daily that children were starving to death 'over there'.

'There's people a lot worse off than you, so stop complainin',' Mum would say, if I turned up my nose at anything.

Perhaps Auntie Nell and Uncle Dil laughed when I brought the burned loaf home, but they thanked me and explained, 'There's no need to bring the burned bread home, Iris. It will be put to good use feeding the pigs over yonder at the farm so that we'll have meat and bacon to eat.' They assured me that the farmer collected the burned bread daily and added it to the pig swill. Happy to know it wasn't wasted, I felt a little guilty that I'd been eating the pigs' dinner.

I already knew the importance of feeding pigs. On almost every street corner in England there stood a large, galvanized-metal bin, known as the 'pig bin'. People were encouraged to deposit edible kitchen waste in it. Then, once or twice a week, special trucks collected the contents of those stinking, fly-infested bins and transported them to area farms and 'pig clubs' to be fed to the animals. Mum told me pigs would eat anything. After hearing that, I sometimes wondered how anyone could eat a pig.

The shortage of meat, along with most other commodities, forced many people to seek alternative sources of food, both during and after the war. As well as the allotments or victory gardens in which we grew vegetables, groups of people pooled resources and purchased pigs. They'd either build a small piggery and share the care of the animals, or arrange to board them with a local farmer in exchange for some of the meat. The idea of pig clubs seems strange now, but the British have always loved their pork and bacon.

It was in Wales that I first experienced the celebration of Hallowe'en. Considered a pagan practice, I suppose, Hallowe'en received no recognition in England at that time. We children didn't know or care what was or wasn't pagan and thought it great fun to bob for apples in a tin bucket filled with water. We'd roar with laughter at each other's snorting, spluttering efforts to grab an apple under water with our teeth. We all ended up looking like drowned rats. Auntie Nell didn't complain about the water we spilled all over the kitchen floor. She laughed along with us and, to our amusement, even tried it herself. I'm sure Hallowe'en involved more than bobbing for apples, but that's the only thing I remember about it.

Christmas was also more fun in Wales. We went carolling up and down the streets of Maerdy, each holding candle-lit lanterns. People invited us into their cosy kitchens to sing for them. They'd give us hot cocoa, and sometimes gave us pennies to treat ourselves. Every house had a Christmas tree, and colourful paper chains or streamers decorated the ceilings of the tiny cottages. We had never had a Christmas tree at home in London. To me, Christmas in Wales was like living in a fairy tale.

The Cooper family's Christmas dinner was an amazing sight. I had never seen so much food in my life. While preparations were under way, the buzz of activity, chatter and laughter reminded me of a story I'd heard about life inside a beehive.

All the relatives came on Christmas Day. We had fun from morning until night. Everyone joined in playing games and singing songs, between all the eating and drinking. Some of the older folk nodded off in their chairs. When they awakened, they ate and drank some more. In later years when I read *A Child's Christmas in Wales* by Dylan Thomas, each scene he described seemed familiar. I found myself grinning and felt a warm tickle inside. At times such as this, I sensed no sadness in the Cooper house, but there was always a tiny spot of it deep in my heart.

I experienced my first heavy snowfall in Wales too, and I will never forget stepping outside the front door on that first blizzard-like morning. I found myself standing in a freshly shovelled pathway, cut through snow so deep I couldn't see over the top. It was like being inside a rabbit warren, and I knew how it must have been for Alice in Wonderland. I, too, felt as though I had shrunk, or that the world around me had magically grown larger. What fun we had, running up and down the streets through the tunnels of snow, pretending to be rabbits and chasing each other.

That snowfall marked the first time local children allowed me to play with them. They even let me have a turn on their makeshift sledge. I don't remember feeling cold at all, although we were building snowmen and pelting each other with snowballs for hours on end. It made me feel, for the first time, that I was part of the village family and that perhaps they might accept me after all.

Living with my foster-family, I'm certain I was cleaner than I'd ever been before. Each night, we children received a top-to-toe wash in a tin tub in front of the fire. I loved to feel the warmth of the flames and the water. More than that, though, I loved the gentle touch of hands as they washed me, followed by arms that enfolded me in a warm dry towel.

That kitchen had something special about it. A small dark room, it was lit by just one lamp in the evenings. But the flickering orange glow of the fire cast dancing shadows on the walls and ceiling, creating a special warmth and brightness. Perhaps that feeling also came from something else: perhaps it radiated with the glow of a loving family simply *being* together.

Other than when one of the aunties washed and dried me, I recall no physical contact with or from anyone. There were no cuddles, no hugs and no kisses. I don't believe people showed a great deal of physical affection in those days. I suppose they showed their caring in other, more practical ways. But I believe all children can see love, caring or disapproval in the eyes of their caregivers, and I always saw caring in the eyes of my Welsh family.

Water for our baths, laundry and dishwashing was heated in heavy iron kettles on top of the black cast-iron stove, in which a coal fire was always kept burning. The kettles, filled with ice-cold water from the one tap outside, were set on the stove's back burners at all times. Hot water was always ready for use.

Miners received all the coal they needed at five pounds a ton and were not subject to shortages and rationing. I don't know if they realized how lucky they were to have a guaranteed source of heat. I suppose that was the one benefit of living and working at the source, while risking their lives daily.

After bathing the children, clean hot water refilled the tin tub, ready for Uncle Dil when he came home from the pit. I'd watch the miners marching down the road, black as coal themselves, swinging their lunch pails and brass miner's lamps. Sometimes they'd be singing.

In the middle of his jolly black face, Uncle Dil always had a big pink smile for us. After he had left his dirty clothes in the washhouse behind the kitchen, we all sat around the kitchen table while he had his bath and chatted with us. We never saw what my mother called his 'naughty bits'. I don't know how he managed to conceal himself from our inquisitive eyes. I was horrified when Eileen told me he had hair growing under his arms. I refused to believe anything so disgusting about my Uncle Dilwyn. It was another reason I was glad she'd run away.

After he had finished his bath, we would all have our supper. Then it was time for us girls to have our hair done up in rags. The Cooper girls had naturally curly hair that formed ringlets with ease, but my short, stick-straight mop was a different story. It must have been quite a challenge for Auntie Nell or Auntie Dorothy to twist it around the rags.

Before I'd come to Wales, I'd worn my hair in a short bobbed style. It looked as though I'd had it cut with a bowl over my head. I envied Ann's and Christine's beautiful ringlets, but Auntie Nell told me, in her usual reassuring way, 'Don't you worry, lovely girl, we'll soon have you with ringlets too.' She kept her promise, even through the trying head-lice invasion.

With all the dozens of rag curlers in place, it was time for prayers and sleep. We often had warm bread and milk before going up to bed. 'I'll not have my girls waking up hungry in the night,' Auntie Nell said.

My prayers were always the same. 'Please God keep everyone safe from the bombs,' followed by a litany of blessings. 'God bless Mummy, God bless Daddy, God bless Peter,' and on through everyone I could think of. The length of my blessing list depended on how tired I happened to be, but I always ended with, 'God bless everyone, except the Germans. Amen.'

Many years later, I confessed my wartime prayer ending to a German friend. He laughed. 'Don't feel bad, Iris. We said the same thing about the English!'

The children of war learned to hate at an early age.

10

Trauma in Maerdy

Maerdy had no cinema so when news of a real 'moving picture show', to be shown at Maerdy Working Men's Club, reached the ears of the community, the village buzzed with excitement.

The film, *Kidnapped*, from the book by Robert Louis Stevenson, was deemed suitable for children, and because I was now six, Auntie Nell said I could go alone.

Early on the day that the film would be shown, people of all ages began lining up outside the hall. I was one of the first. When the doors opened, the hall soon filled.

Pushing my way through the crowd, I found a seat in the back row where I could lean against the wall. The capacity audience was crammed together on rows of wooden benches and folding chairs, and the air soon became thick with the odours of cigarette smoke, sweat, cheesy feet and farts. I held my nose, hoping the film would make me forget the stink.

At last the lights dimmed, and all eyes focused on the tattered screen. After a few false starts, accompanied by impatient booing, whistling and catcalling, the film began.

At about the halfway point, engrossed in the story, I felt a hand on my bare leg. I pushed it away thinking little of it at first. A short while later, an arm pushed behind my back and I felt the hand grab my coat. I tried to stand but found I could not. In the pitch dark, I squinted to see who had me. Was someone I knew playing tricks on me? No, this was a complete stranger. The light from the film flickered on his face making him look grotesque. Now, he put his other hand on my leg, this time pushing it further up between my thighs.

'Stop it,' I whispered, trying not to disturb the people around me.

'Be quiet, and I'll not be hurting you,' he hissed into my ear.

Hurt me? What might he do? My mind and pulse raced. The man was big. He loomed over me, so close that the rough edge of his coat chafed my cheek and I could smell his foul, beery breath.

Paralysed by fear, I tried to think. I wanted to scream but could not. My throat felt tight. It held back my voice, just as he held me from behind. He forced his fingers inside my underpants and I felt his jagged fingernails at the place I knew no one was ever supposed to touch. I wriggled to get free and heard a whimper. It had come from me.

'Shush,' said someone in front of me, without looking back.

At that moment, I knew once again that I was alone, that only I could do something.

I squeezed my eyes shut, tensed every muscle and then, with all my strength, threw myself forward, out of the man's grip and onto the floor. Then, pushing my way through the forest of legs I crawled in the sticky darkness to the end of the row and away from the nightmare. Stumbling, I ran to the back of the hall, pushed through the dusty velvet door-curtain and out through the double doors onto the street. Tears streaming down my face, not daring to look back, I raced towards home.

Safe once more inside the house, but unable to tell anyone what had happened, I sobbed. Auntie Nell and Uncle Dil begged me to tell them what was wrong. 'Was it the film that scared you?' they asked. I shook my head. Clinging to Uncle Dil, I couldn't control my trembling body.

For several days, I cried off and on. Uncle Dil tried to comfort me. He held and rocked me in his strong arms, stroking my cheek with his gentle reassuring thumb, soothing me back to stillness.

Old messages played in my head, telling me I'd been violated, so why did I still feel that I had done something terrible, that it was my fault? My thoughts were reinforced by the memory that this had happened to me before. But why? I questioned myself repeatedly. I had never talked to strangers, would never have accepted sweets from someone I didn't know. Was there something wrong with me? Why had it happened again?

I couldn't tell anyone or talk about what had happened. It was far too shameful. I knew I had to bury it somewhere deep inside, then try to forget it, but I never could. It seems such things stay with you for ever, like an extra layer of skin; dirty skin.

Many years later, on a visit to Maerdy, I went with Auntie Nell to a tea party in the old Working Men's Club. It had become a community centre for the villagers.

'I've been meeting the Guild Ladies every month for years,' she said. 'We get together for tea and biscuits to celebrate birthdays and catch up on the gossip. They know all about you, Iris, and they want to meet my little evacuee. They can't believe you still come to see me.'

When she told me where we were going, my skin prickled. Long ago, I had made a vow never to go near that place again, but I went for her sake. I would never have disappointed her. An ugly building, it now stood in near-derelict condition and I found it still evoked powerful black memories. They receded, though, at the sight of the bright Sunday-best dresses worn by the Guild Ladies. They had all dressed up and someone had baked a cake.

To be there on that unexpected return visit was a gift – a gift of healing. As we sat in that dilapidated hall, with its crumbling plaster, smoke-stained walls and the shredded remains of velvet curtains, I felt as though we were sitting inside a ray of sunshine, or in the bright beam of a spotlight on a darkened stage. Within that circle of laughter and love, the darkness of the building and its memories were held back by a protective shield of colour and light.

On that same visit to Wales, I learned from an elderly villager how Maerdy had come to be widely known as 'Little Moscow' (as was the town of Chopwell, then in County Durham). This quiet little village in the mountains had more history than I would ever have guessed. The coal-mining areas of South Wales were a hotbed of Communism for many years, the party head-quarters being in the Maerdy Working Men's Club. A large Soviet flag hung outside the building. Maerdy became notorious when it became the first town in Britain to elect a Communist mayor.

Later, in one of Maerdy's bleakest times, during the miners' strike of 1984–5 when village families were starving, a delega-tion of Russian miners visited the area. They brought money and food parcels from the Soviet Union to help their striking 'brothers'. Perhaps their kindly actions were thinly veiled propa-ganda, meant as a slap in the face of the British government.

In a 2003 interview, a reporter for the *Moscow Times* quoted one of Maerdy's lifelong Communist residents. 'It's called Little Moscow, because it's full of Communists and it's fucking cold in winter,' he had said.

I also discovered that during the Second World War, the Luft-waffe had made a bombing run over South Wales in an attempt to cripple the coal-mining industry, Maerdy being a specific target. The raid was unsuccessful: not only did they fail to hit Maerdy, they also lost a number of planes. In a radio broad-cast, Germany later warned, 'We have not forgotten you, Little Moscow.'

The Soviet flag has long since gone, but perhaps more ghosts were present in the dreary old building than that of my own experience.

During my two years in Maerdy, Mum came once to see me. For days before her arrival, the Cooper household buzzed with nervous activity, in anticipation of a visit from a 'foreigner', which I learned was what the Welsh considered anyone from outside Wales.

Excited about Mum's visit, I became shy when she arrived and unsure how to act. She was prettier than I thought I remembered her, but I wasn't sure if I really remembered her at all. She and her Cockney accent were like strangers: they seemed out of place in that house. Neither the aunties nor Gran wore makeup but Mum sported bright red lipstick in the shape of a bow. I couldn't take my eyes off those perfectly shaped lips.

Mum and I slept together in Auntie and Uncle's big bed, under their puffy quilted eiderdown. I don't remember if she cuddled me but she had brought me a golliwog, and I know that I cuddled him. He wore a little red jacket and blue striped trousers, and he had hair made of thick curly wool that stuck straight out from his head. His eyes were big pearl buttons and he had a smile almost as wide as his happy black face. I wasn't sure why his face was black. I thought perhaps he was a coal miner, but the clothes were all wrong. I had never heard of *The Story of Little Black Sambo*, and my golliwog was nothing like the starving African children I had seen in pictures at Sunday school.

Mum also gave me something that became my most treasured possession. It was a tiny gold ring with my initials, 'IJ', inscribed on its heart-shaped front. Over the years, I had it enlarged several times. Then, when its shank had worn as thin as a razor blade, often cutting into my knuckle, I had new shanks applied. In a final effort to preserve 'my heart', when the heart itself was paper thin, I had the whole ring cut open and welded onto a thick, wide gold band. I wore my precious ring for more than sixty years until one day it slipped from my finger in soapy water and simply disappeared. With the help of others, I searched, not for hours but for days, to no avail. I cried uncontrollably and, yes, grieved for the one thing that connected me to my mother; the only tangible evidence of her love for me. To this day, I console myself that the loss of the ring signified it was time to break free from an often-painful childhood, but I would still give anything to have it back – anything.

Mum stayed for one night. She said she had to get back to London to take care of Dad, and to her job at the parachute factory. I took her for a walk up the mountain and showed her the sheep and the place where we picked berries. We had a little time to reconnect, but after she left, it felt as though she hadn't been there at all. I wondered if it had been a dream but my golliwog and my little gold ring told me it was real.

Dad also visited me once. I think he stayed for more than one night. He and I went by bus over the mountain to the town of Aberdare in the next valley and, oh, how proud I was, walking beside him. I thought he was the handsomest man in the world.

He took me to visit a woman friend of his, who happened to be in Aberdare visiting her mother. The woman, who I was to call Auntie May, was pretty. She had a Welsh accent but said she lived in London. I guessed her to be a friend of Dad's from work.

The three of us went on an outing to Barry Island, the closest seaside resort, but I have little recollection of the events of that day. What I do remember is that we stayed overnight with this new auntie, and that her husband was away, fighting in the war. I had to sleep with her smelly old mother in a lumpy bed and listen to her snoring and blowing off all night.

I can only guess that this auntie was another of Dad's many 'indiscretions' that fuelled Mum's jealousy throughout the sixty-two years of their marriage.

When Dad returned to London, he went with an extra piece of baggage. He took all the coal he could carry in a sack to have 'one decent fire' at home. I wanted to hold his hand as I accompanied him to Maerdy station, but he needed both hands to carry his heavy load. I hung on to the edge of his jacket and trotted along beside him, trying to keep up with his long-legged stride.

Fuel was scarce during the war, and for a considerable time after. I learned of times when Dad had had to chop up pieces of furniture to build a fire for warmth. Mum's breadboard, which she used for over sixty years, had axe marks all around the edge, evidence of her unsuccessful attempts to chop it up for firewood. I'm glad her attempts failed. That old breadboard remained a reminder throughout our lives of the hardships we had all suffered and survived.

The Welsh were a fiercely religious people at that time. There were chapels everywhere. I attended chapel every Sunday and loved to hear the singing. The Welsh are renowned for their beautiful voices and choirs, especially the all-male-voice choirs. I believe the tradition began in the coal mines, much as it did for the field slaves of America. Often the men would sing as they made their way home from the pits. The richness of a Welsh choir has never failed to bring tears to my eyes or a lump to my throat, especially when they sing the old traditional hymns.

Later, Negro spirituals became a part of their repertoires; perhaps the men related to the plight of America's black slaves, which, ironically, was exactly what the coal miners were. They, too, slaved and died, but in the bowels of the earth, bringing coal to the surface to make the bosses rich.

With coal mining no longer deemed viable, the last of Maerdy's pits closed in 1990. With no industry, the Rhondda Valley became home to thousands of unemployed, disillusioned men. With the closing of the mines, the once-happy and thriving valleys became nothing but barren slag heaps. Religion died with hope, and now only one chapel remains open in Maerdy. There is no sign of the railway station, once the pride of the valley when I arrived all those years before. The railway went, along with everything else.

On a more recent visit, I was pleased to see that vegetation had begun to hide some of the filthy, dangerous slag heaps. Others no longer existed, bulldozed away for safety's sake. I say 'dangerous' slag heaps because of the frequent slides, the most tragic of which took place on 21 October 1966. It resulted in one of the worst disasters in Britain's history.

In the nearby village of Aberfan, following heavy rainfalls, a virtual mountain of slag collapsed and slid down into the valley. The avalanche of mine detritus buried two of the village's schools, killing 144 people; 116 of the dead were children under the age of ten. Sadly, it took that terrible incident to spur the government into action, to begin ridding the valleys of those monstrous eyesores and the danger they threatened.

The mountains are now in the process of reforestation, and one of the larger mines has become a mining museum, but that is a pittance when set against what the valleys need. Crime and vandalism are rife, there is graffiti everywhere, and unemployment statistics remain among the highest in Britain.

The elderly are saddened to see forestry taking away their old berry-picking places and fewer sheep grazing on the hillsides; walking on the many ancient footpaths is no longer permitted. Yet in spite of the changes to their village and the surrounding mountains and valleys, those elderly people maintain the beautiful heart and spirit that I choose to remember.

During the two years of my evacuation, letters from home were rare. I heard news of my big brother and learned that Mum no longer worked at the parachute factory but was now a postwoman, delivering letters and parcels all over Dagenham. She sent me a photograph of herself in uniform. I thought it most strange to see her wearing what appeared to be a man's clothing.

Women were not supposed to wear trousers and a cap, were they?

That reminds me of one of my happier days. It was my birthday and I received a parcel from Auntie Iris: the first postman-delivered parcel I had ever received. I jumped up and down with excitement – it was hard to stop long enough to open it.

Auntie Iris had made me a floral satin blouse and a checked, pleated skirt. They were the first new clothes I'd had for a long time. Everyone laughed at me as I opened the parcel. I couldn't stop grinning.

'Well, there's lucky you are, Iris, they're beeyootiful,' commented Auntie Nell – they always talked like that. 'Now go on, lovely girl, show us how they look on you.' My new clothes fitted perfectly, and I did indeed feel 'beeyootiful'.

I wish it were possible to write in the same singsong way the Welsh speak, but I would have to write it as a composer writes a musical score: the language is purely lyrical.

Before my evacuation, and for some time after the war, all my clothes came from the Women's Voluntary Service (WVS). It ran a clothing distribution and exchange service. Some clothes came all the way from America and I remember how proud I was of a red plaid dress they gave me. It had a 'Made in America' label inside the collar. I hated outgrowing that dress.

People could also take clothes that their children had outgrown and exchange them for something that fitted. Mum would never let me have any of the shoes, though. She always said the same thing: 'You'll get crippled wearin' someone else's shoes, Iris. Besides, you don't know what 'orrible feet's been in 'em.'

Mum was always funny about shoes. I guess she never thought about the ''orrible bodies' that might have worn the clothes.

I was so proud of my new birthday clothes that Auntie Nell curled my hair and dressed me in the new outfit. 'We're goyen over the mountain to Aberdare to have your photo made at a real picture studio,' she said.

Mum and Dad had not seen me for more than a year, and Auntie Nell worried because I had grazed my knee the day before the 'sitting'. 'Whatever will your mam be thinkin' of me, letting you get your pretty leg hurt like that?' I loved the way she called me 'lovely girl' and my leg a 'pretty leg'. She always talked like that to her girls, and it made me feel happy.

'It's all right, Auntie. It won't show,' I told her, but it did. I remember having that photograph taken as though it was yesterday.

'You're going home, Iris,' they told me one day. Home, I thought. Where was home? Why couldn't they just leave me alone? Why did I have to go? I wanted to ask why I couldn't stay there, with them, but once again, no words would come.

Tears blurred my vision and I ran from the house and headed for my special safe place on the mountainside.

I stayed there until dark, and then, knowing I had to go home, that Auntie would be worried about me, I made my way back down the mountain. Uncle Dil was waiting at the door for me; he scooped me up in his arms. 'We've been waitin' for you to come home,' he said. 'Come and have a nice cup of tea. Everything's going to be just fine.' I hung on to him and attempted a smile, but a silent scream inside me was tearing me apart.

I have no recollection of hearing that the war had ended. Neither do I remember saying goodbye to my lovely Welsh family. Those memories lie buried in the deepest recesses of my mind, and somewhere on a mountainside in the Rhondda Valley.

I remember Dad coming for me, and walking hand in hand with him down Maerdy Road towards the railway station. Did anyone come to see me off? Did anyone cry when I left? I would like to think they did but, then, I wasn't their child, was I? In later years, I had many opportunities to ask those questions but did not. I was afraid of the answers, afraid of what the truth might be.

I only know for sure that leaving home, leaving both places I had come to call home, was the greatest pain of all.

11

The Long Journey Home

It was the summer of 1945 and I was now seven. Six years of war in Europe had ended and, at last, it was safe to bring Britain's children home; time for families to celebrate long-awaited reunions.

The journey back to London was long and confusing. I stared out of the window of one train, then another. Dad and I said little; it seemed that neither of us knew what to say to the other. He asked questions and I answered. He tried to make me laugh, but there was a knot tied somewhere between my stomach and my face. If I allowed it to come undone, I'd cry and I didn't want to. Dad pulled me close and put his arm around me but I inched away, afraid to get too close to my own father. The father I no longer knew; he felt more like a stranger to me.

I watched in silence, as mountains became gentle hills, hills gave way to rolling countryside, and villages grew into towns. At last, all green disappeared, replaced by ever-deepening shades of grey. As we neared central London, bomb damage marred the scene increasingly, and I wondered what I would find when we reached what Dad called home and I tried to remember.

'Well, that's the last train ride for us today, thank God,' Dad said, as he helped me off. Good, I thought. I'd had enough of smoky, smelly trains. He picked up the suitcase, grabbed my hand and we headed down the long platform and into the terminus. Once inside, Dad stopped and put the suitcase down.

'Now, let's see,' he said, scratching his head and looking around.

'Don't you know which way to go, Dad?' I asked.

'Of course I do, silly. Come on. This way.' And off he marched again, with me trotting beside him, like a puppy. It wasn't easy for me to keep up with him: I had to take two steps to every one of his.

'We're going the wrong way, Dad,' I said, pulling on his coat.

'No, we ain't,' he said, and kept on walking. He didn't even look at me.

'Dad, Dad, over there, look it says "Way Out". We're going the wrong way.'

'Well, I'll be blowed. If you hadn't seen that sign, we'd be on our way back to Wales now, wouldn't we?' He grinned down at me.

'Yeah,' I said, and for the first time since leaving Maerdy, my face relaxed into a cautious smile.

Outside the station, shock soon replaced my new sense of relief. Here was my first close-up look at London's bombed-out buildings. It was terrible. I remembered seeing bomb damage before my evacuation but had no idea of the devastation that had followed.

Although most streets were now clear, there remained mountains of bricks, timber and other debris all around, and 'DANGER – KEEP OUT' signs hung on barricaded sites. As we passed the ruins of a church, sadness gripped me. All that remained were sections of the outer walls, and just one corner of its bell tower. What had once been the sanctuary was now nothing but blackened rubble from which the charred remains of massive wooden beams protruded. As I gazed up at the dark, angular shapes silhouetted against the sky, they reminded me of an enormous black skeletal hand, pointing towards Heaven, and I wondered if God could see it too.

'Are we nearly there, Dad?' I asked, as we walked on, along London's unfamiliar streets.

'Just about,' he replied. 'It's not far now.' I hoped he was telling the truth: my legs were beginning to ache and I was hungry and tired. Then, just when I thought I could go no further, Dad stopped.

'You can have a little rest, Iris. Here's our bus stop. It won't be long now. I don't know about you, but I'm dying for a cup of tea.'

'Me too,' I replied, as I perched myself on the suitcase, then read the sign on each bus as it approached.

'What's the number of our bus, Dad?' I asked.

He told me a number, which I no longer remember, then added, 'You'll know it when you see "Dagenham" on the front, but don't worry, mate, we'll get there.'

It had been a long day and all I wanted was to get home, but at that moment, home seemed strangely remote.

'Here it comes,' Dad said, as he nudged me off the suitcase. 'Hold on to me jacket when the bus stops so I can 'ave a free 'and to get on.'

I looked up at the sign on the bus. It said 'DAGENHAM', and that was when I knew we really were almost there. Dagenham was where my family lived, and I kept saying it over and over in my head, adding the name of the county, just as I had written it on letters: Dagenham, Essex; Dagenham, Essex; Dagenham, Essex.

We boarded the big red double-decker bus, found two seats and sat down, each letting out a sigh of relief.

'Fares, please, fares, please,' sang out the conductor, as he passed down the aisle.

'One and a half to Martin's Corner,' said Dad.

'Thruppence, please, mate,' replied the conductor. Dad handed him three pennies. *Ka-ching, ka-ching*, went the ticket machine, as the conductor cranked the handle on its side. Tickets appeared, as if by magic, from the front. Dad handed them to me.

I looked down at the two pink pieces of paper. One said '2*d*', the other '1*d*'. Twopence for Dad and a penny for me. Hmm, I thought, that means it won't be a long journey.

I must have dozed off because it seemed we had just sat down when I heard someone shouting, 'Next stop, Martin's Corner.'

'That's us,' Dad said, as he grabbed the suitcase and my hand. 'Thanks, mate,' he called to the conductor, as we jumped from the bus.

'Welcome home, young lady,' shouted back the conductor, as the bus pulled away.

'How did he know, Dad?' I asked.

'I'm sure he's seen lots of kiddies coming home lately, Iris,' he replied, as he pulled his handkerchief from his coat pocket and wiped his eyes. He sniffed, stuffed the damp handkerchief back into his pocket and said, in a funny, quivery voice, 'Come on, let's go home.'

As we walked away from the bus stop, Dad tightened his grip on my hand. It should have felt good, but then everything began to feel like a strange dream. It felt as though my head and body were a balloon and that my hand and arm were the string. My father's hand, wrapped around mine, was the only thing keeping me on the ground; I was afraid that if he let me go I'd fly away.

Perhaps I was just tired, but tired had never felt like that before. I closed my eyes and shook my head, hoping the feeling would go away. When I reopened my eyes, I was dizzy, but began to feel anchored in the real world again.

Crossing the road at Martin's Corner, I looked around at all the shuttered shops. They were strangely familiar, and suddenly I began to remember. This was where Mum had done her shopping.

As I absorbed the scene, my throat tightened in that telltale warning and I began to cry. Dad stopped walking and crouched beside me. 'What's wrong, Iris? Do you feel sick? Do you want me to carry you?' I buried my head in his bony shoulder and sobbed.

'No, Dad, I'm crying because Mum's shops ain't open any more. Why did the Germans do that?' He threw his arms around me, and laughed aloud.

'You silly twerp, the shops are shut because it's Sunday.'

'Is it?' I sobbed. 'Are you sure?'

'Yes, of course I'm sure. If it wasn't, I'd be at work, wouldn't I?' Dad reached into his pocket and, for the second time in ten minutes, pulled out his rumpled handkerchief. 'Here, blow yer nose, wipe yer eyes and stop worryin'.'

'Thanks, Dad,' I said. Then, after handing back his soggy, stained hanky, I took his hand and we resumed walking. I wanted to tell him I was tired, but I was seven years old and seven-year-olds didn't let their dads carry them, did they?

As we rounded the last corner and entered our little street, I was happy to see that Carey Road had survived the war unscathed. According to Dad, one small bomb had fallen into a neighbour's back garden but had failed to detonate. Disarmed and removed safely, it had left nothing but a hole where their garden shed had once stood.

Dad unlatched the gate, and we walked up the path to 'our house'; the house I was now beginning to remember.

'Here we are, then, home at last,' Dad said. He released my hand. 'Go on,' he urged, giving me an encouraging shove, and I ventured through the open front door.

There in the front room sat my family, including my grandparents. I looked from face to face, but tears blurred my vision. I knuckled my eyes and blinked hard. Everyone was grinning, except me: my face had frozen.

I wanted to run and hide, but my safe place was far away. I had dreamed of this moment, but now that it had arrived, I was frightened. My family were like strangers.

Were there hugs and kisses? I don't remember any. Mum, who looked the same as I remembered, now sat in a straight-backed chair, her hands clasped in her lap and red-bow lips slightly undone – she had never been the cuddly type.

Time seemed to stand still. Then Nan reached out and patted my arm. 'Don't she look healthy?' she said, to no one in particular.

'It's lovely to have you kiddies home,' said Granddad, dabbing his eyes with a red-spotted handkerchief.

'Look, here's Peter, your brother,' said Dad, pushing me towards him. 'He came home yesterday.'

''Ello,' we said at the same time, then quickly looked away.

So this is my big brother, I thought. I'd written to him once, and sent him sixpence, but he hadn't written back. He looked nothing like the one old photograph I had of him. Now eleven years old, he had grown tall and his face had changed.

When at last I felt comfortable enough to speak and answer questions, everyone laughed at me and Peter tried to mimic me. Apparently, I had come home from Wales with a Welsh accent.

After a while, Mum and Nan brought out fish-paste sandwiches, rock cakes with currants in, and a steaming pot of tea. We drew our chairs up to the table and tucked in. It was getting late and I was tired after a long day of travelling. The food, hot sweet tea and smiling faces comforted me.

When we had finished eating, Dad ushered me out of the front room. He was grinning from ear to ear.

'I've got a surprise for you,' he said, as we walked into the kitchen.

'Can't it wait till tomorrow, Ted? She's tired and probably wants to go to bed,' Mum said. She was standing at the kitchen sink, washing dishes. Dad ignored her. I glanced at her: she looked as if she was about to cry. Now what? I thought, as we stepped out into the garden.

There on the lawn stood my surprise. Dad had built me a swing from steel pipe, which I later learned he had nicked from work. It was a beauty. He picked me up, sat me on the wooden seat and started pushing me. Higher and higher I went, and in the deepening darkness, I could see over the tall fence next door into the surrounding back gardens. I remembered having friends here and wondered if they still lived in the same houses, if they, too, had just returned from faraway places. My stomach felt queasy, but suddenly it felt good to be home. Then my mind wandered back to Maerdy. I could hardly wait to tell everyone there about my new swing.

VE Day and the Aftermath of War

Soon after our homecoming, the air began to buzz with excitement. Every street in every town in Britain was planning a victory party and Carey Road was no exception. People began hauling junk of all descriptions into the middle of the roads; they were building bonfires. Men, women and children were chopping up old furniture, tearing down derelict sheds and old fences, adding anything they could find to the growing piles. Effigies of Hitler appeared, to be placed on top of the fires. I thought watching him burn would be the best part of the celebrations.

Later, people brought chairs and tables into the streets. Flags and banners flew from every window, fence and lamp post. A stage, festooned with lights and Union flags, went up at the end of our road. Someone rolled a piano out into the street; accordions and other musical instruments appeared. There was sure to be a good old knees-up that night.

The women were responsible for providing food; they must have used up a month's coupons, but in spite of rationing and scant supplies, there was plenty to eat at the party. Piles of sandwiches appeared, as well as fairy cakes, sponge cakes, jellies and blancmanges. There was lemonade for the children and, of course, plenty of beer for the adults.

That celebration was like nothing I have ever experienced since. Everyone was in the streets and their joy was palpable. After hearing a few brief speeches, we sang 'God Save The King', then sat around the tables to enjoy the feast, all wearing traditional paper party hats and waving little Union flags. Later, with tables cleared and moved off to the sides, the real party began, and what a party it was. The singing and dancing went on all night, and when the leaping flames of bonfires engulfed Hitler's likeness, we cheered and hugged each other. The air was thick with smoke. No one seemed worried about where the sparks might land: they were too busy enjoying the long-awaited celebration. People mounted the stage and performed their party pieces, but I remember one performance in particular.

With a great deal of help, an enormous woman climbed on to the stage. She belted out 'You Are My Sunshine', kicking her fat legs up as she sang, then suddenly she stopped, did a half-turn and fell off the stage. She was dead drunk and it took four men to carry her away. Everyone, including me, laughed and applauded.

'Crikey,' said Mum. 'We shouldn't laugh. The silly cow might be dead.'

'Well, at least she woulda died happy,' someone else chimed in, and we all laughed some more.

I don't remember how the party ended but I do remember Mum dragging me into the house and upstairs when I refused to leave. She sat on the top stair, turned me over her knee and smacked my bottom, hard. At that moment, I hated her for spoiling everything.

The next morning the streets were a mess, and stayed that way for several days, the air still thick with the smell of beer and bonfire smoke. Mum mumbled something about everyone being hung-over, whatever that meant.

When we returned to school, each child received a beaker, to commemorate the end of the war, and a letter from the King. I remember thinking how nice it was of him to write to us all when he was so busy.

The war had ended, but the tough times were not over. There were terrible shortages of almost everything. We were underfed and poorly clothed, and I can still see Dad coming down the road one day, pushing an old sewing machine ahead of him – the squeaking of its small iron wheels had brought me running to the front window. God only knows how far he had pushed it. This was something else he had magically acquired.

He taught himself how to sew on that old treadle machine, then made Peter and me winter coats out of army blankets. We still laugh about those coats. They were so stiff they stood up on their own in the corner. Dad was one of many people who tried making clothes out of parachute silk, but that didn't prove at all successful. If the silk got wet, it became transparent, which proved disastrous for one of Mum's friends. She had used it to make herself a swimming costume.

'Wish I'd been there,' chuckled Dad.

Mum shook her head. 'Men,' she muttered, followed by the usual tut-tut-tut of disapproval.

The next thing Dad tried involved a large bundle of leather scraps. Well, he said they were scraps, but they looked like complete animal skins to me.

'Where'd you get that, Dad?'

'Nosy, ain't you?' was all he offered in reply.

Along with the leather, which smelt disgusting, he had an enormous pair of scissors called shears, a heavy-duty hole-punch, and skeins of what he called 'thonging', which looked like plastic or leather string.

'Whatcha gonna do with all that stuff, Dad?'

'I'm gonna make women's handbags and sell 'em at work,' he said. 'They can't buy leather bags nowadays so I bet they'll sell as fast as I can make 'em.'

'How'd you learn how to do it, Dad?'

'I took Mum's old one apart and made a pattern out of it. She wasn't 'alf cross, but I'll soon 'ave a new one for her, don't worry.' And, of course, he did.

I watched him cut the shapes out of the leather. Next, and grunting with each squeeze of the punch, he made holes around the edge of each piece, then 'sewed' them together with thonging and finally attached the handles with a metal rivet.

'There,' he'd say, each time he finished one. 'Another happy woman.'

He'd been right too: the handbags sold as fast as he could make them – the women where he worked went crazy for them. Then the supply of leather ran out and his handbag-making days were over, but his giant shears and the hole-punch stayed in his toolbox for as long as I can remember, and I can still picture him, hunched over, making his precious black-market bags.

The next thing Dad made on the side was hats, but that endeavour was even more short-lived. Again, he made his own pattern, this time copying the design from a picture in the newspaper. I think it was his mother, Nanny Jones, who had given him an old black astrakhan coat. Astrakhan, I learned, was a soft curly fur that came from unborn lambs. It was very popular in its day, but the government banned its use in later years.

The little fur hats were, as I recall, similar to the caps worn by American soldiers, and considered very smart. Dad managed to get quite a few of his 'high-fashion' hats out of the old coat, and he sold them quickly, again to the girls at work.

'I wish that coat had come from a circus Fat Lady,' he said. 'I coulda got a few more hats out of it. I've still got one woman who's dyin' for one.'

'Well, don't you be lookin' at my hat, Edward. You ain't sellin' that one,' said Mum. 'You just find yerself another old fur coat to cut up.' She later told me she'd had to hide it to stop Dad nicking it.

At that time, Dad was able to buy pieces of shoe leather, and he repaired all of our shoes. However, the time came when Peter's could no longer be patched up. The only shoes Mum could get for him were wooden clogs, the type worn by mill workers. I wanted clogs too: I liked the sound they made when you walked, like a horse coming down the street: clip clop, clip clop. Mum wouldn't let me have them. 'They'd be bad for your feet,' she said. Not only was I disappointed, but I also thought it unfair that she allowed Peter to have bad feet and not me.

Dad went back to his old job soon after the war ended; I think he worked at a company called May & Baker but I don't remember what he did there. As we sat by the fire in the evenings, he began telling us about his work at the arsenal and some of his experiences there. We were fascinated to hear of all his adventures, especially the story of him being a hero when he helped catch a spy. One thing in particular piqued our interest: his journey to work each day, and how it involved crossing the River Thames on the Woolwich Ferry.

'Please, Dad, will you take us for a ride on the ferry one day?' I begged.

'I suppose I could. Yus, I think we could afford that. The ferry's free,' he said, with a chuckle. 'As soon as I have enough for the bus fare, we'll go.'

I'm not sure how long it took him to save up, but he did eventually take us to London, where we rode on the free ferry. It wasn't much of a ride, but the fact that we were with our dad, on a boat, crossing the River Thames, made it a grand adventure.

We also learned something of the Woolwich Ferry's history. In one form or another, it has transported people, livestock and traffic across the Thames for hundreds of years, the earliest records being from 1308 when Woolwich was just a fishing village.

Our day out with Dad was fun. He even took us on another bus ride, right into London, where the enormity of the bomb damage around the dock areas was shocking. Six years of war had changed London's skyline, but there, through the watery sunlight, we could see the domed outline of St Paul's Cathedral.

'There you are,' Dad said, pointing. 'The blighters didn't get that, did they?'

'How come the Germans didn't bomb it, Dad?' asked Peter.

'Dunno,' he replied. 'It did get some damage but maybe they were afraid to bomb it because of God and everything.'

'Oh,' we said, nodding in apparent understanding.

Mum kept working for a while after our return home. She was still delivering mail. I believe she had to, until more ex-servicemen re-entered the workforce. She hated houses with dogs. She'd been deathly afraid of them since she had been bitten by one some years earlier.

She also related a number of funny incidents, one of which happened during the war, just as she was putting mail through someone's letterbox.

At that exact moment, a bomb exploded nearby and the blast blew Mum and the front door into the resident's hallway. Down the stairs flew the lady-of-the-house.

'What the bloody 'ell did you do that for?' she shouted at poor Mum, who was struggling to her feet and brushing broken glass and plaster dust off herself.

'Well, of all the cheek,' said Mum. 'You can just get your own letters now. They're underneath your bloody door.'

There was something satisfying about that story: our mum had actually stood up for herself, and had used a swear word. Peter and I curled up with laughter, especially since Mum looked very serious as she told us about it.

During all that time, Mum had to queue up at the butcher's, sometimes for hours, just to get a marrowbone, which she would boil all day or overnight.

'It gets all the goodness out of it,' she informed us. She'd add a few vegetables to the broth and make soup. She still made those horrible suet puddings too, with a few bits of fatty bacon and some chopped cabbage rolled into it. 'Well,' she'd say, 'it makes a meal, don't it?' Yes, it did, but I still hated it.

For some time after the war, the government tried to get people to eat whale meat. We tried it once, and once was enough. As I recall, it was very chewy, had a strange colour, and although it sort of tasted like meat, it also sort of tasted a bit fishy. The fact is, it was terrible. I have talked to people who liked whale meat, but perhaps that had more do with how it was cooked, or disguised.

I thought of my Welsh family almost every day. I missed having good food and being well cared-for. I was back to having only one bath a week, and no one tucked me in at night or said prayers with me. I missed many things I had come to take for granted in Maerdy, and still felt unsure of who my parents really were . . . or was it that I was unsure of who I wanted them to be? I did like watching Dad work, but other than that, I wasn't sure if I felt at home there, or if I was wanted even. Mum sometimes acted as though she didn't know what to do with Peter and me. I thought perhaps she wasn't used to or didn't like having children around. On several occasions, I asked her when I could go to visit the Coopers in Maerdy. It seemed to upset her, so I stopped asking. I kept thinking that I might get a letter from Wales, but I didn't – at least, not for some time. I guessed that they, too, had become used to me not being there.

I had only lived away for two years, yet it seemed a lifetime. Peter had been away for five or six years, and must have felt even more estranged than I did.

Those feelings stayed with me for many years. I battled with a sense of not belonging, of being unwanted, and had relationship and separation issues throughout my life. Peter remained bitter about his terrible experiences, and I know he never truly healed.

13

An Assortment of Aunties

Around the time of the great VE Day celebrations, I walked into our front room one day and found we had a visitor. It was Dad's sister, Rose, whom I had never heard of before. I learned that she would be staying with us until Dad could make alternative arrangements for her.

Apparently, Auntie Rose had come to us directly from what Dad called 'the loony bin'. Her husband had had her committed to it after she'd knocked him unconscious with a frying-pan. Dad hastened to assure us that she had hit him in self-defence after putting up with years of drunken abuse from him. The husband had recently died and it was only then that Dad was able to obtain her release.

Auntie Rose shared my bedroom, sleeping in Peter's bed while he slept on the floor in Mum and Dad's room. Thankful for the temporary respite from Peter and his bogeyman stories, I was now apprehensive but intrigued by the mysterious aunt, who had appeared out of nowhere and smelt of mothballs.

At night, when she thought I was asleep, I'd watch her from under the covers. Wearing a voluminous white cotton nightdress, she'd sit on the end of her bed and release her hair from its prison-like bun. Then, using an ornate tortoiseshell comb, she'd brush her thick, wavy black hair, until it fell about her shoulders and down to her waist, like a silken cloak. There, silhouetted against the moonlit window, she looked ghost-like. Sometimes in the night, I'd hear her sniffing and know she was crying. I wondered what was making her sad. I wanted to talk to her, to ask her questions, to hold her hand, but I dared not.

Her presence in our house was more sensed than felt. She appeared to float from room to room as she helped Mum with a few household chores. Her mind seemed to be somewhere else. When she wasn't helping Mum, she'd sit gazing out of the window, or on a chair in the garden, just looking. I would watch her, feeling somehow connected to her sadness.

Secretly observing her one day, I had the odd feeling that if I crawled under her long black skirt I would become one with her in our mutual loneliness and sense of abandonment. I couldn't have put words to it then, but it was some kind of knowing.

She wasn't with us for long. I'm sure she knew we didn't have room for her, but I missed her when she was gone. I missed that shared emptiness, the emptiness where somehow we had connected.

Shortly after Auntie Rose left us, and family life had settled down again, Mum told me some good news.

'Auntie Iris and Uncle Walter have moved back to London. They're not livin' in Scotland any more and she's invited you to come and stay with her while Uncle Walter's away working. Do you wanna go, Iree?' Did I? What a silly question. Of course I wanted to go. I was elated.

'Yes, please, Mum,' I replied, perhaps a little too enthusiastically.

'Yeah, I thought you would. You can't wait to get out of here, can you?' Mum said. Sadly, she was right. 'She's comin' to get you tomorrow, so make sure you've got clean knickers on.'

'Your mum and her toffee-nosed sister are as different as chalk and cheese,' Dad used to say, and he was right.

To begin with, Mum was short, chubby and fair. Her sister was tall, slender and dark. Mum was not a great housekeeper or cook; Auntie Iris was house-proud and an excellent cook. Mum paid little attention to me, while my beloved aunt was all about attention. I know now that life circumstances had much to do with their differences, but how would a child of eight, nine or ten discern such things?

For me, the 'self-centred kid', it was about comfort, attention, feelings and pride, plus all the little things in between. Loyalty can sometimes be lost when such basics come into play in a child's life. Yes, Mum was right: I couldn't wait to go home with her sister.

My aunt's house was always sparkling clean. It smelt of lavender furniture polish. She used real bone-china dishes and linen napkins at meals. There were books of every description at my disposal. Sometimes she even read to me. In addition, when Uncle Walter was working away from home, she allowed me to sleep with her. She used hand-embroidered pillowcases on her sweet-smelling bed, and sleeping there, with her, made me feel special. I felt like a princess as I snuggled down under the soft pink woollen blankets and the puffy eiderdown. Our blankets at home were dark brown, probably army surplus, coarse and stiff.

Auntie Iris had, I'd heard, always enjoyed a more exciting social life than Mum had. For me, the primary evidence of that were the beautiful evening gowns, and the real fur coat in her wardrobe. 'Please, Auntie, can I see your party dresses?' I'd ask, each time I stayed with her.

She would laugh. 'Of course you can, silly, don't you ever get tired of looking at those old things?'

How could I? Grinning from ear to ear, my response was always the same. 'Nope, they're the most beautiful dresses in the world.'

She'd take my hand, and together we'd run up the stairs to her bedroom, to the wardrobe with its delicious contents.

'There,' she'd say. 'Would you like me to take them out?'

'Yes, please, Auntie.' With a swish, she'd swirl them out of their scented hiding place and lay them on her bed. Then she'd tell me the stories of each special occasion she had attended, wearing one of the elegant gowns.

I loved the look, feel and smell of those magical dresses, and loved to bury my face in the softness of the fur coat. I'd close my eyes and imagine how it might feel to wear such elegant clothing, and a real fur coat. My favourite was a floor-length, lipstick-red georgette gown with long puffed sleeves. It had tiny pearl buttons down the back and at the cuffs, and yards of material in the skirt. She promised it would be mine some day, when I was big enough to wear it. I had dreams of waltzing around a dance-floor in my diaphanous gown, while crowds of people gasped at the very sight of me.

Many years later, I asked her about it. 'What happened to my red dress, Auntie?' At first, she didn't know what I was talking about, but after a while, she remembered.

'Oh, my Lord, fancy you remembering that. I don't know what happened to it, Iris. I probably gave it away to a church jumble sale.'

I was sad that she had forgotten my love of the red dress and her promise that I should have it. From that day on, I understood the importance of remembering promises made to children; perhaps it has something to do with validating a person's worth. To me, and my 'child-within', she had forgotten her promise, but she had also forgotten me and the happy times we had spent together.

Another of her belongings I coveted was the tiny gold watch she always wore. I thought it elegant, with its mother-of-pearl face and fine gold mesh band. She promised to leave it to me in her will, that it would be mine when she died. Another promise I never forgot.

Again, many years later, I confessed to her that I had sometimes wished she'd hurry up and die. Morbid perhaps, but innocent; I was simply anxious to receive my inheritance. She and I shared a good laugh about that. She knew how much I loved her. I am equally sure she never guessed how much I had wanted that watch, all those years before.

After her death, I told my cousin Robin, her second son, the story of his mother's gold watch. He disappeared into the attic for a while and emerged eventually with a box that contained some of her things. He opened it, and there it was, exactly as I remembered it.

'Would you still like to have it?' he asked.

'Yes, I would, Robin, very much. You'll never know the memories it holds for me.'

Auntie Iris had given birth to Robin quite late in life. He'd had no idea that I had spent so much time with his mother before his arrival.

That little mother-of-pearl watch-face remains a sweet reminder of the special relationship I had with my mother's sister, and of the night I curled up next to her in bed and tapped her on the shoulder. 'Auntie, may I please call you Mummy?' I whispered. She turned to face me.

'I suppose you could,' she replied hesitantly. 'But only while you're here. We mustn't let your mum find out, Iris. It would hurt her feelings terribly.'

How I wished I had a mother like her, someone who paid attention to me, who bathed me every night as they had in Wales, gave me little presents, read stories to me and took me to special places. She even held my hand tight, without me having to ask.

After spending an idyllic week, with Auntie Iris spoiling me, it was time for me to go home. I didn't want to go, but knew I had to.

I had no idea what a big surprise lay in store for me.

14

Lindsey Road and My Own Bedroom

My visit to Auntie Iris was over. The day I'd dreaded had arrived. My beloved aunt told me there was a surprise waiting for me at home, which made leaving her a little less painful. Holding her hand, chattering away and skipping along, I failed to notice that we were in unfamiliar territory.

'Here we are,' she announced, and we stopped. I glanced about me. Nothing was familiar. We were standing at the gate to a house I had never seen before, and I was sure she had made a mistake.

'Whose house is this, Auntie? I thought you were taking me home.'

'You'll soon see,' she said, and gave my hand a squeeze.

We walked up the path and Auntie Iris reached for the knocker, *tap tap tap*. Footsteps echoed on the other side of the door. I clung to my aunt's hand, and remained half hidden behind her. The door swung open.

'It's about time,' said Mum, a big smile creasing her face. 'This is our new house, Iris. We moved while you was away. Come on in. I've just made a fresh pot of tea.' Auntie Iris was grinning too; they both looked down at me, expectantly.

'Are you surprised, Iris?' asked Auntie Iris. I wanted to answer but the ache in my throat gave way to tears.

'I thought you were sending me away again,' I said between sobs.

'Aw,' they chorused.

Mum and Dad had moved from 10 Carey Road to 62 Lindsey

Road, also in Dagenham, but it seemed a world away from our old home. I later discovered we had only moved a mile or so. The strangest thing was that there was no bomb damage here. I guess it had not been in the Luftwaffe's flight path. In that respect, it really was another world.

The war had been over for little more than a year, yet much had happened in that time. Memories of it were fading – or, at least, becoming buried, now that we lived in a different house on a different street. Maybe it was easier to forget, without the daily reminders of destruction around us. We now lived closer to Nan and Granddad. I liked that idea; we all did.

Our new house, again let to us by the London County Council, was odd. The kitchen was at the front. Kitchens were supposed to be at the back of the house, weren't they? But Mum liked that: it meant she could see out to the street while working at the sink. She could keep an eye on the neighbours' comings and goings and see what we children were up to, providing we stayed close to the house. Of course, if we were doing something we shouldn't, we made sure we were well out of window range. She would have killed me if she'd seen me sitting on the kerb, near the drain, where 'dirty old men spit', and eating pilfered dog biscuits with my new friends.

This house, as the last, had a dark pebbledash finish. Other than that, it was different. The front door was at the side, and it had no covered porch. It was a semi-detached house, while our previous home had been in a terrace.

We shared a front gate and pathway with the house next door, the one that was not attached to ours. Hence, our side-facing front doors faced one another. This arrangement of doors and knockers provided endless entertainment for us children. We'd tie the knockers together across the path, then knock on one door and run away. When the occupant of the first house opened their door, it pulled the string and knocked on the facing door. And there they'd be, pulling at each other's doors while we hid in the bushes, laughing and listening to them swearing and yelling.

'Them little blighters, I'll 'ave their guts fer garters if I ever catches 'em.' They'd be promising all kinds of cruel punishment to us 'little sods'. The funniest threat was when one old bloke screeched at us, 'I'll kick yer arse'ole up between yer shoulder blades.' Did the threats deter us? No, they never did. I believe that game was called Knock Down Ginger, but for the life of me, I can't imagine why.

The best difference between this house and the last was that it had three bedrooms. The time had come for Peter and me to have separate rooms – hooray!

Mine was tiny. Called the box-room, it was also the coldest room in the house. It was above the staircase and on the corner of the house so it received the worst of the cold wind. Most of the time, I had to wear a cardigan and socks to bed, and sometimes even a woolly hat.

With no toilet upstairs, we had to take a bucket up with us each night. Placed on the landing, it saved us having to go downstairs in the dark. Mum said it was easier emptying one bucket rather than three 'gazunders', which was what she called chamber pots.

'You know,' she explained, with a chuckle. 'It "gazunder" the bed.'

Another nickname for chamber pots was 'Jerries'. Why? Because Londoners called German soldiers Jerries, and chamber pots looked like German soldiers' helmets, if you turned them upside down, which, of course, you wouldn't, especially if they were full. It's little wonder people think the English language is strange.

I learned how to wee in the bucket without making too much sound; it embarrassed me to think someone might hear me. The men didn't care who heard them. It sounded like a waterfall out there on the landing, and they splashed wee all over the floorboards.

In this house, the kitchen walls were again bare brick, but this time Dad painted them light yellow instead of dark green. Although the room wasn't much bigger than our previous kitchen, it seemed enormous, with a larger window and a bright colour.

I knew the kitchen was a little bigger because of the old table. Once placed against the wall by necessity, it now sat in the middle of the room and we could walk all around it. The rest of the furniture remained much the same, too. However, Dad again surprised us with his know-how. He reupholstered our old couch and armchairs with off-white canvas, obtained from some dubious source, I'm sure. It made the room, with its new linoleum-covered floor, look very posh. There was also enough space in the living room for a dining-room suite.

Our 'new' suite was in fact second-hand. It had an extendable table, six chairs, with brown leatherette seats, and a sideboard. The sideboard had a green felt-lined cutlery drawer and a wine cupboard, both of which we used for storing junk and Dad's tools. We had little cutlery and Christmas was the only time a bottle of wine appeared in the house.

A cast-iron combination fireplace-stove was set in the living-room wall. The fireplace, again our only source of heat, had a boiler built in behind it to heat water for the kitchen and bathroom. If no fire was burning, there would be no heat or hot water. When the fire was burning, a drying rack, draped with wet laundry, usually obscured it. Again, this made for a damp house, causing rust to invade the surface of the iron stove, and once more, Mum had the chore of keeping it under control. I can still see her kneeling on the floor, scrubbing first with a wire brush to remove the rust and then, after applying black-lead polish, she'd buff it with a soft brush to make it shine. I can also hear her muttering unrepeatable words under her breath. Mum was not fond of that stove.

We ate most of our meals at the little table in the kitchen, but on Sundays, we had dinner and tea at the dining-room table, which was also where Dad now did some of his odd jobs, one of which was repairing radios. Mum finally drew the line, however, when he tried repairing our shoes on 'her' table.

'Oh, no, you don't, Edward, not on me nice new table. You just find yourself somewhere else to do your dirty work.' She didn't mind him repairing radios on her table, 'Cos you don't use no bloody hammer to mend a wireless,' she said.

Later, after Dad dug up the air-raid shelter, he used the sheets of corrugated steel to build a workshop in the back garden. It was a beauty. It had tool racks and a workbench where he could do his odd jobs, including shoe repairs, safely. Dad removed his tools and other 'clobber', as Mum called it, from the kitchen and the sideboard and at last the furniture was safe from 'that bloody hammer'.

I loved spending time with Dad in his workshop. Perhaps it was because he was away from home so much. I also loved the smells of wood, paint and oil, and of him. When he was at home, I was his shadow. Full of questions and curiosity, I'd watch and praise everything he did. He always took time to explain things to me.

'She wants to know the ins and outs of a cat's behind, she does,' Mum used to say. She was always too busy to talk to me and often became impatient if I asked too many questions.

I'd watch Dad for hours as he built, cleaned or repaired things. We'd chat endlessly and I was in awe of all the things he could do. In fact, I believed there was nothing he could not do.

'He's a clever old cock but he can't lay an egg,' was another of Mum's regular comments. I wasn't sure what that meant but people always laughed when she said it.

One day, while rummaging around in his workshop, I found some wedge-shaped pieces of wood. They looked like the heels on women's wedge shoes. I brought them and my school shoes to Dad.

'Will you put these on me shoes, Dad, so's they look like wedges?' He shook his head as if I was crazy, and his answer shocked me.

'Don't be daft. You can't put different heels on shoes.'

'Why not, Dad? Why can't you?' I whined.

'Well, first of all you'd 'ave nails stickin' up in your feet, wouldn't you, and you'd be fallin' all over the place and breakin' yer flippin' neck because they'd be all wobbly, wouldn't they? No, it can't be done, sorry, love.'

'Could you just try, Dad, please?'

'It'd ruin your shoes,' he said, 'and your mum would shoot both of us. You'll have to wait till you grow up to get wedges, Iris. Sorry.'

I'm not sure I believed him. I still thought my dad could do anything if he really wanted to, even if he couldn't lay an egg.

The image of that dining-room table conjures many memories. One such is of our Sunday dinners where there was always a jug of water in the middle of the table, but only one glass, which we shared. Did we own just one glass? I don't know. If that was the case, I suppose we could have used jam-jars, as other people did in those days. Then again, perhaps Mum's pride was involved. Maybe she would rather use one proper glass than stoop to jam-jars. Also, you got a penny back if you returned the jars to the shop and, as every child hears at some time in their life, 'A penny saved is a penny earned', or, 'Every penny counts', or then again, 'You take care of your pennies and the pounds will take care of themselves.' I never did understand all those adult sayings but I do remember how I rolled my eyes in boredom every time I heard them.

Sometimes on Sundays we'd have dessert, 'afters'. When we did, it was invariably stewed prunes and custard. When Mum was able to get dried fruit, we considered it a treat. Prunes were always a forum for sibling rivalry and squabbling at our house. Mum had to be careful how many prunes she gave to each of us. When we'd finished eating, Peter and I always counted our prune stones. God forbid Mum should ever miscount when doling them out.

'Tinker, tailor, soldier, sailor, rich man, poor man, beggar man, thief,' we'd chant. If we didn't come out with the same profession, we'd know that one of us had had more than the other. Poor Mum.

'Stop muckin' about, you two,' she'd say. 'I counted the bloomin' prunes. One of 'em didn't have no stone in it.'

Prunes and custard was good, but for me, the most memorable 'afters' I ever ate was when the greengrocer received his first delivery of bananas since the war. According to Mum, the queue outside his shop went down one street and halfway down the next. When she got her ration of two bananas it meant we each got a half. Peter and I had a contest to see who could make the most sandwiches out of half a banana. Instead of slicing it, we scraped it and spread it on the bread, as you would jam. I don't recall how many sandwiches we made, but it was a lot, and we both felt a bit sick afterwards.

Sunday afternoons were also when Mum and Dad took their dreaded naps. That meant we had to be quiet; we couldn't even have the wireless on. I hated having to sit in that dark, silent living room, listening to the two of them snoring. How I wished they'd go back to taking their naps in bed.

Finally, relief would come. The winkle man coming down the street was the sound of reprieve. He came every Sunday afternoon, pushing his big green flatbed wheelbarrow on its noisy iron wheels, the barrow piled high with boxes of fresh seafood.

'Cockles and winkles. Come and get yer lovely fresh cockles. Cockles and mussels, fresh off the boat. Just up from Southend,' he'd sing out, in his rich Cockney accent – Southend pronounced 'Sarfend'.

Southend, the nearest seaside town to London, is located at the mouth of the River Thames where it flows into the North Sea. With its large amusement park, called the Kursaal, its famous pier and not-so-famous beach, Londoners have always gone there on day trips; I suppose you could call it the Cockneys' Riviera.

Mum would be the first to jump up from her snooze. She'd grab her handbag, scoop out some money and send us to buy our Sunday-evening meal of cockles and winkles. The winkle man sold his wares by the pint and we had to provide our own containers. I loved the smells that wafted from that old green wheelbarrow; they made my mouth water. Sometimes, if money permitted, Mum might also buy a pint of prawns, considered a special treat.

Teatime would find us sitting around the table, each with a plate and a straight pin. In the middle of the table there would be a mountain of bread and margarine and the bowls of seafood. With the pin, we picked the little hard covering, 'the eye', off the end of the winkle shell, then dug out the black worm-like winkle. We always ate them smothered with malt vinegar and pepper. Mum and Dad would sometimes buy themselves a few whelks, mussels or jellied eels, but those slimy things, considered adult fare, were too expensive to feed to children. Anyway, I could never have eaten whelks: they still reminded me of that 'thing' Mr Easy used to wave at me.

We all loved those tiny delicious crustaceans. However,

I'm not sure I could eat them today. Perhaps I could, if I closed my eyes and didn't have to look at them.

It was heaven having my own bedroom. It may have been small and freezing cold, but it was mine. Life was good, with no big brother to plague me. However, his evil nature prevailed. He would sneak into my bedroom ahead of me, hide under my bed and then, after I'd climbed in and the light was off, he'd begin his ghoulish moaning, and he'd tug on the edge of my blanket while fear paralysed me.

From an early age, he had instilled in me a fear of monsters in cupboards and under beds. Certain that something was about to get me, but unable to shout for help, I would lie there, crying softly, my head buried under the covers.

Thankfully, I discovered it was Peter and not the bogeyman when, one night, he could not control his laughter. In spite of his threats to bash me if I told on him, I told Mum.

'You just wait till your father comes home, Peter, you're gonna get a good hiding.' That was her usual threat. Peter called me a rotten tell-tale, but I didn't care.

'Wait till I get you outside,' he hissed.

'I hate you,' I said defiantly. 'I hope Dad kills you.'

The joy of having my own room was short-lived.

'You're gonna have to share your bedrooms again for a while, and I don't wanna hear no moanin',' Mum announced.

'Oh, no, Mum,' we moaned.

'I said no moanin', didn't I? Dad's brother, your uncle Joe, and his lot have to come and stay. They don't have nowhere else to go, so stop lookin' miserable. It ain't gonna be for ever.'

'Where are we all gonna sleep, Mum? Ain't they got three kids?'

'Yes, we'll just have to bunk up and make do.' And that was what we did.

Mum and Dad moved into Peter's room, Uncle Joe and Auntie Vi went into my room and all five of us children went into Mum and Dad's room. The three boys, Joseph, Peter and Alfred, slept in a double bed, and Cousin Violet and I slept in a single, she with her head at the top of the bed and me with my head at the bottom.

It's a wonder we ever got any sleep for the high jinks that took place in that room. It was bedlam at times, especially if our parents were out. We had pillow fights until one of the pillows exploded and feathers spewed everywhere. It looked as though it had been snowing in our room. We were terrified of being found out, but laughed at one another: we had feathers in our hair and ears, and even up our noses. I don't know how we managed to get all the feathers back into the pillowcase, but we did. Then Violet sewed it back up before anyone found out.

Our older siblings teased the two younger children, namely Alfred and me, unmercifully. They scared us with ghost stories and put us up to things our parents would have killed them for, had they found out.

Once they tried to get us to say, 'Fuck', but we refused.

'I'm never going to say "fuck", are you?' Alfred said to me later, out in the garden.

'No,' I replied. 'I'm never going to say "fuck" either.' Then we both fell to the ground, laughing and saying, 'Fuck, fuck, fuck.'

That incident came to mind many years later, as I watched *Hope and Glory*, a film set in the Second World War in London. In one scene, a gang of older lads tries to get a young boy to say that very special word in order to become a member of their gang. I laughed aloud.

Having an extra family in the house must have been a strain on Mum. Dad and Uncle Joe worked for the same company and were often out of town for weeks at a time. When one was gone, so was the other, leaving discipline to our mums. Auntie Vi had a job so she was gone all day; when she was at home, all she did was sit and smoke cigarettes. Mum had to deal with us kids by herself, and she wasn't very good at it. Her idea of discipline was the usual threat, 'Just wait till your father comes home.' We knew she'd never tell him and took full advantage of her impotence.

Poor Mum: she'd had to make many adjustments. First, her mum and dad had had to live with her when they lost their home in the Blitz. After the war, Peter and I returned home. Then Auntie Rose moved in for a while and now another family had descended upon her.

On occasion, I'd hear her crying in her bedroom. She must have been overwhelmed. One day I overheard her tell Mrs Peckham, our next-door neighbour, 'Me home's not me own no more.'

When Dad's family moved out, we all moved back into our own bedrooms. At last, life could return to normal. Although by then I doubt that any of us remembered what normal was.

While we were living at Lindsey Road, I attended Stevens Road School. It was there that I attracted my first male admirer. His name was Billy Brown, and I hated his guts. He would chase me home from school almost every day; a young version of a stalker, I suppose. I believe 'the chase' is a common demonstration of affection when one is eight or nine. I also recall my excitement, and Mum's apprehension, when a boy invited me to his birthday party and I was to be the only girl there. What a hussy I was, even at that age. It wasn't much fun. None of the other boys wanted me there. I just ate my cake and went home. Nobody even noticed.

Shortly after that social disaster, I came to the realization that all boys were horrible. It was on a night when I had been left in Peter's care: a situation we both hated. He was under strict orders to take care of me until Mum and Dad got home, and not to leave me alone under any circumstances.

I tagged along with him and some of his mates to the allotments. There, we picked a load of ripe tomatoes and proceeded to throw them at houses down the street. Aware that food was still scarce in those early post-war days, and knowing how people relied on their allotments to supplement their food supply, I felt guilty, but didn't want them to call me a big baby. What we were doing was terrible: I knew it and was ashamed.

Later that night one of the boys shouted, 'Come on, boys, let's throw 'er in the 'orse shit.' Before I could think of running away, they grabbed me and shoved me into a deep ditch, which was full of compost material, most of it being horse manure. The boys disappeared into the darkness, laughing their heads off, leaving me alone to die, or so I thought. It stank, they stank, and so would I.

Somehow, I managed to crawl out and ran home, crying. When Mum and Dad returned, I told them what had happened, and begged them not to leave me with Peter again. I did not tell them about the stolen, wasted tomatoes. Peter claimed he had had nothing to do with throwing me into the ditch. Maybe he hadn't, but he'd done nothing to stop it, had he? I don't remember if they punished him, but I hope so.

Another of Peter's larks that frightened me was when he tried smoking. It was a rainy day and we were both playing in the small back porch. He had pieces of paper, newspaper perhaps, about twelve inches long, which he rolled into a tight cylinder. It looked a little like a cigar except for the colour. He produced matches, lit one end of the paper, put the other in his mouth, and then the whole thing burst into flames. We both fell back on our behinds, scared half to death. The flames singed his eyebrows and the front of his hair; it would have been far worse, had the paper been shorter.

'Blimey,' I said, fanning the smoke out of the porch.

'Don't you dare tell no one,' he threatened, as he brushed the nasty-smelling, shrivelled bits of hair from his face.

Later, he enlisted my help in going around the streets collecting dog-ends, as we had done during the war. Then he and his mates would make cigarettes, using papers pilfered from someone's dad. I tried a puff of one of their 'fags', and once was enough. The smoke seared my throat and burned my eyes. I thought I was about to die. I couldn't believe people enjoyed smoking. Our parents and grandparents all smoked, and to hear them say, 'Ooh, I'm dying for a fag,' made me wonder if they were all bonkers. Almost everyone smoked then, and I cringe when I think of Mum or Nan cooking dinner with a cigarette hanging out of the corner of her mouth.

On another evening when Mum and Dad were out, Peter and I once again caused an incident. We decided to surprise Mum by tidying the house and polishing the living-room floor.

After applying paste-wax to the floor, Peter came up with a brilliant idea.

'I know,' he said. 'Wouldn't it be fun if we polished it by sitting on cushions and spinning around?'

'Good idea,' I agreed.

We sat on the cushions and began, but after spinning for some time, I began to feel ill. When I stopped, the room kept going. Round and round it went. I looked at Peter, who appeared to float up and down in front of me. His usual rosy complexion was now a yellowish green. We both clutched our stomachs and threw up all over our lovely clean floor. We were clueless about the effects that spinning might have on the equilibrium.

We were still retching when Mum and Dad arrived home. I don't think they even noticed that we'd tidied the whole house.

'Get to bed, you two,' was all they said, as they set about cleaning up our mess.

'It serves you right,' mumbled Mum, handing us our toast the following morning. Peter and I glanced at one another across the table, and ate our breakfast in silence.

I wished she could have said something different. Why couldn't she, just once, thank us for trying to help her?

Before leaving the subject of nausea, another thing stands out in my mind. It was during that period that I had terrible bouts of vomiting, the cause of which was thought to be acidosis. I never did understand what that meant, but I do remember that it resulted in me having to eat large quantities of glucose, obtained from a clinic; it came in powder form and we had a dozen boxes of it at any given time. What stands out most clearly, though, is the vision of me leaning over the toilet, heaving my insides up until the only thing coming out was bitter green bile. In spite of the pain and the foul taste in my mouth, I didn't really mind. I have since realized that those were the only times I remember my mother holding me. As I clutched the edge of the toilet bowl, she would have one hand on my tummy and the other on my forehead. I can still feel the comfort of those precious moments and my mother's hands.

15

Unexpected Company and Purple Grapes

As I prepared to leave for school one morning, Mum gave me instructions.

'Go straight to Nan's after school, Iris. You're stayin' there overnight. Be a good girl, and whatever you do, don't ask for an egg. You mustn't eat Nanny and Granddad's rations.' She always said that.

'What am I goin' there for, Mum? Are you goin' away?'

'No, of course I'm not. Don't be daft. Stop askin' questions and just do as you're told.'

I'd never stayed at Nan's overnight. This would be a new adventure and I could hardly wait. The end of the school day couldn't come soon enough.

When it did, I ran all the way to Nan's house. Reaching my hand in through the letterbox, I fished out the dirty piece of string with the key on the end, and let myself in. I could smell dinner cooking.

'I'm here, Nan. Hello, Granddad,' I shouted.

'Hang your coat up and come and have a nice cup of tea,' said Nan. 'Warm yourself by the fire. Dinner'll be ready soon.'

The food I'd smelt cooking was egg and chips. I wouldn't dare tell Mum about the egg. She'd think I'd asked for it, which, of course, I had not.

There wasn't much to do at Nan's house, but after dinner, I busied myself cutting up newspaper and threading it on string to hang in the toilet for toilet paper. Then I found some old magazines, called *Esquire*, to look at. They contained pictures of glamour girls and Nan said they belonged to my uncle Peter who was away in the air force. We never had magazines at our house, just boring newspapers.

'Why am I staying overnight, Granddad?' I asked.

'Shush,' he said, as he turned the wireless on. 'The news.' Hmm, I thought, I wonder why grown-ups never tell kids anything?

'Can I turn the light on, Granddad? I can't see to read no more.'

'Not yet, love, it ain't dark enough. We'll turn it on after the news. We can't waste the electric. Now shush.'

That night I stayed in Uncle Pete's bedroom. He was Mum's youngest brother and was in the RAF, stationed somewhere in India. I wished he'd hurry up and come home; I bet he'd let me turn the light on early, and he'd probably let me listen to some of his records too. He had three records with Nat King Cole's picture on the front; he must have really liked him, but Nan said we mustn't touch Uncle Pete's record player.

I hadn't packed anything for my overnight stay. I slept in my underwear and wore the same clothes the next day, which was what I did at home anyway. I still didn't own a toothbrush, so that was another reason I hadn't had to pack anything. All the grown-ups in our family had false teeth; I suppose they didn't think about our dental hygiene.

The next morning, after breakfast, Nan was helping me put my coat on in the hallway. 'You're to come here for dinner again this afternoon, Iris. Don't forget, straight 'ere after school, and no hangin' about.'

'Again, Nan? Do I really get to come again?' I asked. 'Whatcha makin' for dinner today?' I added. I could feel myself grinning.

'I haven't thought about it yet, Iree, but I'll try to think of something that don't 'ave an egg in it. Now go on, get going.' She gave me a shove and laughed. She knew Mum worried about Peter and me eating their egg rations.

Speaking of eggs reminds me of another story, or two. It was around that time Mum managed to buy some eggs from a neighbour who kept chickens. She wrapped two eggs in newspaper, placed them in a string shopping bag and sent me off to deliver them to Nan, her final orders being to carry the bag carefully and make sure I didn't let it bang against anything. Off I went, skipping happily along. In my vacant-minded pleasure, I began to swing the bag up and over my head – and then CRASH! Down came the bag, on top of the churchyard wall. I stood for a moment, paralysed with fear at the inevitable fate of the two precious eggs. I arrived at Nan's house, tears streaming down my face, and handed her the bag. I don't remember much of what happened next, but from then on Nan called me 'Eggy'. She assured me that it would be our little secret but I'm sure Mum suspected the truth, especially now that Nan had a new nickname for me.

Nan usually rolled her own cigarettes. They were skinny little things that burned fast, and I can honestly say I never met anyone who could smoke a cigarette down to the length that she could. There would be no more than a quarter-inch dog-end left, clamped in her mouth and still burning.

Yes, Nan was a champion when it came to smoking. In all the times I watched her preparing meals, I never once saw her drop ash into the food. That mangled dog-end just hung between her narrow lips as if it was glued there. Granddad told me she sometimes used a pin to make it last longer, but I never saw her do that. It would have been like eating winkles.

That evening, after baked beans on toast and a sausage, but no egg, Nan surprised me again. 'Get your coat on, Iris. I'll walk home with you.'

What? I thought. What was going on? Nan had never done that before. 'It's not dark, Nan. You don't 'ave to go with me,' I said. 'I'm not a baby any more. I'm eight.' But she already had her coat and hat on. I shrugged my shoulders at Granddad and he shrugged his at me.

'Ta-tah,' we said, and I saw Nan wink at him. I gave him what he called a 'kiss on the whiskers', and he pinched my cheek. Poor Granddad. He'd hardly left the house since having his leg amputated after the war. The only times I saw him outside was when he'd sit on a low box in the garden, tending his geraniums, and the one time, using crutches, he took me to the pictures to see *Bambi*. He had tried using a wooden leg but hadn't liked it; I remember seeing it propped up in the cupboard under the stairs.

I skipped along beside Nan, still wondering what all the fuss was about, but enjoying it.

When our house came into view, I noticed a woman coming out of our front gate. She was dressed in a nurse's uniform and pushing a bicycle.

'I wonder who that is, Nan? What's she doin' at our 'ouse?'

'Dunno,' was all Nan said.

As we approached, the woman stopped. She leaned her bicycle against the gatepost and appeared to be waiting for us. When we arrived, she smiled down at me. 'I bet you can't wait to see your new baby brother, can you? You can go in now, dear.'

'Baby brother?' I said. 'I ain't got no baby brother. You're at the wrong house, Miss.' She and Nan laughed.

'Go up and see for yourself if you don't believe us,' said Nan.

I raced up the stairs, burst into Mum's bedroom and, to my surprise, they were right. It wasn't even bedtime but Mum was sitting up in bed, in her nightie, holding a baby in her arms. I was flabbergasted. Leaning in to look at the baby, I sniffed. He and Mum smelt nice, but everything else smelt like disinfectant.

This new situation took a lot of explaining, and an interesting story it was too. Something about a stork, as I recall. There was even a white feather on the bed to prove it. Seriously!

It was 21 November 1946. I now had a baby brother whose

name would be Robert Clive, after some famous bloke in India, I learned later.

Robert, and we always called him Robert, was a dear little baby. I was allowed to hold him if I promised to be careful, which of course I was. I was eight years old, for goodness' sake.

One thing I could never understand, though, was why Mum kept sticking the baby's head inside her nightie.

'Whatcha doin' that for, Mum? Why do you keep hiding him?'

'Stop askin' questions. It's just what you do with babies,' she said. Mum was never forthcoming with information. No wonder I thought she was starving my poor baby brother. I never did see her give him any food. Well, not for a very long time. It's amazing he survived, really, but I was glad he did.

Soon after Robert's birth, Mum again appeared sad. She began crying a lot; it frightened me and made me cry too. She was remote and didn't seem like Mum at all. Why was she sad? Why wouldn't she talk to me? Did she hate me? Had I done something wrong? Why wouldn't she let me come near her? Those were some of the questions I asked myself. I wished I could have asked Dad, but he was away working again. Sometimes, sobbing, Mum would call me to her. 'Go and get Mrs Peckham, Iris. Tell 'er I need 'elp.'

I'd put my hand on her shoulder and try to comfort her. 'I'll help you, Mum, just tell me what you want me to do and I'll do it.' She'd just shake her head, push me away and tell me to do as I was told.

Mrs Peckham, the next-door neighbour, would come running, all the time mumbling something about 'that poor woman'.

'Tut, tut, tut, you poor thing,' Mrs Peckham would say, and she'd sit holding Mum's hand, talking softly to her. Sometimes she'd help with the baby, which Mum wouldn't let me do. I felt useless.

Most of the time I had no idea where Peter was, but I discovered later he'd been at Nan's house. He helped her and Granddad do things that I couldn't. He was also Nan's favourite: she let him take jam-jars back to the grocery shop and he got pennies for them. Lucky bugger.

'Don't worry yer mum,' Mrs Peckham instructed me. 'She's depressed. She can't be worryin' about you now.' But what about me? I thought. Why doesn't anyone care about me? Inside, I felt like Mum looked. Did that mean I was depressed too? Who could I send for when I was crying? No one.

Confused and feeling very much alone, I tried to work out what Mum was unhappy about, hoping it wasn't me, and wondering if the new baby had anything to do with it. She still cuddled him, though, and stuck his head under her dress, so I was sure she liked him.

I tried eavesdropping on her conversations with Mrs Peckham, but the only thing I ever heard was something about having 'piles'. Piles of what?

'They're like a bunch of purple grapes,' she said. 'They keep pouring with blood.' I saw a lot of blood in the toilet one day and thought Mum had flushed some of her grapes down there.

At the time, I didn't know what grapes were; there was still very little imported fruit in our shops. It was several years before I discovered what piles were, and to this day, when I see purple grapes, I think of poor Mum and the agony she must have suffered. Undoubtedly, she was also anaemic from all the blood loss, but women rarely discussed such things with their male doctors. Mum wouldn't even buy sanitary napkins; she was far too embarrassed to ask for them at the chemist's. She used cut-up pieces of cloth that she washed and reused.

But that wasn't the only thing I was ignorant of. With Dad working away, often for weeks at a time, Mum again had reason to suspect him of infidelity. She had always been jealous of the attention he received from, and gave to, other women. Her jealousies and suspicions, I learned later, were, in most cases, well founded. However, at the time, I had no idea that Dad's missing cufflinks had anything to do with it.

16

Infidelity and the Missing Cufflinks

The story of the missing silver cufflinks is well known in our family. It is one of the great unsolved mysteries that lie hidden, and perhaps grinning, within the pages of Jones family lore. This is what I know and heard about it.

Dad's landlady at the boarding-house where he stayed when he was working away from home had presented him with a pair of engraved silver cufflinks. Dad, being a bit of a show-off, showed them to everyone, including Mum, which was a big mistake.

A short time later, the precious cufflinks went missing. No one knew what had happened to Dad's pride and joy; they had simply disappeared.

'They couldn't 'ave just vanished into thin air,' stormed Dad.

'Well, don't you look at me, Edward. I don't know what you done with 'em,' replied Mum.

'I ain't done nothing with 'em, Kitty. You must 'ave moved 'em. They couldn't 'ave moved themselves, could they?'

'You shoulda put 'em in a safe place,' Mum chided.

'I did put 'em in a safe place, Kitty. I left 'em on top of the dressing-table, not out in the flippin' garden.' Dad was fuming.

'Stop askin' me, Ted, and stop makin' accusations. I ain't seen your precious cufflinks, and that's the end of it.' Mum rarely raised her voice but it was obvious that she was on the verge of doing so.

I don't remember hearing them discuss the matter again, but I know it remained an issue for a very long time.

Over the years, we often teased Mum about what might have

happened to the infamous cufflinks, but she never let on that she'd had anything to do with their disappearance.

'Dad must have flogged 'em. I don't have the foggiest idea what 'appened to the bloody things,' was all she would say. And that was that. We knew Dad hadn't 'flogged 'em' though: he'd been far too proud of them.

Many years later, on one of my last visits to Mum, when she was about eighty, I asked her to tell me the truth.

'What really happened to Dad's cufflinks, Mum?' I coaxed. 'Come on, you can tell me. It'll be our little secret.' With a hint of a smile, she still pleaded innocence, much to her credit and my frustration.

For a while, Mum's younger brother, Tom, and Dad worked together. They often went out of town on extended job assignments and lodged at the same boarding-houses.

My father's blatant philandering during those periods, and Uncle Tom's love for his sister, caused a rift between the two men that lasted throughout their lives. Dad's dalliance with their landlady in Great Yarmouth, and the fact that he chose to stay with her rather than go home to his family at weekends, was for Uncle Tom the proverbial straw that broke the camel's back. I didn't learn the truth until my adult years when Uncle Tom's widow told me what had happened.

'Your uncle Tom gave up his job because of it,' she said. 'He couldn't work with your dad no more. He was afraid he'd kill him for what he was doing to your mum and you kiddies.'

It saddened me to know that Dad's behaviour had kept Uncle Tom and Mum apart for all those years, but fortunately, shortly before they died, we managed to get them together, without my father, of course. It was a touching, bittersweet reunion.

I'm sure that, in her heart, my mother knew why she never saw her brother, but she refused to acknowledge the situation. She was loyal to my father, in spite of his constant liaisons.

Perhaps Dad did attempt to be a better, more loyal husband: not long after Robert was born and christened, and when Mum was going through her breakdown, he began attending a nearby Methodist church; something he had never done before.

This occurred after the minister, Mr Groves, began calling on us. He was what Mum called 'a lovely man', and Dad seemed to have great respect for him. I suspect a family member had interceded, and was responsible for this turnaround in his behaviour.

Subsequently, Dad became increasingly involved in church activities and even began teaching in Sunday school.

'Ted? Teaching in Sunday school? Well, I'll be blowed.' That was Nan's reaction, and perhaps that of many others who knew him.

So Dad had found a new spot in the limelight, and Mum had new jealousies to cope with. She occasionally attended church with him but, shrinking violet that she was, she preferred staying at home.

The person I suspect responsible for interceding on Mum's behalf was her youngest brother, Peter, who had recently returned from India. He was young and handsome, still single and lived at home with his parents, Nan and Granddad. I adored him, and I will never forget the day he came home from overseas; I was overjoyed.

As I often did, I popped in to see Nan and Granddad after school on that particular day. Reaching through the letterbox, I snared the front door key-on-a-string and let myself in. When I poked my head around the living-room door, there he was, handsomer than ever and brown as a berry. He stood, arms extended, beaming from ear to ear, as was I, and then he scooped me up in his arms.

'Are you still my girl?' he asked.

Hah, what a silly question, I thought. 'Of course I am.' I giggled.

When, at last, my excitement subsided, and reality brought me down from the clouds, I realized something was missing. Uncle Peter had come home alone: he had not brought me a monkey.

Some time earlier, Nan had shown me a photograph she had just received from India. It was of my uncle, and on his shoulder, secured at the end of a leash, sat a small monkey. Apparently, it was his squadron's mascot. Thinking it would make a fine pet, I wrote and asked him to bring it home.

'Where's the monkey, Uncle Pete?' I asked. Seemingly lost for words he turned to Nan, who immediately had the explanation.

'Ooh, you can't 'ave a monkey for a pet, Iris. It's too cold for 'em in England. Besides, they've got 'orrible ugly bums that look like lumps of raw meat.'

'Ugh,' I said. I didn't really mind, especially when I saw all the lovely exotic presents he'd brought us from India.

Later, my handsome uncle walked home with me, to surprise Mum. He opened our rarely locked front door, and shouted a greeting, in what I guessed to be Indian. Mum came running down the stairs, tears streaming down her face, and threw her arms around him. I stood watching their happy reunion, grinning so hard my face ached. It was wonderful to see Mum looking so happy.

Now out of the RAF and home for good, Uncle Pete soon learned of Dad's infidelity, family neglect, and Mum's unhappiness. I am not sure what happened but Dad suddenly seemed to make more effort with his family. I'm sure it was because of Uncle Pete. Later I wondered if he, and perhaps Uncle Tom, had given my father an ultimatum, in spite of their gentle nature.

All of our family was now involved with the Methodist church. My brother Peter was in the Boys' Brigade, I was in the Brownies, Mum *occasionally* attended services or mothers' meetings with baby Robert and, of course, Dad was becoming very self-important with his growing role.

My experience with the Brownies was a strange one. It was there that I suddenly became disruptive. Was it because I was getting almost no attention at home now that the new baby had arrived? I suspect so. I remember, with shame, a Brownie meeting when I was made to sit on the Big Toadstool in the middle of the room. The other Brownies marched in a circle around me and, pointing accusing fingers, they sang a song about bad Brownies. I wanted to disappear, but also felt anger rising within me.

Fortunately, we must have had an unusually perceptive Brown Owl: she took me aside one evening, after I had been particularly naughty, and told me I was to become a Sixer.

Brownie troops were divided into small groups of six, with each group having a different name, such as Fairies, Elves, Pixies or Gnomes. Hence, the girl in charge of each small group was the Sixer, and I became Sixer of the Fairies. What a brilliant piece of psychology that turned out to be. I never again behaved badly; in fact, I was determined to be the best Sixer ever.

As I've said, I loved watching Dad in his workshop, but I also loved being in there even when he was not. I loved the smells, especially those of sawdust and the new leather used to mend our shoes, of paint and varnish. All delicious smells to me, they *were* my father.

I'm not sure why I went in there on one particular occasion but my eyes and heart almost popped out when I spied, half hidden on his workbench, a complete set of doll's house furniture. I had never had many toys and could hardly contain my excitement, but I knew I must. I couldn't let on that my curiosity had spoiled the surprise. Christmas was coming. Soon the big day would be here. I would feign surprise as I opened the magnificent gift, the gift my beloved father had made with his own clever hands.

Shortly after I made my wonderful discovery, and just before

Christmas, the church held a holiday fair. There were raffles, games, a refreshment stand, people selling homemade Christmas puddings, mince pies and cakes, and all kinds of hand-made items. In the evening, there was to be a Christmas concert, concluding with Father Christmas drawing names for some wonderful grand prizes. The church had planned it as an all-day Christmas party, and it was great fun – until my world turned inside-out.

There are no words to describe my feelings upon discovering that what I'd thought Dad had made for me had, in fact, been donated to the Church for a raffle.

Displayed on a table at the front of the church hall sat my beautiful set of doll's house furniture. Beside it a sign read:

HAND MADE AND GENEROUSLY DONATED BY MR TED
JONES WITH THE SINCERE THANKS OF THE
CHURCH BOARD AND CONGREGATION

I ran from the building into the alley behind the church and there, hidden behind the rubbish bins, I sobbed my heart out. I wondered how I could ever face my father again.

The hurt of that bitter disappointment gouged deep; it stayed with me for many years, but I told no one. Perhaps I kept it buried because I was afraid the pain had been self-inflicted by my own selfishness, or perhaps because I was afraid to face the reality of my father's egotistical callousness.

Throughout all this time, our family remained financially challenged. Poorly fed and dressed, often ill, we enjoyed little in the way of recreational activities. We still played the street games when we were not attending church-sponsored functions, which for me now included membership of the Junior Missionary Association (JMA). We learned about all the good works the Church was doing for the heathens in Africa, and how they'd go to Hell if we did not bring them to Jesus. Our job was to go from door to door, begging for money for the missions. On Sundays we handed in the collection box, and whoever had collected the most money would get a gold star. My own missionary work was a complete flop. I never did get a star. I hated knocking on doors asking for money, and have ever since, because people would be unkind.

'Buzz off and don't you come back no more,' they'd say.

'You can't get blood out of a turnip,' Mum told me. 'You don't live in the right place, Iris. No one round 'ere's got money to give away. We could do with a bit of missionary money ourselves.'

At last, a ray of sunshine entered my life when a lone roller skate came into my possession. Rust had immobilized the wheels, though, and as hard as I worked on it, I could never get them to work properly. In retrospect, I suppose a little oil would have helped but it never occurred to me to ask Dad; I had stopped going into his workshop. With difficulty, I'd propel myself up and down the street on my precious skate, thinking it a little like having the scooter I'd always wanted.

A pedal car was the only other thing I'd ever longed for, but I knew that was out of the question and never asked for one. Once I mentioned it casually to Mum.

'Don't be a baby,' she said. 'You're too big to 'ave a pedal car.'

It just wasn't fair. I was always too old or too young, too big or too small for anything I wanted, according to Mum.

Uncle Pete gave my brother a bike for doing well at school. It was his old one but still lovely and shiny, so Peter wasn't around much any more, lucky boy. He wouldn't even give me a ride on the handlebars either, the selfish pig.

The Christmas when I didn't get the doll's house furniture Auntie Iris gave me my first ever pair of slippers: they were blue. She also took me to London to see *Aladdin*, my first pantomime.

Mum surprised me, too, by taking me shopping at Gamages Department Store where she allowed me to pick out a book for Christmas. That was a first, and I wondered later if she and my aunt knew of the doll's house furniture incident and its effect on me. I'd like to think so.

It took me for ever to choose the book I wanted. It was called *Our Friends Next Door*. Now, with renewed interest in Christmas, I could hardly wait to feign surprise that Father Christmas had brought me the very book I had selected, as well as the usual orange, nuts and sweets stuffed into an old sock. I loved and treasured that book and must have read it a thousand times.

At that time, we still had milk, bread and coal delivered by horse-drawn carts, and I liked to visit the nearby United Dairy stables to see the horses. I'd sneak in and wander up and down the rows of stall doors, wallowing in horse manure and urine, patting the horses' noses and talking to them. There was a kind of mystery about the place, and I savoured the warm smell of the animals and hay; they reminded me of Wales.

Once, the council made street repairs in our neighbourhood, which caused great excitement among us children. We loved following the work crews as they went from street to street, laying new tarmac and stone. The massive steam-rollers, painted bright green and embellished with stripes of blood red and shiny gold, sparkled in the sunshine. They made me think of dragons, searching for food, as they plied back and forth over the fresh tar. More exciting than the steam-rollers, though, was the day we made an astonishing new discovery.

We discovered that when the horse that pulled the tar wagon did a wee, a big long thing came out from under his belly and hung almost to the ground. Well, that's how I remember it. We had to call it a thing since we had no other word for it.

For days, we followed the work crew up and down the streets, sitting on the kerb for hours on end, waiting and hoping for the re-emergence of the animal's strange protuberance. When it had finished weeing, there we'd be, equally mystified by the thing's disappearance, wondering where he kept it when it was not in use. We suspected it was something naughty and I suppose that was exactly what made it so fascinating, and why it made us giggle.

For the most part, I enjoyed school and remember some of the teachers well. My favourite was Mrs Gare, who I adored: she was patient and kind, unlike Mrs Hill, who was as wide as she was tall and just as strict.

Once, after we'd had a snowfall, which was rare in London, we made an ice slide in the playground and had great fun sliding and falling all over the place. For several nights after that, I dreamed that Mrs Hill sneaked onto the slide after school, and every time she did, she fell down with a crash, her fat legs straight up in the air and showing off her bloomers. That was when I discovered that my mind could be evil and creative, on both levels of consciousness, both waking and sleeping.

Our headmistress, Miss Buchanan, was a tall woman with flyaway reddish hair, worn in a loose bun. She always dressed in mannish tweeds and sported a large hairy wart on her chin that waggled when she spoke. We had great difficulty stifling our giggles and paying attention to what she was saying at morning assembly once that wart started its tricks.

It was at Stevens Road School that I became acutely aware of something sorely lacking in my life, and that was having parents involved in my daily activities. I still envied children whose mothers met them with umbrellas on rainy days. I also envied children when their parents came to see them perform in plays or concerts, or to inspect their schoolwork on open days. I don't remember Mum and Dad ever being there.

Once, at church, I was to recite a poem. Auntie Iris made me a long floral dress to wear for the performance and I practised my poem endlessly in preparation for the big day. When that day and my turn came, I stepped onto the stage and scanned the audience for my parents. Realizing they were not there, I forgot every word of my poem and ran from the stage in tears, embarrassed and ashamed.

It seemed that nothing much had changed in my life since the war and my evacuation. I still had to rely on myself, not others. I had to stop expecting things to be different. I had to accept the situation; after all, I was nine.

17

Almost Family Holidays

During the early post-war years, the Jones family made two attempts at taking a holiday together. Unfortunately, things did not go as planned.

'Sure sign the Joneses are going out,' Mum would say. That usually meant it was raining, but other things could, and usually did, go wrong.

Peter and I stood there with our mouths hanging open.

'Well, don't just stand there with your bare faces hangin' out. What do you think?' said Dad.

'Oooh, goodie,' I said, clapping my hands.

'Is it by the sea, Dad?' Peter asked.

'Nah, I wish it was, mate.'

Dad had just announced that Mum had arranged for us to spend two weeks in Hampshire, visiting her relatives who were tenants on a large farm.

We were ecstatic at the thought of two whole weeks in the country. We'd never been on a holiday before so were understandably excited. We drove poor Mum round the bend with our constant questions.

'How many more days, Mum? Do they live in a big house, Mum? Do they have kids, Mum?'

'Wait and see,' was all she ever said.

'She never tells us nothin',' I whispered to my brother.

At last, the big day arrived. We were going on holiday, hooray. Dad locked the house, latched the front gate, then turned and waved at Mrs Peckham, whose head was sticking out of an upstairs window.

'Ta-tah, mate. Keep your eye on things while we're gone,' he called to her.

'Ta-tah, Mr Jones. Ta-tah, Mrs Jones. Have a lovely time. Hope the weather stays nice for ya.'

'Some hope,' muttered Dad, as a drop of rain fell on his face.

'Sure sign the Joneses are going out,' said Mum. She was laughing. Dad was not.

We trudged off down the road, first to catch a bus and then a steam train to Hampshire. With all our belongings stuffed into carrier-bags, we were travelling for the first time ever as a family.

Mum was in her glory. She'd been born and raised in the country, and had grown up with the relatives we were going to visit. The rest of us would be meeting them for the first time, but Mum would be seeing aunts and cousins she hadn't seen since her family had moved to London when she was a teenager.

We arrived at the station to find the train standing at the platform. Dad, leading the way, looked for an empty carriage. The engine belched thick black smoke from its fat funnels and it wafted back, engulfing us in its stench. I squinted and held my nose as we made our way along the platform. The smell of the smoke reminded me of another train ride I'd taken, during the war, when I was evacuated. This train was also taking us to an unknown destination, but this time my family was with me; I was not alone.

Dad found an empty compartment; it was close to the engine. He pulled open the heavy door and we all piled in.

'Keep them windows closed for now, or we'll all choke on the blimmin' smoke,' he said, as he pulled up the window sashes.

We had the whole compartment to ourselves. Dad hefted our bags onto the brass overhead luggage rack. Mum propped baby

Robert up in the corner and put her handbag and shopping bag on the seat next to him.

'Sit down, you two, and behave yourselves,' she told us. 'They'll throw you off at the next stop if you don't.'

As the train groaned and chugged into motion, it was almost impossible to sit still. The excitement in that railway carriage was palpable: you could have cut it with a knife and spread it on bread.

I glanced at Mum. She looked content as she gazed out of the window at the passing scene. Dad, on the other hand, appeared tense: he said hardly a word on the journey and didn't seem at all excited. Born and raised in the slums of London, he was a real city boy and I'm sure he had misgivings about our holiday in the country, but I suppose it was all he could afford at the time.

After what seemed like several hours, we approached our station. I'm not sure what its name was, but our ultimate destination was the village of East Meon, Mum's childhood home.

'Quick, hurry up. Pick up all your stuff. We're nearly there,' Mum said. She sounded panicky.

'Calm down, Kitty. We ain't going to miss our stop,' Dad said impatiently. He shook his head and tutted. 'Dear, oh dear, oh dear,' he muttered. Dad said that a lot, usually to express impatience with Mum.

We gathered our belongings quickly. My brother and I stuffed as much as we could into our pockets. The rest, we poked into Mum's shopping bag; we were soon ready.

'Thanks a lot,' said Mum, sarcastically. 'I'll carry it for you.'

'It's only rubbish, Mum.'

'Oh, lovely, that's very nice of you. Ta very much.'

After we'd clambered off the train, Mum looked up and down the platform to see if anyone had come to meet us, but they had not. A few people stared at us through the grimy waiting-room window.

'Them people over there must think we're a bunch of wandering Jews,' said Mum. I didn't know what that meant, but Dad laughed.

'More like gypsies,' he said. Then, more seriously, 'Too bad nobody cared enough to come and help us.'

'Farmers are busy this time of the year,' Mum explained. 'Not to worry, though, I know me way. It don't look like anything's changed around here. Come on, you lot.'

She appeared to know where we were and where we were going so, for a change, Dad let her lead the way. Following close behind her, we trudged off down a shady, tree-lined lane. Mum carried Robert, her handbag and a shopping bag, but I could hear Dad behind us, grumbling, as he lugged our heavy bags.

'Are we nearly there, Mum?' I asked, several times.

'Shuddup, Iris. We'll get there when we get there, and I don't care if we never do,' griped Peter. I glared at him, and wondered why he always had to be so hateful.

After walking for what seemed a hundred miles, but was probably only one or two, we reached the farmhouse. Ivy, Mum's first cousin, and her daughters must have been watching for us: they greeted us at the gate.

'Where was they when there was bags to be carried?' muttered Dad.

'Shush, they'll hear you, Ted,' whispered Mum.

Following a tearful but happy reunion, we gathered around the long kitchen table, drank two pots of tea and ate lots of Ivy's home-made cake. After that, Dad appeared to be in better spirits, thank goodness. Cousin Ivy then showed us all where we'd be sleeping.

Peter was to sleep in the corner of Mum and Dad's bedroom. His bed, an old leather settee, was covered in cracked black leather; its horsehair stuffing was coming out underneath and a spring stuck out of the seat, right in the middle.

'How am I supposed to sleep on that thing?' he moaned.

'If you start complainin', we're goin' straight home,' warned Mum.

'Cor, my dogs are barking,' groaned Dad, who was sitting on the edge of the bed, taking his shoes off.

'Humph,' grunted Mum. 'You don't know what barking dogs are, Ted. You should've seen mine when I took me shoes off. There was steam comin' off 'em.'

Robert, still an infant, was to sleep on the floor in Mum and Dad's room on a pallet made up of old blankets. He was too young to complain.

I'd be sleeping with Joan and Christine, my cousins, on hay-filled mattresses on the floor of a small attic room. Enormous cobwebs, like frayed, dirty curtains, hung from the room's rafters, and one tiny window high in the eaves let in little light.

We three girls were not the room's only occupants. I soon discovered that we shared our quarters with a multitude of creepy-crawlies, including mice. Later, I also discovered that one of my new cousins wet the bed every night. Thank goodness, they changed the hay in the mattresses every few days, when it started to get soggy. Our crowded room smelt like the stables at the old United Dairy, but I didn't care: I was having fun.

The cottage had no running water: it had to be hauled in a bucket from a well in the garden. The well water smelt like rotten eggs, and there were always slugs trailing their silvery slime up the sides of the bucket. It didn't bother anyone except our dad. Auntie Ivy appeared to take great pleasure in scaring the daylights out of poor Dad. Each morning, before breakfast, she'd show him the bucket with its livestock.

'Get that bloody thing away from me,' he'd shout.

We'd all laugh our heads off, but Dad was not amused.

The farmhouse was hundreds of years old. Full of nooks and crannies, it was perfect for games of hide-and-seek. An enormous inglenook fireplace dominated the room that served as kitchen, dining and living room; all manner of iron pots hung over it. Dozens of old horse brasses hung from the room's stout wooden beams, and pretty ornaments stood on the mantel above the fireplace. Faded family photographs, some in fancy oval frames, decorated the walls. It was a typical farmhouse of its era and I loved everything about it.

I spent the early mornings watching the milking, and once, from a safe distance, I stood on a fence to watch a farmhand lead a snorting, bellowing black bull out of the barn on a rope that was attached to a ring in his nose.

'You'd be screaming bloody murder, too, if you had a ring stuck through your nose,' said Mum, when I told her about it later.

It was now late summer, harvest time, the days idyllic. We could go nutting, and filled buckets with hazelnuts, picked from the hedgerows. We ran behind the men as they cut the wheat, and helped form it into sheaves. Later, after it had been threshed, our reward was the unleashed joy of climbing and sliding down the stacks of straw, all the while shrieking with laughter.

We chased rabbits as they dashed out of hiding. Our cousins had the horrible job of bashing them over the head with clubs, killing them for family dinners. I could never have killed a rabbit, but I did enjoy eating them.

When our holiday was only halfway through, Dad announced that we had to go home. He told us he had received a telegram summoning him back to work because of an emergency. At first, no one said a word. We were devastated.

'Well, then, we'd better start gettin' our things together,' said Mum, stoic as always. She shooed us upstairs to begin gathering our belongings, while Dad sat in a rocking chair, reading the newspaper.

What we didn't know at the time was that Dad had walked to

the next village and sent himself that telegram. He hated being in the country and wanted to go home. I couldn't understand why we all had to leave. Why couldn't he go by himself? We could come later. I dared not ask. Reluctantly, we packed up to leave.

It was a sad scene on the morning of our departure. No one said a word. Auntie Ivy stood at the door, dabbing a handkerchief to her eyes. Mum kissed her goodbye, and then grabbed Robert's hand. Lips pursed and eyes filled with tears, she strode off ahead of us. She did not look back.

Peter and I glared at Dad as we set off for the station, and the miserable ride home.

I'm unsure how much time passed between that first failed holiday to the country, which Dad had sabotaged, and the next, but I was probably ten, and Peter fourteen, when we learned we were going on our second family holiday.

Dad worked with a woman whose family leased a permanent site at a campground near the sea. He had arranged to rent it from her. Yes, we were going camping at the seaside. Peter and I were excited and hopeful. Maybe this time things would go better.

'I think Dad likes the seaside,' Peter said. 'I remember him saying he wished we was going to the seaside instead of the country when we went away last time.'

'I hope so,' I replied. 'If he spoils it this time I ain't never gonna to talk to him again. Won't it be fun, Pete, stayin' in a tent?'

'Yeah, but Mum don't look all that excited. I heard her say she don't like the idea of traipsin' across a field in the middle of the night to go to the toilet.'

'Why can't she use the bucket like the rest of us?' I asked.

'She don't want no one to see her big fat bum,' he replied, and we dissolved into fits of laughter.

Early one Saturday morning, Dad and I travelled by train to a halfway meeting place to meet his friend. There, on the railway platform, we took possession of an old pram, piled high with stuff. It was an old Silver Cross baby carriage, the kind posh people used. It sat high, on huge wheels, but it had definitely seen better days. The chrome was rusted, the hood in tatters, spokes stuck out of the wobbly wheels, and we heard it squeaking before it came into view.

'Bloody hell,' Dad muttered, as the conveyance rattled and creaked towards us.

Dad's friend had previously explained to him that the campsite was set up each year for the summer season, and had assured him it was well organized.

The site consisted of two large, ex-military bell tents, with a connecting kitchen tent stretched between them. The bell tents contained camp beds, and the kitchen tent a Primus stove, worktop and storage cabinet. Also provided were a folding table and chairs, and there was an old sink for washing the dishes and ourselves.

As well as transferring the perambulating relic into Dad's hands, she gave him a hand-drawn map, directions to the campsite and added last-minute instructions and explanations.

'Oh, by the way, Ted, the sink ain't connected to nothin'. It's got a plug and a plug-hole but you have to fill it with buckets, and it just empties onto the ground.'

Dad listened intently.

'There you go, then, Ted,' she said, grinning from ear to ear. 'There's your new home by the sea, all packed up nice and neat in the baby's pram, but without the baby, ha, ha, ha.'

The pram contained pots and pans, sleeping bags, and other camping paraphernalia.

'Thanks, mate,' he said. 'I'll send you a postcard.'

Mum, Dad and me looking very
smart at a family wedding in 1941.

Me aged one and a half and Peter aged five
and half, taken at Blackwall Pier.

Granddad leading evacuees at the station where he worked.

My Welsh foster parents, Nell and Dilwyn Cooper, a year or so
before I arrived on their doorstep.

Me shortly after I arrived in Wales.

Dad and Uncle Tom before their big fall out over Dad's infidelity.

Mum in the 1940s, with her bow lips
and clamshell necklace.

Mum, during the war, wearing her
postman's uniform.

School photo of me, aged eleven.

Me, aged twelve, wearing too-big hand-me-down
clothes held up with safety pins.

Mum, Christopher, Robert and me, aged fourteen,
on our almost perfect holiday to Clacton.

My Wedding Day, 16 October 1954.

My new husband, Bob Irvine, on board ship on our way to America, 1955.

Me dancing with my wartime foster mother, Nell Cooper,
on her ninetieth birthday.

'I'll look forward to it. Ta-tah, love,' she said, as she walked away. When she was halfway down the platform, she turned again and blew us a kiss. Well, I think it was for both of us, anyway.

We loaded the pram into the baggage car of the train and off we went. It all sounded perfect to me, but Dad already looked apprehensive.

Mum burst out laughing when she saw us coming up the path with our load. She had tears rolling down her face. Then Peter appeared, and he started laughing too.

'What's so funny?' barked Dad.

'You should've seen your face, Ted,' she replied. Then, with one hand on the wall, the other clutching her stomach, she was laughing all over again, which started Peter and me off. 'Ooh, stop it, Ted,' she said.

'I ain't doin' nothin', and it's not bloody funny.' Dad tried to keep a straight face, but then he was laughing too. 'Yes, I suppose I can see the funny side, but I'd like to watch you lot trying to push that ruddy pram.'

The next day we readied ourselves to embark on our holiday.

'Don't nobody laugh,' warned Dad. 'Or else!'

'No, Dad, we won't,' we promised. We didn't want anything to upset him today.

'We're gonna leave early in the morning,' he had announced the previous night, as he put the finishing touches to his packing. 'I don't want nobody seein' us with this lot. I ain't gonna be the laughin' stock of Dagenham, and that's what we'd be if the neighbours saw us.'

Mum and Dad had repacked the pram to make room for food, clothing and other supplies. Now, piled twice as high as it had been the day before, they'd had to secure it all with rope, to make sure nothing fell off.

We left early in the morning. Again, we travelled by train and we looked like gypsies, except that gypsies usually had much nicer vehicles for transporting their belongings.

Huffing and puffing, we loaded the pram into the baggage compartment, then found seats for ourselves in a passenger carriage.

'Phew,' said Mum. 'I wouldn't wanna do that every day.'

'You can say that again. God knows why they call this kind of thing a holiday. It's bloody hard work,' grumbled Dad.

'I'll have a go pushing the pram when we get there, Mum,' offered Peter.

'You and whose army?' Dad asked sarcastically.

It was a glorious sunny day when we arrived in Shoeburyness. Peter and I whooped with delight as we retrieved the pram. Even Mum and Dad were smiling – at the weather, not at the prospect of having to push the pram again.

Shoeburyness was on the east coast of England. We had never heard of the place before, but it was a seaside town, which was all that mattered. We were here. Now we had to find the campground. Dad reached into his pocket and took out the map his friend had drawn.

'It don't look far,' he reported.

'Hooray. We're nearly there,' I said.

'"The Campbells are comin', oho, oho."' Mum sang the familiar line from the old song, and we all laughed, but not for long.

The three-mile walk from the station to the campground wasn't too hard on Peter and me. Mum and Dad, however, were both red-faced and panting as they took turns pushing their heavy load. I could see the sweat trickling down their faces and dripping off their chins. Peter tried to help. First, he had a go at pushing the pram, but could barely budge it. Then, for a short while, he carried Robert, who was two, piggyback style. I trotted along beside our small, pathetic caravan, all the time scanning the surroundings for a much-needed oasis. There had been little conversation as we trudged along, but then, Mum broke the silence.

'That map was a bit deceivin', wasn't it, Ted?'

'You call that a bit?' growled Dad. Mum winced. You could see she wished she'd kept her mouth shut.

At last, a tired, bedraggled group of holidaymakers arrived at the campground. We soon found our tent-site, unpacked the pram, and moved in. It was exactly as Dad's friend had described it, and, to me, it was perfect. Mum found the kettle and made tea, which put everyone in a better mood.

Then Peter and I went for a walk to find the sea. Along the way, signs with arrows pointed us in the right direction: 'To the Sea' or 'To the Beach', they said.

From the edge of the campground, the path led us across a field and along the top of a cliff; it was about half a mile. Peter and I stood on the edge of the cliff and stared. The beach stretched out before us, and beyond that, the glorious sparkling sea. Seagulls circled above us, and all around, wild flowers dotted the ground. At that moment, I thought this must be Heaven, and with arms stretched high, I twirled ballerina-like, in a little dance of joy.

'Ain't it lovely, Pete?' I said, returning from Dreamland.

It was getting dark: we couldn't stand gawking any longer but we didn't mind – we had a whole week ahead of us to enjoy it. We headed back to camp and I could hardly wait to go to sleep so that I could wake up in the morning and start having fun.

That first night, as I snuggled down in my camp bed, there was a tickle of excitement in my stomach. To think, we were really, really camping. Here we were in a tent, lit by nothing but a kerosene lamp. I loved the smell of the burning oil, and the ground beneath us. What an adventure. Exhausted, I must have fallen asleep quickly.

Suddenly, a rumpus outside awakened us – I can only describe it as bedlam.

'What the hell?' Dad shouted.

'Oh, my God, Ted, what's happenin'?' said Mum.

We could hear people shouting all around us. Loud banging and metallic pinging sounds seemed to be coming from every direction, punctuated by an occasional agonizing scream. I thought pirates or murderers might be attacking the campground. My heart was pounding as we jumped from our beds and ran outside to investigate.

Instead of a band of marauders, we found that an enormous swarm of hornets had invaded the camp. Something must have disturbed them and they were on the warpath. Dozens of people were outside, flailing frying-pans and other forms of weaponry, trying to kill them. The bizarre scene was terrifying.

'Get back in the tent,' shouted Dad, and we did – he didn't have to tell us twice.

We jumped back inside and did the flaps up tight. It was obvious that our dad was not pleased.

'Get back to sleep,' Mum said. 'Thank God that's over.'

Dad grunted something inaudible and we all settled down again. After the unexpected excitement, we were now more than ready for sleep. That was when the rain started, and it was torrential. We all sat up again.

'Sure sign the Joneses . . .' Mum began, but Dad's face stopped her. Ooh, if looks could have killed.

'Don't say it, Kitty, just don't bloody say it.'

The tent leaked, badly. Not knowing any better, each time we touched the places that leaked, they became worse. In some places, water streamed in. No one dared to speak. I looked at my brother and, as our eyes met, we read each other's minds. We moved our camp beds away from the tent walls, pulled the covers over our heads and slept.

The following morning, after our miserable night, we woke to find Dad repacking the pram. We were going home. He was not about to give it a second chance.

'Please don't make us go home, Dad. Maybe the sun'll come out again tomorrow,' I begged.

'It ain't going to come out, Iris, and we ain't gonna have another night like the last one. I'm fed up with this lark. We're goin' 'ome and that's all there is to it.'

Peter stared at the ground. He didn't say a word. He just stood next to the tent pole and kicked at it. Mum also said nothing; she knew better. I started to cry.

'For pity's sake, stop your snivellin' and help your mum,' said a grim-faced Dad. He wanted to be at home in his nice dry house, in his nice warm bed. No amount of crying or whining was going to change his mind, and that was that. At that moment, I hated him; and I hated Mum too, for not saying anything. She never did stick up for us.

I remember nothing of the journey home. It's almost as though someone erased that part of my memory, and I'm sure it's just as well.

What I do remember is that it was a few years before Dad attempted to take us on another holiday.

Before I leave the subject of the Jones family's failed holidays, though, I'll jump forward in time as I feel it's only fair to tell you of our one almost perfect holiday.

After those two failed holidays, the Jones family was about to embark on what Dad called 'a real holiday'. He had hired a caravan at a campsite in Clacton-on-Sea. 'It's been highly recommended,' he told us.

'Are you sure, Ted?' asked Mum, who was understandably dubious after previous reassurances.

'I wouldn't say it if I wasn't, would I, Kit?'

Mum shrugged her shoulders and rolled her eyes. I knew what she was thinking. I was thinking the same thing: here we go again.

Then, Mum added her own surprise: she took me shopping for a brand-new summer dress and sandals for our holiday. That shopping trip remains crystal-clear in my memory; it was the one and only time we ever shopped together, except for when she had let me choose a book for Christmas. Other than school uniform, my clothes had usually been second-hand. She made sure I knew that my new holiday clothes were purchased on the never-never, which was what we called credit because many poor people were never able to pay off their debts.

'You'd better take care of them new clothes, young lady. It's gonna take a long time to pay for them. I don't want them ruined before they're paid for.'

'Of course I'll take care of them, Mum. I'm not a baby, am I? You don't have to keep tellin' me that.' She was such a nag sometimes.

'Well, I'm just sayin',' she said.

At last the time arrived for our long-anticipated 'real' holiday, and off we went. This was the first time we'd be travelling with real, if borrowed, suitcases. I prayed that Dad wouldn't find anything wrong with this holiday, and made promises to God in exchange for its success.

'There's a first time for everything, Iris,' Mum said.

'Yeah, and who knows, Mum? Maybe it won't even rain when the Joneses go out this time.'

'Some hope.' She chuckled. 'I'm takin' me umbrella, just in case.'

I remember nothing of the journey to Clacton. All I remember is that the sun was shining when we arrived.

'Touch wood and whistle, whoo whoo,' said Mum.

'Daft,' mumbled Dad, but I noticed he touched a tree and whistled for luck, as did I.

The campsite was pleasant and well maintained, and the caravan, although small, was clean and well equipped. It was close to the sea, the bathhouse and the site's grocery and, best of all, the weather was perfect during our two-week stay.

On the first day, I discovered that a girl who appeared close to my age was staying with her family in the caravan next door. Her name was Pearl, and although she turned out to be several years older than I was, we became fast friends and were inseparable throughout our holiday.

I haven't a clue what the rest of my family did all day during that holiday. I don't remember asking and I don't remember them telling. The deckchairs were always out, so I suppose they just sat in the sun and drank cups of tea while I was enjoying myself with my new friend.

On one of our promenades along the seafront, Pearl and I met two nice-looking young men. It was obvious that they were a lot older than I was, but since I hadn't even told Pearl I was only fourteen, I certainly didn't plan to tell them.

The young men were of working age, probably in their early twenties. They appeared to have plenty of money, and seemed pleased to spend it on us, taking us to all the seaside attractions and to the cinema, buying us balloons and silly hats and no end of other seaside treats. We did everything there was to do in Clacton, and we did it together. Pearl and I were gone from morning until night. Mum and Dad knew I was with Pearl, and since she was older, and we hadn't told them about the men, they didn't seem worried about me.

There was never any sexual contact in those days, except for some kissing and cuddling, but I remember feeling very grown-up as we strolled along, holding hands with our new boyfriends, Frank and Jack.

Towards the end of that near-perfect holiday, we decided to pay one last visit to the fairground, and that visit almost turned into a tragedy.

The four of us went on a ride called the Screamer, and we soon to found out why. The individual cars were attached to the engine by large swivel bolts at each end. As the ride sped around the track, they swung out, as a hammock would. Pearl and Jack were in the car in front of us, and as we zoomed round, screaming with laughter, we heard a loud SNAP. Their car had broken loose at one end. It swung back and caught under our car, throwing us onto its floor. Then we heard the second bolt snap. Their car had now broken completely loose, and we watched in horror as it went sailing through the air. I will never forget the sight of Pearl and Jack's bodies hurtling, like rag dolls, towards the ground.

The ride screeched to a halt and I heard ambulance bells. We were all taken to hospital, but Frank and I, although badly shaken up, suffered only minor cuts and bruises. Pearl and Jack stayed there for the next two or three days. They had arrived unconscious and were more seriously injured. They had numerous cuts and bruises and both had had teeth knocked out. Pearl also had concussion, broken ribs and a fractured leg.

When I got back to the caravan and told Mum and Dad what had happened, they were shocked.

'Oh, Iris, you didn't rip your new dress, did you?' said Mum. Typical, I thought.

'Make her a cup of tea, Kit. I'll go over to see Pearl's mum and dad,' Dad said.

'Don't bother, Dad,' I told him. 'They're not there. The police came and got them and took them up to the hospital.'

Mum started to nag, about what I should or shouldn't have been doing, but when she began the 'It serves you right' routine,

Dad told her to shut up. I said a silent thank you to him. Still shaken by what had happened, I didn't feel up to being nagged.

We were grateful that the accident happened at the tail end of our holiday, and that we had had so much fun with our new friends. When we said our goodbyes, we all looked as though we had been in the wars. Poor Pearl's head was bandaged, her leg was in a cast and she was walking with crutches.

We stayed in touch for a long time and I often visited her during her convalescence. The last time I saw Pearl was at her wedding. No, she didn't marry her holiday boyfriend. It turned out she was already secretly engaged to someone back home, whom she eventually married. I noticed, as she walked down the aisle, that she still had a slight limp.

I also stayed in touch with Frank for a while; we saw each other a few more times, but I decided he was much too old for me, especially when he said he wanted to take me home to meet his parents. That scared me. I'm sure if he had discovered I was still at school, he would have been mortified, and I would have died of embarrassment.

I still have a photograph of him, hanging by one hand from a lamp post, scratching under his arm with the other, imitating a chimpanzee; he was such a fun, and funny, person. He was also very thoughtful, if not tactful. He sent me a lovely headscarf for Christmas that year and I was thrilled – until I read the note that came with it. It said, 'I was going to buy you some nylon stockings but when I looked at them I thought they'd be too baggy on your thin legs.' Now, I was fully aware that I had skinny legs, but hearing it from someone else made me feel even more self-conscious. The only thing that saved me from becoming a recluse at that time was that long skirts were in fashion. I could face the world, skinny legs and all.

18

Mud, Glorious Mud:
the Joneses Move West

In late 1947 the London County Council offered our family the opportunity to move to a new house. It was located north-west of London, on a new housing estate near Watford, in Hertfordshire. The government was trying to relocate as many families as possible after the war, the first priority being to house those who had lost their homes in the bombings. Next was to move as many people as possible out of the city so that the clearing and rebuilding of London could begin. It was an enormous undertaking. Many Londoners refused to budge, and of those who did move, large numbers flocked back at the earliest opportunity: they did not adjust well to suburban or country life.

Dad decided it was time for the Jones family to move again. Watford would be closer to where he worked most often; he would no longer have to travel through London to get to the majority of his assignments. He accepted the council's offer of the new house, sight unseen.

'Maybe a move like this'll be good for us,' said Dad. 'We ain't never gonna improve our lot if we stay here.' He was talking about living conditions, and the social class system that existed in England at the time.

I was excited to be moving such a long distance, into a brand-new house, but sad about leaving Nan and Granddad. I would miss them, and I knew Mum would, too.

On May Day 1948, all of our belongings, including sacks of coal, were loaded into a borrowed van. It almost turned out to be too small, even for our little household, but somehow Dad managed to pack everything in. Fascinated as usual by my father's ingenuity, I watched him struggle to wiggle each item into position and wondered, as he muttered, what some of his words meant. Eventually he stood back and scratched his head.

'Blimey, Ted, are you sure that's safe?' asked Mum, who had come outside to check on his progress.

'Well, I was hopin' I wouldn't have to leave the tailgate down,' he said. 'I've tied it up with lots of rope, though, and the weight of the coal sacks should stop stuff shifting.'

'Where are we all gonna sit, Ted? 'Ave you remembered to leave room for us among all that lot?'

'Crikey,' he said. 'I forgot about Peter.' Mum went back into the house, shaking her head.

'Oh, I know what we'll do,' I heard Dad say to himself.

I sat crowded into the front seat with Mum, Dad and two-year-old Robert. A dejected Peter had to ride in the back of the van perched on top of the coal. That had been Dad's good idea. 'He can keep an eye on things. You know, make sure nothing falls off.'

'Yeah, and who's gonna keep an eye on me, to make sure I don't fall off?' moaned Peter.

'I'll put a rope around you as well if you like,' offered Dad.

'Oh, goodie. If the ride's awful, I can just hang meself.'

'Ooh, don't talk like that. That's wicked,' said Mum.

'Come on, stop rabbitin', you lot. We ain't got all day.' Dad's tone told us he was losing patience. It was time to shut up and get going.

Off we went on our top-heavy, slow and bumpy ride. We were on our way to face life in what was to us foreign territory. Sadly, we waved goodbye to 62 Lindsey Road and headed north-west.

'"My old man said follow the van, and don't dilly-dally on the way,"' sang Mum. She often broke into song when she was nervous; Nan did the same thing. This was one of their old music-hall songs.

Dad joined in. '"Off went the van with me home piled in it, I followed on with me old cock linnet . . ."'

I was grinning. I loved it when they sang those old songs: it always cheered everyone up and eased tension.

We were travelling at what Dad called 'snail's pace' through London and its suburbs, so the journey seemed to take for ever. Then the density of buildings began to thin. We were almost in the country, driving along tree-lined roads and lanes. All I could think about was that Dad hated the country. I looked up at him. So far, he appeared happy.

Carrying all of our worldly possessions, including ourselves, the rickety van trundled down the last country lane. We crossed an ancient, single-lane railway bridge. With each lurch, as the wheels crashed into a rock or dropped into a water-filled pot-hole, I was sure our over-burdened vehicle would topple over the bridge's low parapet and we would plunge to our deaths on the rails far below. Dad drove slowly. With white knuckles, he grasped the steering wheel. It was as though his and our lives depended upon his driving, and they did.

Thank God, it was a sunny day. We found ourselves in a sea of mud as we approached a hand-painted, temporary sign bearing the name of our street: Lundin Walk.

'There it is,' I shouted.

And, yes, there it was, our new house, a big '10' painted on a plank, leaning against its side wall.

'That's the second time we've had a number ten,' chirped Mum.

'Brilliant, Kit, that's just brilliant,' said Dad.

'Don't you be sarky with me, Edward,' she said.

'Come on. Let's get out of this bloomin' van. Me legs'll never be the same after that drive,' he complained.

'Mind the mud,' cautioned Mum.

Little did we know how often we'd hear *that* over the next year or two.

Crawling out of the van, we stepped onto some conveniently placed sheets of plywood. We all stood and stared at the house. None of us had ever seen anything like it. It was nice, but odd. It was modern.

The lower half of the two-storey house was white stucco, and the top was corrugated iron painted bright yellow. Large grey asbestos tiles covered the roof, and there were many large windows. The living-room window was about six feet square. Even the front door had glass panels on the top half. Our two previous houses had had tiny windows that let in little light.

'Crikey. It'll take all me sheets to cover them whacking great windows.' Mum was already thinking of her privacy, but I couldn't wait to see inside our new home.

Carefully, stepping on the boards laid over the mud to form a temporary path up to the house, we made our way to the front door. There, crowded onto the four-feet-square front doorstep, the five of us stood waiting expectantly.

An official envelope from the London County Council was pinned to the door. In large letters, scrawled on the front, it said, 'To Mr E. R. Jones.'

'That's us,' said Mum, immediately regretting it. Dad often made fun of her when she stated the obvious.

Dad reached for the envelope, tore it open, removed the contents and read. 'It says the keys are inside on the draining-board in the kitchen.' He tried the door handle. The door was unlocked.

'Don't bring all that mud inside the house. Leave yer shoes on the doorstep,' Mum ordered. In spite of the wooden planks, we had been baptized with mud.

Slipping off our shoes, we dashed in, going off in all directions to explore. It was wonderful. The kitchen had cupboards all around. The sink was stainless steel and had hot and cold taps. There was a separate dining room.

'Ooh,' said Mum. 'That's posh. And, look, we won't need to

buy no lino either.' Shiny brown asphalt tiles covered the floors, at least on this level.

Through a set of double doors, we found the living room, complete with fireplace and that enormous picture window. The house was light, airy and seemed enormous.

Outside the back door there was a small covered porch with a door on the right that led to an outside toilet.

'Ooh,' said Mum, again. 'Fancy havin' an outside lav as well. That'll be handy if I get took short when I'm hangin' out the washin'.'

On the other side of the porch, a second door led into a shed, handy for storage and as a workshop for Dad.

'Look, Dad, you won't have to go out in the rain no more when you need somethin',' said Peter.

'No, nor to get coal. Look, the coalhole's in there too. It looks like they thought of everything,' chimed in Mum.

Inside the front door there was an entrance hall that was bigger than my old bedroom, and upstairs there were three bedrooms and a bathroom with tub and sink. The toilet was separate, the only room in the house with no window.

The bedrooms had built-in wardrobes, with hanging-bars and shelves. I didn't have any clothes that went on hangers. The master bedroom also had a linen cupboard that housed a modern miracle: an electric immersion water heater.

'We can have hot water all the time,' said Mum.

'If you can afford the electric,' griped Dad.

The master bedroom also had an electric fire built into the wall.

'Why don't the other bedrooms have fires, Mum?' I asked.

'Because kids don't need 'em, that's why. Kids have thicker blood. They don't feel the cold so much,' she said, ending that conversation.

It was a wonderful house, the pleasure of it visible on everyone's faces. We all got busy unloading the van, setting up beds, hanging sheets over the windows, and finding the kettle.

Outside it was another story. The streets and footpaths were unpaved. The mud we found ourselves dealing with was in reality heavy clay. It clung to our shoes, accumulating with each step taken, resulting in feet that could hardly be lifted. I felt like a zombie in a Boris Karloff movie as I clomped about with all that squelching clay on my shoes. It was dreadful, the bane of our lives for a long time.

The new housing development, called Oxhey Estate, was one of the first post-war efforts to rehouse Londoners. It was built on land purchased by the government from the Blackwell family estate, of the famous Crosse & Blackwell Company, 'By Appointment, Purveyors of Preserves to the Royal Family since the early 1700s'.

Sir James Altham had built Oxhey Hall, in the early 1600s. He was a judge, and had been Baron of the Exchequer to Queen Elizabeth I. The manor house, private chapel, family graveyard and beautiful gardens were still in existence when we moved to South Oxhey, but only the chapel remains today. One further note, of minor historic interest, is that when the roof of the chapel was replaced in the 1960s, the original roof tiles were sold to Yehudi Menuhin, the late violinist, for use in his house in London.

Open countryside and woods filled with rhododendrons and bluebells surrounded the manor. Many of the fields around the estate were still part of working farms, and used as pasture for livestock.

I remember the excitement of finding our back garden filled with cows one morning. They had trampled down the flimsy fence.

'Blimey,' laughed Mum. 'Those are big sparrows.' We sat with our noses pressed to the kitchen window, staring in amazement.

'Don't be daft, Mum. They ain't sparrows, they're cows,' I said, grinning.

We were fascinated, but a little frightened, to find that German prisoners of war had been responsible for most of the construction on the new housing estate.

'I hope they lock 'em up at night,' whispered Mum. 'I wouldn't trust them buggers any further than I could throw 'em.'

'Bastards,' muttered Dad.

Dad made enquiries. He told us the council had assured him that, at the end of each day, 'our' prisoners returned to the Oxhey Lane Internment Camp, in Hatch End, Middlesex. Many years later, I learned that the Oxhey Lane Camp was just one of more than three hundred such camps in Britain during the 1940s.

'Thank Gawd for that. I'll be able to sleep at night knowing they're not on the loose,' was Mum's response.

We soon realized there was nothing to fear from the German soldiers, and we children would chat to those who could speak English. The prisoners told us about Germany and their families.

'I haf girl and boy of your age. I haf not seen zem for long time. Zey vill be grown-up ven I go back to my home,' said a young prisoner. He had tears in his eyes as he spoke and I felt sorry for him. I was surprised to learn that they had children, wives and mothers, just like the British. They almost sounded like normal people.

One day, as we sat around the edge of a ditch the men were digging, one of them beckoned to me.

'Hey, leedle girl, haf you za beeg seester at home?' he asked.

'No,' I replied. 'But I've got a big brother if you wanna meet him.' All the other men laughed.

Later, when I told Mum about it, I thought she was going to explode. 'Bloody cheek. First, they bloody well try to kill us, and then they want our girls. They should have all been shot,' she spluttered. I loved seeing Mum get flustered like that. She was so funny.

'Don't get aerated, Mum. He was only asking. He wasn't gonna take anyone, was he? He's a prisoner, ain't he? Where would he take someone?'

'Just the same, they shouldn't be thinking things like that, let alone saying it to children. It shouldn't be allowed, cheeky buggers.'

The prisoners wore khaki uniforms with 'P.O.W.' stamped in large letters on the sleeves, jacket backs and the seats of their trousers. The letters on their trousers made us laugh: they looked as though their bums were saying 'POW POW POW' as they walked away.

'Pow Pow Pow,' we'd chorus, as we skipped along behind them. I don't think they had a clue what we were talking or giggling about. We would curl up laughing and they would just smile back at us. Sometimes they said something in German. We could only guess what they meant.

'Very kind,' I told Mum. 'They say we're very kind. Nice, ain't it?'

'Very kind?' she said. 'They don't know what they're talking about. Kind, my eye. That'll be the day.'

'I wonder if they know what we're laughing at, Pete.'

'Nah, they just think you're all bonkers,' he said, and he was closer to the truth than we knew.

We later learned from a friend that what those poor harassed prisoners were saying was '*Verrückte Kinder*' which meant 'crazy children', somewhat different from 'very kind'.

'That's more like it,' said Mum.

We were one of the first families to move to South Oxhey. The housing estate was still in its early stages of construction, with only half of its planned streets and houses completed. Not only were the roads unpaved, there was no school or shops.

We learned we would have to travel by bus to a school in the nearest town, Watford. To make matters worse, our mothers would have to walk almost three miles to buy groceries from Brazier's, the local farm. The only alternative was a one-mile walk to the railway station to take a train into Watford, and that cost money they could ill afford.

'They call this progress?' Mum said, to no one particular. Then, to Dad, 'I wish I was back in Dagenham, that's what I wish, mate.'

The nearest railway station was Carpenders Park. Considered a 'halt', not a proper station, it had originally been built for the exclusive use of residents of the St Meryl Estate, a small exclusive community of privately owned bungalows, and for golfers who came to play at the Oxhey Golf Club. The halt consisted of two narrow wooden platforms and a ticket office housed in a wooden hut no bigger than a newspaper stand. To catch the London train, you had to walk across live electric rails. The halt soon began to sway under the weight of hundreds of rehoused Londoners, but I don't remember how long it took to get a 'real' station.

There were many hardships to overcome in those early days on Oxhey Estate. It did help when Brazier's Farm began taking orders door-to-door and making deliveries. That didn't happen for quite a while, though. We often had to push our old pram up those bumpy country lanes to get supplies. On nice days it was pleasant, but in bad weather, it was hell.

On the way to the farm, all along Little Oxhey Lane, the hedgerows were full of blackberry bushes. We would pick berries along the way for Mum to make into jam or pies. The first time we kids picked berries, we ate as many as we put into the bucket. Later, at home, Mum put the berries in water to clean and prepare them for cooking. Hundreds, if not thousands, of maggots floated to the surface. We were horrified when we realized what we had been eating. Mum gave us each a pill to make sure we didn't end up with the dreaded 'worms'. 'Just in case,' she said.

I had nightmares about maggots crawling around in my belly – ugh! Mum just laughed. She had been brought up in the country so things like that didn't bother her. I recall the time she was picking what she thought was mud off her shoe with her fingernails. Suddenly she stopped and sniffed.

'Pooh,' she said. Then, 'It don't matter.' She laughed. 'A little bit o' shit's lucky if you don't get mad with it.'

After roads and pavements had been constructed, life became easier. Once more, we were able to get staples, like bread and milk, delivered daily. Travelling shops began to show up once or twice a week, including Barker's, a general grocery shop, and the Co-op butcher. They'd toot their horns and women would come dashing from every direction with their shopping baskets hanging over their arms. They all seemed to look the same in those days, at least on our side of the tracks. Most would appear without their false teeth, wearing floral aprons, bedroom slippers and turbans knotted over hair and curlers. Sometimes it was difficult to recognize them if they had their hair combed out, their teeth in and were not wearing an apron.

I believe it was about two years before we got our own shops on the estate; fortunately, they were built at our end of the 4,200-house development. Things were definitely looking up.

19

Watford Fields School and How to Break Your Arm Down the Toilet

Moving to South Oxhey at the beginning of May meant that I would only have to go to school for three months before I was free to enjoy country life. I could hardly wait. I told Mum I didn't think it was worth going to school for just three months but she did not agree, worse luck.

The first day of school arrived. It was time to take the bus to Watford Fields Primary School. I headed for the bus stop, not knowing what to expect.

As I stood there, other children began to arrive; at least now I knew I wouldn't be alone. Nervously pondering my fate, I thought I heard someone call my name, but who could possibly know it on the first day of school? I turned and thought I was dreaming. There, waving and grinning, was Sheila McDonald, my old friend from Dagenham; her family had moved to the Oxhey Estate too. We jumped up and down with excitement and my fears of the unknown dissolved.

Watford Fields Primary School looked like all the old schools in London, dark, oppressive, Victorian, and I learned that it had rules to match. Our new school and the inhabitants of Watford did not receive us well. Considered undesirables from the slums of London, people made fun of our accents and grammar. We also had the stigma of thick mud on our shoes: the locals knew who we were and where we lived. I felt ashamed.

I have scant memories of Watford Fields Primary since my attendance there was brief, but I do remember going to Cuffley School Camp for a week. I believe I was one of the poor kids that went free of charge. Cuffley Camp was in a place called

Potters Bar; we travelled there by bus. Upon arrival, the members of our rag-tag group each received a large canvas bag, which we learned was to be our mattress. We then trooped to a barn where we filled the bags with straw. The barn was crawling with spiders, mice and rats; it gave me the willies. With that chore done, off we went, dragging our lumpy straw mattresses behind us, to find our assigned, two-person tents.

We ate our substantial meals in a community hall. I thought the food was great, but others complained. Some kids cried to go home, and my tent mate ran away because no one believed her story that she owned a real lion. I was happy to have the tent to myself for the rest of my stay.

We went on hikes and nature rambles, played games and sang songs around the campfire, and each day we had to do our chores. My favourite was cleaning the wash-house; I had volunteered for the job. I'm sure everyone thought me strange, but I had never enjoyed competitive sports or games, and had never learned to swim. If cleaning the toilet got me out of those activities, I was delighted. I enjoyed learning about nature, loved listening to folklore and ghost stories around the campfire but was happiest when reading, which I did by torchlight for hours on end after lights-out.

I was sad when it was time to go home; I wished I could have stayed longer.

When our bus arrived back at school, a crowd of parents had gathered outside the gates to welcome their children home. I scanned the crowd for Mum, but she wasn't there; I'd known she wouldn't be – she never was. I would have been so happy to find someone waiting for me.

I caught the regular school bus home, and when I walked back into our kitchen, it was as if I had never been away. I heard Mum clomping down the stairs. She stuck her head around the kitchen door. 'Oh, it's you. I thought I heard someone come in. Go and put your things away, Iris. Did you have a nice time?' She didn't wait for my reply.

On my way home, I had envisaged her welcoming me home with open arms, and giving me a cuddle. I felt sad and disappointed; I had so wanted a different kind of homecoming. Mum was always too busy to think of things like that, I supposed. Sometimes I tried to imagine what it would be like if I ran away. I wondered if she'd miss me, or if she'd even notice I was gone. Yes, I must confess, I often felt sorry for myself in that respect.

It was in a sewing class at Watford Fields Primary that I learned to embroider. My first big project was a set of chair-back covers. We had to pay for all our own materials, and Mum was not happy.

'No. We don't need chair-back covers, Iris,' she said.

'But, Mum, they stop men getting Brylcreem on the backs of the chairs. They keep your furniture nice and clean.'

'I can't afford something that big. Can't you make something smaller?'

'I already told the teacher – please, Mum.'

'You kids think money grows on trees,' she grumbled.

After much pleading, she gave in. I don't know where she got the money from; she must have found that money tree.

The three-piece set had little rabbits, surrounded by flowers, embroidered in each corner. I thought they were beautiful and was proud to have the finished product displayed on the school open day. When I was allowed to take them home, the new covers went straight onto the living-room suite. At least, they did for a while.

Two or three months later, I was lying on my bed reading when Mum, hands planted on hips, appeared in my bedroom doorway. 'Iris, do you know what happened to me new chair-back covers?' she asked.

I knew from the look on her face that I was in trouble.

'Yes, Mum. I gave 'em to Nan.' Nan had recently moved from Dagenham and now lived nearby.

'You done what?' shouted Mum. She had a look of total disbelief on her face. Her hands left her hips and flew up in the air. For a moment, I thought she might strangle me. 'Well, we'll just see about that,' she muttered, as she stomped back down the stairs. I continued to lie there, puzzled by her outburst. I could still hear her in the kitchen, banging things around and talking to herself, saying something about 'bloody kids', which I knew meant me.

I truly thought that, because I had made the chair-back covers, they were mine, and having nothing else to give, I had wrapped them up and given them to Nan as a birthday present. She'd looked almost as pleased as she had when I gave her a signed photograph of Bing Crosby, which I had sent away for knowing he was Nan's favourite film star and singer.

'Don't you ever give anything away before asking me again, Iris,' Mum ordered. 'Especially if it ain't yours to give. Do you hear me?'

'Yes, Mum, I hear you,' I said. I'd given up trying to convince her that they were mine, that I'd only been letting her use them for a while.

I don't know what, if anything, took place between Mum and Nan after that, but it did eventually become a long-standing family joke, just as the infamous missing silver cufflinks had.

Those chair-back covers, which Nan called 'antimacassars', never did find their way back to our front room; they stayed on Nan's furniture until she died, more than twenty years later.

The only other thing I remember about Watford Fields Primary was that I broke my arm there in a freak accident. Breaking a bone is normally an unremarkable event for a youngster, but the way I broke mine was somewhat unusual.

It happened during morning break. We were all running

around the playground as usual when I had an urgent need to visit the toilet. It was against the rules to run inside school buildings, but I was in a hurry. As I ran into the toilet stall, someone put their foot out and tripped me. My left arm went into the toilet bowl as I tried to stop my fall. I heard a snap. The pain was immediate and excruciating, and I fell to the floor screaming. Several teachers arrived on the scene to examine my arm, and the gym teacher, who seemed to know something about first aid, decided that it might be broken. He took me to the hospital by bus.

There, the nurse in Casualty asked, 'And how did you injure your arm, young lady?'

'I fell down the toilet, Miss,' I replied. She looked up from her paperwork. Then, seeing that I was serious, she burst out laughing. That was when I knew it had been worth all the pain: I'd get lots of mileage out of my strange but true story.

An X-ray showed that my arm was broken. The nurse told me I was to have a plaster cast and I knew, for a while at least, that I'd be the centre of attention.

At school, everyone gathered around me to autograph my cast. I also received extra attention at home. I loved having a broken arm, and when it stopped hurting, I pretended it still did.

The itching under the cast almost drove me crazy. I thought God might be punishing me for pretending that it still hurt, but good old Nan saved me. She told me to carry a knitting needle with me so that I could reach under the cast to scratch the itch.

After the cast had been removed, my arm was weak, the skin discoloured and peeling. The doctor had warned me about dead skin, but I was unprepared for its disgusting smell.

'Pooh, blimey, what a pong,' said Mum. 'It smells like something died.' Of course, she was right. 'You'd better soak that arm in disinfectant or dogs'll start howling.' Well, I thought, at least someone thinks it's funny.

I don't remember how long I was at Watford Fields Primary School, but eventually the time to move on approached and I learned that next term I'd be attending Victoria Girls' School, also in Watford. There would be no school bus: we were 'big girls' and would need to start making our own way to and from school. We'd have to commute by train, and I was not looking forward to that. However, in the mean time, we had six whole weeks of freedom, plenty of time to enjoy life in the country.

It was an idyllic summer. We played from morning to night, tramping through the woods, chasing through fields, picking wild flowers and building tree houses; we hadn't a care in the world. I made new friends, mostly boys, and there was never a lack of new things to do or places to explore. At one time, I was the only girl in an otherwise all-boys gang. I liked that. It meant they wouldn't pick on me, or tease me, as they did most other girls. We also played on construction sites, which reminded me of playing on London's bombsites, but without the fun of finding treasures as we had in the rubble of bombed-out houses.

That was one of the happiest summers of my life. At that time, we were on double daylight-saving time and the days seemed endless. It stayed light until after ten o'clock at night, and often we'd still be playing outside at that hour, before our parents realized the time and called us in. That was the summer of my tenth birthday, and I remember wishing it would last for ever.

I only recall feeling frightened once, when I was walking alone in the woods. Suddenly a man jumped out from behind dense bushes, exposing himself to me. He was the classic flasher, I suppose, complete with trench coat.

I ran away from him, as memories flooded my mind of the family friend who had terrorized me years before, and of the man in Wales who had molested me.

There was no one at home when I got there, and I was glad. I didn't have to tell anyone what had happened. Had they known, they might have forbidden my visits to the woods, especially alone.

Another time, when Maureen Tring, the girl next door, and I were picking berries in the lane, I became aware of someone riding back and forth behind us on a bike. I turned to see who it was and there was a man, perhaps the same one I'd seen in the woods, exposing himself.

'He's got his whelk hangin' out,' I whispered to Maureen. She screamed, and we ran. Fortunately, Maureen's dad was at home.

'Mr Tring, Mr Tring, there's a man up the lane with his whelk hanging out,' I blurted. Maureen and I were still panting after running all the way home. Mr Tring turned beet-red. He jumped on his bike and pedalled off down the lane to try to catch the offender.

'Bloody pervert, I'll wring his effing neck if I catch him,' he shouted.

He never did find him. Thankfully, we never saw the man again.

'What's a whelk?' asked dumb Maureen later. 'I thought it was called a willy.' She added, as an afterthought, 'I don't think my dad's got a willy, though. I heard Gran say something about his nuts, and she was pointing at his down-there.'

I often wondered why our parents didn't report those incidents to the police. Perhaps they were too embarrassed to talk about it; I know Mum would have been. I always thought she would blame me for whatever happened; she usually did. I could imagine her saying things like 'You shouldn't have been there,' or 'It's your own fault.' What would have been the point of telling if your own mum wasn't on your side?

Anyway, that kind of thing never stopped us playing in the woods. We only knew fear if we came face to face with it, and most of us had experienced far worse things in London during the war.

'Stay away from them gypsies,' our mothers warned us. There were many gypsies about in those days. They went door-to-door selling handmade clothes pegs. Mum always bought a few because she was superstitious.

'If I don't buy some, they'll put a curse on us,' she told us.

We usually ignored our mothers' warnings. Gypsies fascinated us. We would skulk around their encampments trying to catch a glimpse of their mysterious ways. We heard all kinds of scary stories about them, but they just made us more curious.

'Curiosity killed the cat,' Mum warned. She never did explain what cats had to do with gypsies.

Some gypsies still lived in the classic, elaborately painted wooden caravans. Others had begun living in more modern types. I wished I could see inside one of those brightly painted caravans with all the shiny brass things hanging inside. My friends told me if I went in, the gypsies would kidnap and sell me – no one would know what had happened to me.

We saw them roasting a hedgehog over the fire one day. They wrapped the whole thing, eyeballs, spines, feet and all, in wet clay. Then they threw it in the open fire. Later, they removed it and broke away the clay. The skin and spines came off with it, leaving the meat ready to eat. We thought that was clever but still didn't fancy trying it.

'Do you know what hedgehog tastes like, Mum?' I asked later.

'How would I know that? It probably tastes like rabbit,' she said. 'What do you want to know that for?'

'Dunno, Mum. I was just wonderin'.'

I liked roast rabbit – we often had it for dinner – but I don't think I would have liked it if I'd seen it cooked with its fur and ears still on. I was glad Mum didn't ask any more questions.

Another discovery was a tramp's camp in the woods, well

hidden beneath enormous rhododendron bushes. Occasionally, we'd find a tramp staying in there. We were afraid to hang around for long: we had heard that they ate children. A quick look was all we needed to send us running – after we'd thrown a few stones to wake him. We might have been scared but we still enjoyed annoying the poor man. He was probably harmless, but we were taking no chances on becoming his dinner.

That glorious summer ended. It had been the happiest summer of my life but, as adults constantly reminded me, 'All good things must come to an end.'

20

Methodists and Spiritualism

After we'd settled into our new home and become accustomed to our surroundings, Dad began talking about the need for a church. 'We need a Sunday school for the kids.'

'Whatever are you talking about, Ted?' Mum said.

'We should start one.'

'What do you mean, *we*? I ain't having nothing to do with starting a Sunday school. I've got enough to do.'

'I know, I know, I wasn't talking about you, Kitty. I was talking about me, wasn't I?'

'Oh, that's all right, then, but I still don't know where you get off thinking you can just go out and start a flippin' Sunday school. People are gonna think you're mad, Ted.'

'I should have known you'd try to put the kibosh on it,' he said. Then I heard the kitchen door close, and Mum's footsteps going upstairs.

I'd been in the next room listening to Mum and Dad's conversation, and thought, Please don't say anything else, Mum, please don't get Dad upset. I couldn't stand it when Dad turned into what Mum called 'an old rat-bag'.

I think Dad missed being involved. He had spent much of his spare time at the church in Dagenham, but now there was no church, well, not nearby. The closest church was in Watford. Except for the few Catholics on the estate, who I learned *had* to go to church, no one else seemed to bother. I never did work out why the Catholics had to go and we didn't. I asked Mum about it.

'Dunno, really, Iris. I used to know lots of Jews up the East

End, but I don't think I've ever met no Catholics. I think they're all Irish but they sound like a funny bunch. Fancy being scared to stay home on Sundays – blimmin' daft, if you ask me.'

Dad, in spite of Mum's apprehension, took matters into his own hands. He was on a mission, and he had flyers printed at work. Having left his old job, he was now with at Odhams Press in Watford and no longer worked away from home.

'It's handy working for a printing company,' he said. 'These flyers came out nice, didn't they? Now all we have to do is deliver them. Wanna help me do some canvassin', Iris?'

'What's that?' I had visions of putting up tents.

'You daft ha'porth, it's delivering these papers and talking to people about it.'

'Yeah, I don't mind, Dad,' I said. I still wasn't sure what he was talking about, but I knew I shouldn't ask Mum. She still shook her head and walked away every time Dad brought up the subject. I was just glad to be included.

In the evenings, Dad and I began canvassing the neighbourhood. First time around, we stuck the flyers through the letterboxes. Then we went back, knocked on doors and talked to people. I have no idea how many houses we visited, but it was a lot.

The flyer declared, 'NOTHING PROVIDED FOR THE CHILDREN AND YOUTH OF SOUTH OXHEY'. It went on to say that we were trying to determine what interest there might be in starting a Sunday school and possibly a youth club.

Dad was excited when the idea was greeted with enthusiasm, and several people offered to help in any way they could.

'It's about time these kids had something to do besides buggering about in the streets,' said one old woman. 'They're a bloody menace if you ask me.' She handed Dad half a crown. 'Good luck to you, mate,' she said, as she stuck her cigarette back into her mouth and closed the front door. Dad and I just looked at each other and grinned. Half a crown was a lot of money.

One man said we could borrow an old portable organ that had belonged to his missionary father, and since Dad could play the piano and the organ, he accepted the offer. He also acquired several dozen old hymn books; I have no idea where they came from but he was now well on the way to having everything he needed to get started.

The next step was to find a place to hold the meetings. Dad approached the London County Council and asked if he could use a nearby Nissen hut that had been used as a canteen by the prisoners of war and other construction workers on the estate. He explained that it would be ideal for his purposes: the workers used it only during weekday working hours, and it was already equipped with folding chairs and tables. He added that they would also be doing a great public service by allowing the use of the building for such an honourable activity.

After some debate, the council gave Dad permission to proceed. He could use the corrugated-steel building, which looked exactly like an enormous air-raid shelter, free of charge if he guaranteed its maintenance. They even provided him with a set of keys.

Dad and I were excited, but I could tell Mum was worried. She didn't have to say a word. I always knew when she was unhappy or nervous: she would call Dad 'Edward', instead of the usual Ted. Dad, too, knew she was upset, but as usual, he ignored her.

A second flyer, announcing the opening of the Oxhey Sunday school, was printed and distributed, and on that first Sunday afternoon, we set up twenty chairs. Wondering if we were being too optimistic, we sat nervously waiting to see if anyone would turn up, and turn up they did; we even had to set out extra chairs.

I was proud of my dad, and happy to be working beside him, helping to make his community project a success.

His first sermon was a simple message, told with his Cockney accent, in plain language that the children could understand. Then we sang some favourite hymns, accompanied by Dad pumping away on the ancient fold-up organ.

'Who would like to come back next week?' he asked the children.

Every hand shot up in the air. 'I would,' they all shouted.

Dad beamed, and so did I.

It wasn't long before Sunday services, by request, were added to the agenda. Later, a youth club began meeting on Thursday evenings. In all it was a great success, and Dad was in his element. He spent hours studying and preparing sermons and the people loved him.

After a while, I think Dad realized it was too much for him to handle on his own.

'You've bitten off more than you can chew, Edward,' was all Mum said, but her face wore an I-told-you-so look.

'You may be right, Kitty,' he replied, surprising us all.

Although he now had some help from one or two other people, he admitted he was finding it difficult to keep up with such a full agenda. It was especially hard since he was now putting in a lot of overtime at Odham's.

'I've decided to ask the Methodist church in Watford for help and advice,' he announced. 'I'll tell them that we belonged to the Methodist church in Dagenham and I bet they'll be only too glad to help now I've got this one started for them.' He looked relieved to have come up with what I'm sure he thought was the perfect solution.

The church's response to his request came as a great shock to Dad. Instead of being pleased with his efforts, and their results, they were offended and angry: 'How dare you presume to preach

God's word? How dare you think that just anyone can start a church without proper education and ordination?'

Their attitude and rudeness stunned Dad. He came home from the meeting a dejected, disillusioned man. He told us he would have to pray for an answer, for patience and tolerance.

The following Sunday, Dad put on a happy face and held services as usual. Seated in the congregation were several of the Methodist church officials from Watford, the men he had met. If they thought their presence would upset Dad, they were wrong. It had the opposite effect. I was sure he preached his best sermon ever.

After the service, one of the men asked Dad if he was available to meet them, which he did. They told him they had talked to the church hierarchy and explained the situation. They had received the go-ahead to assume responsibility for the new church as soon as possible.

Dad was thrilled – until they informed him that his services would no longer be required 'in any capacity'; that he was not qualified to do what he had been doing at church services, Sunday school or the youth club. They requested that he hand over all his records, then asked him to announce to the parishioners that he would no longer be involved in running the church. They even told him it would be best for all concerned if he attended a different church.

'Different church, my eye,' stormed Dad, when he came home. 'If that's what the Methodist Church calls Christianity, they can bloody well have it. I certainly won't be having anything more to do with them.'

It broke my heart to see him like that. He had worked hard, only to be squashed like a bug by bureaucracy. I felt sorry for him, and for myself, as once more I experienced the pain and frustration of entrapment in the confines of the lower uneducated class of British society, a class in which we would never be quite good enough. For Mum, though, it seemed different. She had always accepted her so-called station in life, and was comfortable with it.

'I told him he shouldn't have done it,' she told me, when Dad wasn't around. 'His big head's got him in trouble again. I knew something like this was gonna happen.'

Too young to realize what Mum was talking about, I still thought my dad was the cleverest man on earth, that he could do no wrong. In spite of how he had hurt me in earlier years, when he had made the doll's house furniture for our old church, not for me, I was yet to learn of, or understand, his inflated ego and his need for attention.

The old saying that 'When one door closes, another opens' proved true at this difficult crossroads in Dad's life.

Dad returned the borrowed organ to its owner, Mr Addison, and explained what had happened with the Methodists. Mr Addison was sympathetic and invited him in for a drink. During the course of their conversation, he told Dad about the church he and his wife attended. It was the Watford Christian Spiritualist Church. They told him not to be disheartened and invited him to go with them to a service some time; he would find their church different from most other denominations, they said. There was no bureaucracy.

When Dad came home that evening, he looked a little less depressed and told us of his interesting conversation.

'I might give it a try once I get over that other miserable lot,' he said.

Not long after his chat with Mr Addison, Dad visited the Spiritualist church, and soon appeared hooked; it was all he talked about, with me his primary audience. What he told me was fascinating. Even Mum became interested and surprised everyone by saying she wanted to go to church with him.

'You go, Mum, I'll take care of Robert,' I said. I thought it would be nice to see them going out together for a change.

At first, they only attended Sunday services. Then they began attending Thursday evening clairvoyance sessions. For a while, it seemed they were always going to church and that I was always babysitting.

I enjoyed taking care of things at home initially. Besides getting Robert to bed, I would tidy the house and do the ironing. At first, Mum seemed to appreciate my efforts, praising and thanking me, but then it became expected and I was resentful. One night I did nothing, just to see if they would notice. The house was still a mess when they came home.

'You ain't done nothing, Iris. What have you been doing all night?' Mum said. Anger and hurt welled up inside me.

'You witch,' I yelled at her. 'All you ever do is nag, nag, nag.'

Dad stepped up to me and slapped my face. Shocked, I ran to my room, sobbing. The slap had hurt physically, but the fact that it had come from Dad was devastating. I blamed Mum and hated her for it; I didn't speak to either of them for days, and they didn't speak to me.

Many years later, it occurred to me that it was the only time I had ever known Dad to defend Mum; in a way, I admired him for that.

Dad's interest in spiritualism was growing. It seemed that he couldn't get enough of what the Church believed, taught and offered. He began attending séances and healing services and read everything he could get his hands on to further his understanding and knowledge of the subject.

With Dad becoming more and more involved, Mum started pulling back. It became too much for her, especially now that Dad was travelling all over the London area, attending lectures and classes.

At the time, Harry Edwards was one of Britain's most famous

clairvoyants and healers and Dad travelled long distances to attend his idol's lectures. Whatever gift Harry Edwards had, Dad wanted it too, and he worked hard to develop his own healing and clairvoyant powers.

It wasn't long before Dad became popular and respected in spiritualist circles. Mum once more stepped – or was pushed – into the shadows; she stopped attending church completely. I think she had learned long before that she could never compete for Dad's attention once he had found his way into the limelight.

After about a year of studying under some well-known 'sensitives', and now recognized as a healer and clairvoyant, Dad began holding séances and healings in our home.

Spiritualism fascinated me. I often went with Dad to church and loved listening to his conversations on the subject. Then, when I was perhaps twelve, Dad invited me to sit in on one of his séances.

'We've got a famous medium coming tonight,' he told me. 'It should be very interesting. Would you like to come?' I was scared at the idea, but curious. I also felt that at last I had become visible: someone actually valued my presence.

'Yes, please, Dad.'

'Ooh, I don't know, Ted. Are you sure it's all right for a kid?' Mum asked.

'Of course it is or I wouldn't have suggested it, would I?' he said, showing his impatience with her. I didn't like causing trouble, but I did like Dad including me, along with Mum.

That evening about ten people gathered in our dimly lit living room. The guest medium sat in a wingback chair in front of us and, after completing the social niceties, she explained that she would be going into a trance, and that her 'guide' would more than likely take over. Of course, I hadn't a clue what that meant.

Closing her eyes, she began rocking back and forth and then to chant. When she stopped rocking and chanting, she spoke, but now her voice sounded nothing like it had before. It was now a *basso profundo* male voice, with a strange foreign accent.

She first spoke to the group using sweeping hand and arm movements. Then she addressed individuals, giving them each messages from people in the spirit world. In the middle of it all, I suddenly became aware that someone, a stranger, was standing behind my mother's chair. I almost jumped out of my skin when I realized that I was seeing a spirit, and I began shaking like a leaf. Then Dad, who was sitting next to me on the sofa, gently placed his hand on my knee and smiled. 'It's nothing to be scared of, Iris. I can see him too. He's just an old friend of your mum's,' he whispered.

I didn't know then, and don't know now, what to make of that experience. It scared me to the point that I didn't want to sit in on a séance again. I was interested in spiritualism, clairvoyance and healing, but I was too young to experience surprises of that nature. It was far too unsettling.

When Dad asked me if I would like to learn more and attend other séances with him, I told him I was too scared of what might happen. Often when I was upstairs in bed, I became aware of strange noises downstairs. I heard stories of tables flying around the room during sessions with the ouija board, and of the sofa levitating across the room with three people sitting on it. No, I wanted nothing more to do with it.

As Dad became more involved in spiritualism, he also became interested in other fields of study. He read voraciously, and became very knowledgeable about the Bible, various sciences, philosophies and most other religions. He wanted to better himself through education, hoping that in doing so he might be able to move within a more intellectual circle of people.

Eventually, he became president of the Watford Christian Spiritualist Church, which made me proud, I suppose. It was an unpaid position, but he was a popular man, especially with the women. It fed his hungry ego but made Mum even more insecure and unhappy. Not only did she stop attending church and meetings with him, she took less and less care of herself.

My father was a handsome man and very sociable. Mum, in her insecurity, became more overweight and decidedly more antisocial; she went for days without putting her false teeth in. He went to dinner parties but Mum usually declined. Dad wanted to reciprocate and invite people home for dinner, but Mum lacked the confidence to entertain his friends. He was gone from home more and more.

'He don't want me with him anyway,' she confided. She thought he was ashamed of her, and by then, I'm sure she was right.

I loved to sit and talk to Dad, and we often talked into the wee hours. I believe I have him to thank for opening my mind to such a wide variety of subjects, and that it was him who inspired me to learn. I know my mother was jealous of our relationship, but Dad said she refused to discuss with him the things that interested him.

'You just wanna make me look stupid in front of all your high-falutin' friends. You just wanna make a fool of me,' she told him.

I thought my dad was the most brilliant man in the world, and hung on his every word. I idolized him and, I'm sorry to say, had very little respect for my mother. I always thought that if she had made an effort to look nice, or to keep a nicer home, things might have been different. Instead, it seemed to get worse. She never wanted to join in discussions around the living-room fire, and usually just stayed busy in the kitchen, doing ironing or other chores. Mum and I argued a lot, which I suppose was normal, but I believe she resented my relationship with Dad. If only she had known how much I had wanted and needed her throughout my childhood. If only she hadn't pushed me away.

But where did I fit into my father's actual church activity at that time? Nowhere, it would seem. I clearly remember asking him if I was invited to the children's Christmas party at the church. He seemed hesitant, but finally agreed that I could go. When Father Christmas handed out a present to each child, there was nothing for me; Dad told me it wouldn't have been appropriate. I never understood why our relationship seemed non-existent outside the home. Was it because, in his lofty position at church where the congregation showered him with praise and attention, he was ashamed of me too?

In spite of the great admiration I had for my father and his accomplishments, something happened, also around that time, that made me question how I really felt about him as a man. He was studying reincarnation and regression, and after explaining its theories and concepts, he asked me to participate in an experiment. Curious, I agreed. Then, as he tried to talk me into a hypnotic state, I felt distrustful and feared he might touch me inappropriately. I could not relax. I completed the exercise and related my made-up dream experience. I could never have told him that I had held back because of my underlying fear of him.

I agonized over that experience for a long time. The only thing I can believe is that I had acquired a deep mistrust of men after the experiences in my early childhood. There had since been yet another incident, at the cinema, where a man had offered me money if I let him touch me down below. Again, I'd run away, but could not tell anyone for fear of reprisal. My mother's and grandmother's words played repeatedly in my head: 'Men, all they ever want is one thing'; 'Dirty old men'; 'Men, I wouldn't give you twopence for a cartload of 'em'; 'Men, I wouldn't trust 'em any further than I could throw 'em.' I suppose all of that contributed to a lasting negative effect on my subconscious, making it impossible for me to lose or surrender control.

Another traumatic incident occurred during our days of spiritualism. I had spent the evening with a school friend, Sonja Oehme, who lived on the next street. Her parents had been to London to celebrate their anniversary, and it was very late when they arrived home.

Sonja's father, who was very drunk, insisted on walking me home, and what happened on that so-called walk scared me and brought me to tears. Once we were outside, he took my hand and started running up and down the street, dragging me along behind him.

'Where is it? Where is it? Where's the house with all the ghosts flying around?' he shouted, as he ran. At one point, he tripped and fell, pulling me down on top of him. By now, lights were going on in windows, and people were looking out to see who or what was making all the noise.

I'm not sure how long it went on, but I was sobbing when at last he left me at my front gate. He staggered off, laughing and shouting something about 'those crazy Joneses and their ghosts'. I despised him, and I wanted to die.

It was then I became aware that certain of our neighbours were making fun of my father and of his beliefs. That particular neighbour had taken it out on me, and I had never felt so ashamed, of myself and of my family.

Little did anyone know that, ultimately, the idol of Watford Christian Spiritualist Church would tumble from his pedestal, once his relationship with a member of the church was revealed. It would then be our turn to be ashamed of *him*.

With all of that, plus Dad's ever-increasing absences from home and family, and Mum's seeming lack of interest in anything or anyone except Dad, I knew I would have to look for support from outside the family. However, in the mean time, I had yet another new school to deal with.

21

Victoria Girls' School, Diseased Fish and Other Capers

I stood outside the walls of Victoria Girls' School and stared up at the tall wooden gates, which had rusting iron struts across them and a giant lock. They seemed to say, 'Keep out,' and I wondered if I'd feel as unwelcome here as I had at two previous schools, one in Wales, the other in Watford. Looking down at my shabby clothes, baggy socks and scuffed, muddy shoes, I already knew the answer.

With a feeling of dread, I pushed open the heavy gates and walked into the playground. Scanning the area for a familiar face, I found none. I knew my friend Sheila wouldn't be there. She had scarlet fever and was in hospital.

Girls in uniform played nearby. They stopped and stared at me. 'We know where you're from,' said one of them.

'Why don't you go to your own school?' said another, thumbing her nose at me.

I wanted to say something back but the words wouldn't come. I hated them, and I hated me. I didn't want to be there, but had no choice. An ache started in my throat and tears stung my eyes. Then I felt the heat of anger rise in my chest. Already hurt, I decided I would not allow their mistreatment or derision to wound me further. Although unsure whether my reaction would be that of fight or flight, I found new strength. I stuck out my chin defiantly and marched forward to face my new challenge, only this time I was wearing a new attitude.

The local children wore uniforms, which made it impossible for us council-estate children to blend in. At the first morning assembly, our shabby presence was obvious.

'You council-estate children will not be required to wear uniforms. We don't expect to have you here for long. We're hoping you'll soon have your own school on the estate,' the headmistress announced, peering down her nose over horn-rimmed glasses. Then, after one or two other notices, she refastened her lips. Her face was like a worn-leather drawstring handbag. She was not an attractive woman; in fact, she looked like a man in women's clothes. She even wore a tie under her brown tweed jacket.

'Good,' someone said behind me.

'Good riddance,' said somebody else. Around me, other girls snickered, and a finger poked me in the back. Clenching my fists, I felt like punching someone but I knew it would just cause trouble for me.

I knew that we estate girls would have to stick together and at break time, like magnets, we gravitated to one another.

'Like attracts like,' Mum always said. She was right, of course, but how could we convince the local girls that we were really just like them? Why did they have to be nasty to us? We didn't want to attend their school, and it wasn't our fault that we sounded different from them.

'"Ain't" ain't in the dictionary "ain't" ain't,' they taunted. 'Don't they have any aitches where you poxy lot came from?'

'Just ignore 'em,' said one of my friends. 'They're just higorant.' We all laughed.

Later, when I told Dad, he laughed too. 'Well,' he said, 'it's true. Cockneys stopped using aitches a long time ago. They thought they were a waste of time and energy. 'Ere, I'll tell you a joke about aitches. A Cockney boy moved to the country and started going to a posh school. The 'oity-toity teacher decided to try to teach 'im 'ow to pronounce 'is aitches. "Repeat after me," she said, strongly pronouncing each aitch. "Hard Hearted Harry Hit His Horse over the Head with a Heavy Hammer." And what do you think the boy said? "Aw, poor 'orse."'

'Now, don't it make you feel better knowin' 'ow it all started and knowin' there's even jokes about it?'

'No, it don't, Dad, not when people are pointin' at you and laughin', but I'll try to think of 'Arry and 'is poor 'orse next time.' And I couldn't wait to tell my friends the joke.

When Sheila recovered from her long illness, we began travelling to school on the train together. It helped to be with someone who was just like me. A number of estate children commuted to school with us and, like sleepwalkers, they'd flop down on the seats. Some looked as though they hadn't combed their hair or had a wash. Half asleep, they'd often still be gnawing their breakfast bread and jam. They made me feel ashamed.

Memories of two teachers remain with me. Each in their way brought joy into the hours I spent in that gloomy, unwelcoming building. Mrs Godden, the English teacher, was an ordinary-looking middle-aged woman; I see grey when I conjure an image of her in my mind. However, there was nothing ordinary or grey about the way she taught.

With the dramatic expression of a professional actor, she would read aloud to us. Each story and character sprang to life. As I followed the lines with her, I was no longer just reading words on a page, I was learning to see and feel them too. Pictures and illustrations were no longer necessary: I could see it all in living colour inside my head, and I couldn't get enough of it.

Mrs Godden was one of those rare teachers who had that special gift of turning children on to learning. I will never forget her, or the love of literature she instilled in me.

For reasons beyond my comprehension, I followed her home after school one day. I stood outside her gate, staring at her closed front door. I wondered what it would be like to have her for a mother. How it would feel to have someone like her to talk to every day. I wanted to go up to the door and knock, to let her know I was there, but I didn't. She might think me a nuisance or, worse, be angry with me. Instead, I turned and began my own long journey home, knowing that no one would notice I was late.

The other teacher I remember was Madame du Brulle. She taught, or tried to teach us, French. She was a tiny woman with flaming red hair, which she wore piled in an enormous bouffant on top of her head. Inside the bouffant you could see some kind of a form, I supposed there to maintain the height of the hairdo. We thought it hilarious since the brown lump was so visible. It looked as though she was trying to conceal a giant wart, and perhaps she was. With an excess of rouge on her cheeks, and bright red lipstick applied haphazardly near her mouth, her face was almost a caricature. She had a nose that curved down, and a chin that curved up; she looked like Punch, of the old Punch and Judy puppet shows.

Madame, as we called her, had a flaming temper to match her hair, and we delighted in getting her riled. I remember well her attempts to teach us a lively French song about *sabots*.

First, we'd sing it with no expression at all, making the jolly folk song sound like a funeral dirge.

'Seeng ze song wiz more ensusiasms and loudness,' she'd shout, beating a tempo on her desk with a small baton. We would then scream it out at the top of our lungs.

'Not zo loud, not zo loud, *s'il vous plaît*,' a quietly fuming Madame would plead. Then, of course, we would whisper it.

Exploding in a fit of rage, our dear, and until then, patient teacher would throw up her hands and storm out of the classroom, leaving us laughing nervously, like a pack of young hyenas. We were sure she'd come back with the dreaded headmistress, but she didn't. She never ratted on us.

Our behaviour was dreadful. It was inexcusable. However, Madame always returned with a smile. She must have been an optimist and, in spite of all the disruption, I remember almost everything she taught me.

It was also at Victoria Girls' School that I first learned to ride a bicycle. I had never owned a bike so I'd never had the opportunity to learn.

Some of the local girls – we called them townies, including a girl named Audrey – rode their bikes to school. They stored them in the school's bike-shed during the day. No one liked Audrey: everyone thought she was stupid because she wore thick lemonade-bottle glasses and had ears that stuck out the way cup handles do. I felt sorry for her; I knew how it felt to be shunned. She was the only townie I ever made friends with. Unfortunately, our friendship was short-lived.

One day, as I ran my hand longingly over Audrey's shiny blue bike, she offered to teach me how to ride. She knew I didn't have a bike and that I didn't know how to ride one.

'I'll show you how at lunch times. You can go along the edge of the playground when no one's looking.'

'Ooh, thanks, Audrey,' I said, trying hard not to jump up and down with excitement.

Audrey was a good teacher and I learned fast. Then, one sunny day, when I was having a go on the bike, I had an idea. 'Can I have a ride outside the playground, Audrey?' I asked. 'I wanna see what it's like riding in the road. I wanna see if I can do it. I promise I'll be careful.'

'Oh, all right,' she said. 'But I'll kill you if you're gone more than five minutes.'

'Thanks, Audrey. I won't be long, don't worry.'

She pushed open the school gates for me and off I wobbled, on my first real bike ride. Grinning from ear to ear, I waved back at her. 'Ta-tah,' I shouted.

'Ta-tah,' I heard, looked over my shoulder and saw the worry on her face.

It was an idyllic day, warm and sunny under clear blue skies. There wasn't a wisp of a cloud in sight. Smiling both inside and out, I rode back and forth on the street, all the while thinking, I can do it. Then, in a moment of daring or madness, I decided to venture a little further. I rode to the end of the street, rounded the corner and kept going.

I was outside those ugly walls, away from the people who seemed to hate me, away from the place where I felt unwelcome yet imprisoned. I wanted to laugh aloud. I felt like a bird that had just learned to fly. I'd been released from my cage and the sensation was exquisite as I pedalled faster and faster with my long plaits flying out behind me.

I have no idea how long I'd been riding, but suddenly, my errant mind re-entered the conscious world. Somewhere, somehow, I had made a wrong turn. Wrong turn, I thought, they'd all been wrong turns. I hadn't made a right turn since I'd left the school gates. The realization that I was lost hit me over the head like a bagful of wet laundry. I hadn't a clue where I was.

Dazed and shaking, I stood by the side of the road next to my getaway vehicle. I couldn't ask anyone for directions. If I did, they'd know I was a truant. I felt sick. My stomach was in knots and my heart was pounding like African tom-toms. Sweat trickled into my eyes and down my back. I knew I couldn't just stand there so I got back on the bike and started out again.

After riding around for what seemed hours, I eventually found myself back at school, and wondered what nightmare lay ahead. I was terrified.

By then school was over for the day. There was no sound coming from the playground, and the grey 'Gates to Hell' loomed. With a growing sense of foreboding, I pushed open the creaky gates and there stood Audrey. She was waiting for the return of her former friend and, of course, her bike. Strangely, she didn't look relieved or angry; she looked as scared as I felt. It was only then that I realized Audrey was not alone.

There, with tree-trunk legs astride and hands planted on

broad tweed-clad hips, was our formidable headmistress. Her face was a strange colour and it looked as though it was about to split right down the middle. At that moment my mind, once again, departed. I vaguely remember Audrey grabbing her bike and heading out of the gate, and then a firm hand grabbed me and dragged me into the building.

Standing before Attila, our nickname for her, I awaited the bad news. Would I get the cane? The slipper? Worse? Maybe the news would be good: perhaps they would expel me. What if I'd broken the law? What if they sent me to an approved school? The whirlwind of thoughts made me dizzy.

'Have you no brains at all, child?' she began. 'Do you not understand rules? Who brought you up? Did they not teach you right from wrong? You are a disgrace.' The lecture was long. She droned on for ever. Her insults were hurtful and cruel. 'You people are all alike. You'll never make anything of yourselves. You must remember your place and start showing some respect for your betters.' What was she talking about? I wanted to die and have it over. The last thing I remember her saying was something about how lucky I was that school policy disallowed the caning of girls. I suppose she was right in a way: I was lucky. I was lucky that my mind had once more absented itself.

The incident was reported to my parents who, although displeased, were surprisingly sympathetic.

The punishment for my crime, besides being forbidden to ride Audrey's or anyone else's bike, was to sit outside Attila's office at break and lunch times every day for a month. I didn't really mind. I was allowed to read, and I loved reading. Besides, I had learned how to ride a bike, even on the street. It had been worth it. Now, I thought, if only I owned a bike.

Not long after that incident, Mum let me in on a secret. 'Your dad felt sorry for you, Iris,' she told me. ''E's put a notice up at work sayin' 'e's lookin' for a cheap second-hand bike. Don't tell him I told you, though, 'e don't want you gettin' your 'opes up.' I promised I wouldn't say a word.

Every day after I'd learned the secret, I waited for Dad to tell me he had good news for me. I'd sit at the front window waiting to see if there might be something different in his walk, or his face, that might tell me he'd had good luck. Two weeks passed. No news. Then one night Dad stuck his head around the back door, and he had a big grin on his face.

'I think you've got yourself a bike, Iris. A bloke at work's givin' it to me,' he said. 'I'm goin' to 'is 'ouse at the weekend to pick it up. 'E told me it needs repairs but 'e thought it was all there. It used to belong to 'is daughter. It's a girl's bike.'

'Thanks, Dad. I never thought I'd ever get a bike of me own. Is it a nice one? What colour is it?'

'Dunno,' he said. 'It's free. Beggars can't be choosers, remember?' I must say, I was getting sick and tired of hearing *that* admonishment.

That weekend Dad carried home my long-awaited bike. When he came around the corner, he had the rusty frame slung over one shoulder, the wheels over the other. The tyres had rotted away on the rims and the rest of the parts were in a burlap sack. How could that rusty pile of bits be a bike? I knew it had been too good to be true.

'In case you was still wondering about the colour of the bike, Iris, it's rust-coloured,' laughed Mum.

'It's not funny, Mum,' I said, glaring at her.

'Don't worry,' said Dad. 'You keep telling me I'm a clever old cock, and now I'm gonna show you what a clever old cock I am. I'll soon sort this out.' Mum rolled her eyes.

Over the next two weeks, in his spare time, Dad soaked all the parts in some kind of liquid. Then, piece by piece, using a wire brush, he scrubbed away the rust until I could see the metal underneath. I still wondered if there was a whole bike there, but Dad assured me there was. He even promised to buy new tyres.

'What colour do you want it?' he asked.

'Blue,' I replied, envisaging the birth of a twin to Audrey's bike.

'Righto, then. That's what you'll get.' He told me to stay out of the shed until it was finished. I could hardly wait to see what, if any, miracle Dad could perform.

The big day came. I stood outside Dad's shed, waiting for the unveiling. Mum waited in the kitchen doorway, watching me. When he wheeled the bike around the corner, I felt my chin and shoulders drop. He had painted it with bright baby-blue bathroom-enamel paint. It was the ugliest bike I had ever seen. How could I ride a thing like that? Everyone would make fun of me. How could I tell Dad I'd be too embarrassed to get onto it?

'Oh, Dad, it's lovely,' I said, hoping he couldn't see my disappointment.

'Do you like the colour?' he asked. 'Mr Tring give it me. 'E 'ad it left over from doing up his lav.'

'Smashing,' I said.

'There's only one thing wrong with it, Iris. It's fixed wheel.'

'Fixed wheel? What does that mean, Dad?'

'Well, it means you can't stop pedalling. If you're coasting down a hill, you have to take your feet off the pedals because they'll keep going round. Here, get on and we'll go out in the street and you'll see what I mean.'

He held on to the back of the bike until I got the feel of it, then let me go. It was fine. There were no hills around there and I wasn't likely to ride anywhere else in case someone from school saw me. On Audrey's bike, you could stop pedalling and the wheels still kept turning. Dad told me that was called freewheeling. On this thing, when the wheels were turning, so were the pedals. I could see what he meant.

'Remember, if you're going down a hill, take your feet off the pedals and hold your legs clear of 'em. Then you won't get your legs all banged up.'

'Don't worry, Dad, I don't think I'll be goin' down any 'ills.' I forced a smile. At least the brakes worked fine. If I could just keep my mind off the bike's bathroom-blue paint job . . . 'Thanks, Dad. You done a lovely job,' I told him. He shoved his hands into his pockets, rolled back on his heels and wore a look of satisfaction.

'Look at 'im,' Mum said later. ''E looks like the cat that swallowed the canary.'

'Clever old cock,' I mumbled, picturing myself flying down a hill, legs extended like bony wings, with the whole world pointing and laughing at the strange blue apparition.

I did ride the bike a few times but after sustaining multiple bruises and cuts from pedals that had a mind of their own, the joy went out of it; it certainly wasn't what I'd had in mind.

As I think about Victoria Girls' School, some of its smells seep out from my memory. Three, to be precise. First there was the overall mustiness of the building. Then there was the pong of the toilets. The third occupied just one small room – well, most of the time it did. This smell lived in the gymnasium's equipment room, but it definitely smelt dead.

In those days, few of us owned our own gym shoes, or plimsolls; the school provided them. Before the gym class out came the box of plimsolls. We had to rummage through the box to find a pair in our size. The rancid smell of that tangle of black canvas, rubber and stale-stinky-feet-sweat was almost unbearable, but we had to endure it. The rule was, no 'plimmies', no gym, and I liked gym.

I doubt that anyone, anywhere, enjoyed buying and owning

their own pair of gym shoes as much as I did. It was many years later, but certainly no less appreciated.

Due to the migration of families from London, Watford schools were seriously overcrowded. At Victoria Girls' School, conditions necessitated the use of an extension comprised of prefabricated classrooms and located about two miles away from the school. The girls went there for art, domestic science and sports. Victoria Boys' School used it for woodwork, art and sports.

The prefabs, situated in the middle of lush green fields, were reached by walking a mile or two along a path that ran beside the River Colne, which flowed through the centre of Watford. I enjoyed the walk if it wasn't raining.

On our way home, we fished for silvery tiddlers. They were easy to catch and put in a jar, because they didn't swim fast. However, we stopped fishing when we learned why the fish swam slowly: they were diseased. They had white lumps all over them. It's no wonder they died as soon as we got them home, or sooner. We hadn't a clue about pollution in those days. All the waste from Benskins Brewery and other factories went unchecked into that little river.

'For Gawd's sake, stop bringin' them diseased fish home, Iris. It looks like they've got leprosy. They might have something we could catch,' Mum ranted.

'Oh, Mum, stop naggin'. It's just for fun.'

'Fun, my eye. You call that fun? Look at 'em, a bunch of dead lumpy fish. Now go and bury 'em up the garden. Get 'em out of 'ere – they give me the willies.'

'Bury 'em under the raspberry bushes, deep,' chimed in Dad. 'It'll be good for the garden. You don't want the cats gettin' 'em, or we'll 'ave dead lumpy cats all over the place.'

'Oh, Ted, don't say that,' worried Mum, but Dad was laughing.

One day as I dawdled along the riverbank, I caught a small frog, and this is a story I am not proud to tell. I put him into my blazer pocket and took him home. He was to be a surprise for my little brother, Robert.

When it came time to extract the frog from my pocket, I panicked. I was afraid to reach in with my bare hand. Suppose he jumped out and scared me? What if he bit me? What should I do? I couldn't just leave him in there, could I? I squished him. Right there in my pocket.

A frog murderer, that's what I was, a frog murderer. It gave me nightmares and I still feel ashamed of that incident. It's hard for me to believe I was capable of committing such a heinous crime.

I sometimes think Victoria Girls' School brought out the worst in me, but that would soon be behind me: our own school on the estate was almost finished. It would be ready for the next school year – hooray!

22

Suspicious Deaths

Now that I bore the guilt of being a frog murderer, I had to wonder if there was something inherent in the Jones family genetics. As I recall, there was plenty of reason to think there might be.

Besides Auntie Rose, who had been in a lunatic asylum, and his four brothers, Dad had twin sisters, known as Carrie and Liz. Those two aunts always seemed old. They must have dolled up for special occasions, but I have no recollection of them in that condition, but perhaps I hadn't recognized them with their faces on. The images etched in my mind are of hair in hairnets, dreadful sets of ill-fitting false teeth, overalls and either tatty slippers or old-lady lace-up shoes. To me, they always looked ancient.

We saw little of Dad's siblings, except at weddings, christenings and funerals. They were all older than he was, and heavy drinkers. Mum did not enjoy their company. It wasn't that she was a snob, far from it. She simply came from a different background and the Jones family intimidated her with their brashness.

I loved the rare visits to Dad's relatives; they were fun, and his people, funny. They were always laughing and telling jokes, unlike Mum, who was tight-lipped and serious. I can picture her now, a cigarette dangling from the corner of her mouth, telling us that Dad's family was too coarse.

'Ooh, they use filthy language, always effin' and blindin', and they don't care who 'ears it neither. When they ain't at work or in bed, they're in the pub. I've seen enough of that kind of life, thank you very much.'

I suppose in a way she was right, but we kids found them

entertaining, such as when Auntie Sally, Dad's sister-in-law, related the sad tale of their pet canary's escape from the cage and his ultimate demise.

'Poor little bugger,' she said, shaking her head in recalled horror. 'There 'e was, one minute 'oppin' along the edge of the stairs, tweetin' his little 'eart out, when that clumsy sod, Jack, comes down the stairs, not lookin' where he's goin'. 'E don't see the fuckin' bird, does 'e, and 'e steps on it. Crushed 'is fuckin' skull 'e did.'

Mum's face blanched. She sat there in a state of shock, while we kids ran off to hide our laughter and to stash that story for future telling.

There's nothing memorable about Dad's sister Liz, perhaps because she was too normal, but Carrie – now she was another story altogether. I don't think I ever met Auntie Carrie's first or real husband, Charlie Watkins. No one referred to her as a widow; perhaps they had simply parted ways. The only uncle I knew in connection with Auntie Carrie was Uncle Percy. He and Carrie lived together 'in sin' for years, but although it was very hush-hush, that was not the big family secret.

The story goes that Uncle Percy came home early from work one day. He was not feeling well, but he had also stopped along the way for a few pints. Unable to make it up the stairs in his tipsy condition, and finding the house freezing cold, he lit the gas fire in the seldom-used front parlour, closed the door to keep the heat in, and lay on the horsehair-stuffed settee to have a snooze.

Some time later, Auntie Carrie arrived home from work, went straight through the long dark passageway to the kitchen at the back of the house. Having no idea that Percy was already at home, asleep in the parlour, she closed the kitchen door to seal out the hallway draughts and proceeded to prepare dinner.

Attempting to light the gas stove, she discovered they were

out of gas. She reached for the old tea-tin, hidden on a high shelf above the stove where she kept her extra shillings for the meter. Percy did not know about the tin; if he had, the money would have gone, spent on beer. Carrie fished out a shilling, popped it in the gas meter, lit the oven and burners, and continued to prepare dinner.

Most houses had metered gas and electricity back then; life for the poor was usually on a pay-as-you-go basis. You always had to keep an extra shilling or two handy. However, there were often frantic knocks on our door from neighbours or, more likely, their children, in need of a shilling for the gas. They would stand on the doorstep, desperation on their faces, with a handful of coppers.

'Me mum wants to know if you've got a shilling for twelve pennies,' they'd say, and off Mum would go, tutting and grumbling about people not thinking for themselves, to rummage in her handbag for the elusive coin. However, that was not the case with Auntie Carrie.

With dinner ready and waiting, Carrie began to fume, assuming Percy was out on the razzle – again. Covering his dinner with a second plate, she put it in the oven to keep warm. Unwilling to wait for him any longer, she ate alone, smoked a cigarette, then noticed the smell of gas. After first checking to make sure she had turned the stove burners off properly, she opened the back and front doors to air the place.

She told Dad that when she opened the kitchen door into the hallway, the fumes almost knocked her down. She rushed down the hall and threw open the front door. It was then that she noticed someone had closed the parlour door, which normally stood open. Now sure that the gas smell emanated from the parlour, she opened the door and found that she was right: she could hear the gas hissing from the fireplace.

Choking, she stumbled across the room to check the gas tap.

It was open. With her apron held over her mouth and nose, she wrenched it closed. Then she turned and saw him. Uncle Percy was half hanging off the settee. He was dead.

Auntie Carrie ran out into the street.

'She was screaming bloody murder,' a witness later reported.

Neighbours and passers-by came to see what was going on. Carrie was on her knees in front of the house, tearing at her hair; she was hysterical. Apparently, it was not unusual to hear yelling and screaming coming from inside 'that house'. Carrie and Percy often had what the neighbours referred to as 'knockdown dragouts', but this time, they said, it was different.

'I've killed him, I've killed him,' she screamed.

The police arrived, soon followed by an ambulance that removed Uncle Percy's body. Officers took the names and statements of possible witnesses, and told them that undoubtedly there would be an inquest and that they would have to testify.

Inside the house, the police questioned Auntie Carrie. Then, certain she was guilty of murder, they arrested her for the crime and a Black Maria transported her to the police station where she was bound over to await trial. At the time, no one doubted her guilt, but she had been in shock: she had not had the time or the presence of mind to think about what had actually happened.

Dad attended the trial. Having heard Carrie's version of events, and reading conflicting newspaper reports, he wanted to be there to learn the truth and to support his sister, regardless of the outcome.

Testimony confirmed the facts. While Percy was sleeping in the warmth of the gas fire, the gas supply had run out. He had been safe until Carrie had come home and put money in the meter to cook dinner. When the gas came back on at the stove, and Carrie ignited it, the gas in the parlour had also come on – unlit. With no flame to consume the gas, it was lethal.

After Percy and Carrie's regular daily routines were established and verified, and all other evidence presented, Uncle Percy's death was ruled accidental. Auntie Carrie, acquitted of all charges and accompanied by Dad and her twin sister, Liz, adjourned to a nearby pub to celebrate her release. However, the story does not end there.

Because of negative publicity, absence from work and the fact that some people still doubted the verdict, Carrie lost her job at the local pub. Unable to collect a widow's pension since she and Percy had never married, and without an income, she was penniless.

Although relieved by the trial's verdict, a grieving Carrie told relatives that she was responsible for Percy's death; that although she did not murder him, she was in fact guilty.

It must have been during that time that Dad took me with him to visit Auntie Carrie, and it was awful. I sat, for what seemed hours, in the corner while he and his sister talked. The house was dark and cold, with no sound except the *pss pss pss* of them whispering. Auntie Carrie gave me a cup of tea and a biscuit, but then they seemed to forget my presence. I wondered why Dad had bothered to take me with him. It was one of those times when I hated being a kid. I had no idea what was, or had been, going on; Dad would not tell me until much later.

When eventually it was time for us to leave, Auntie Carrie said she wanted to accompany us to the bus stop, and the three of us walked together with me holding Dad's hand on one side, and she hanging on to his arm on the other.

She waited with us until the bus came. Dad kissed her on the cheek. 'Take care of yourself, Carrie.'

'I will, Ted. Thanks for coming, mate. I'll be all right, don't worry. It wasn't much fun for you, though, was it, love?' she said, turning to me. She leaned down then, and kissed me, her lips cold as ice, and I saw tears running down her cheeks.

'All aboard, please,' barked the now impatient bus conductor.

'Sorry, governor,' Dad replied.

We climbed aboard, found a seat and waved goodbye to the lonely figure at the bus stop.

'What's wrong with Auntie Carrie, Dad?'

'I'll tell you later,' he said. He took my hand and patted it. That told me he didn't want to talk about it, and for the rest of the journey home, I left him alone with his thoughts.

A week or two later, I was looking out of our front window when a policeman stopped outside. He climbed off his bicycle, propped it against the gatepost, and bent to remove the bicycle-clips from his trouser legs.

'Mum, Dad, there's a copper comin' up the path,' I shouted. There was a knock on the door.

'I'll go,' Dad yelled back. Mum followed him, and I peeped through the door-crack.

'Mr Edward Jones? Brother of one Mrs Caroline Watkins?' the policeman asked.

'Yes, that's me,' replied Dad.

'I'm afraid I have some very bad news, sir. It's your sister, Mrs Watkins. She's been knocked down by a bus, sir.'

'Is she all right?'

'I'm afraid she's dead, sir. She died at the scene.'

I heard Mum and Dad suck in air, the way you do when you're shocked or surprised.

'Can you come in for a minute, Constable?' Dad asked.

'Yes, sir. Take your time, sir. I know this is a shock and I'm sorry to bring the bad news.'

Mum, Dad and the policeman sat at the kitchen table. I was on the other side of the dining-room door, listening.

'There will be an inquiry, of course, Mr Jones.'

'An inquiry?'

'Yes, sir. There seems to be some question as to whether or

not it was an accident, sir. The driver of the bus said she stepped right in front of the bus. He thinks she might have done it on purpose, sir.'

'Oh, God.'

'We'll let you know the details, Mr Jones. I'm sure you'll want to be there but, of course, you don't have to be. I'm afraid I must be on me way now, sir, madam. Again, I'm sorry I had to bring bad news, but it's me job, sir.'

'Yes, of course. I understand, Constable. Thank you for coming.'

'Are you sure you don't have time for a cup of tea, Constable?' Mum called, but it was too late: he and Dad were already at the front door.

Since most working-class people had no telephones, the police usually delivered such news. Telegrams, considered inhumane on such occasions, were rare, with the exception of wartime when there was a shortage of police.

After Dad had seen the policeman out, he and Mum sat in the kitchen, not speaking. I could hear Dad sniffing. It sounded as though he was crying.

The next day, Mum told me that Auntie Carrie had died in an accident, and that was what the policeman had come to tell Dad. She was unaware that I had overheard the entire conversation of the previous evening. I felt my face crinkle, and I ran to my room. There would be time enough for my questions later.

I never learned the outcome of the inquiry into Carrie's death, and many years passed before I discovered the details of the preceding tragedy.

23

Manners and Mah Jong

During my pre- and early teen years, I still jumped at every opportunity to stay with Mum's sister, Iris, and her family. Given the option, I always chose to spend Christmas with them: it was festive and I got more than one present there. I was happy that they had moved back to London from far-away Scotland.

I learned a lot from my aunt; she took the time to teach me things. She taught me the correct and most efficient way to iron clothes, and how to set what she called a 'nice table'. At mealtimes, we used the embroidered linen napkins that lay beside each place, tucked into engraved silver rings. We had to wash our hands before we ate and had to bathe every night, just as I had in Wales, only here it was in a proper bath and not a tin tub. Auntie Iris had lovely smelly stuff to put in the bath water, and perfumed talcum powder for afterwards, applied with a big fluffy puff. It was all so different from how we lived at our house.

'The grass is always greener on the other side of the fence,' Mum would say. That might have been so, and it still applies, but visits to that other side of the fence taught me a great deal. They also showed me that perhaps, as Auntie Iris had, I might be able to make a better life for myself. Perhaps I could escape the trap of what the British called 'class'.

'She's a snob,' said Dad, of Mum's sister. 'She should remember where she's come from. Who does she think she is? Queen Victoria? She ain't no better than us, she just thinks she is.'

'Don't be mean, Ted,' was all Mum said. She knew better than to argue with Dad. He had a foul temper. I knew enough to bite my tongue too.

The best Christmas gifts I ever received from Auntie Iris and Uncle Walter were *Little Women* and *Good Wives*, by Louisa M. Alcott; it was the same year that Uncle Peter spent Christmas Day with us. Obviously, he had conferred with my aunt and bought me a third book from the same series, titled *Little Men*. I loved those books; I read them many times and was scolded often for taking a flashlight to bed with me.

'You're going to ruin your eyesight,' they'd warn me, but I didn't believe them. Once I got my nose in a book, nothing else mattered. I was willing to take the risk.

Besides spending time with my aunt, I also began to visit some new friends of Mum and Dad's, people they'd met at the Christian Spiritualist Church in Watford.

An older couple, Mr and Mrs Vanstone had never had children of their own. They lived in one of the smart privately owned bungalows on the St Meryl Estate, on the posh side of the railway tracks. Sometimes I stayed there when their nephew came to visit too. At other times, I stayed there by myself. Either way, I loved it.

Mr Vanstone was tall, white-haired and distinguished-looking. He had lived in the Orient for many years, where I believe he had been a diplomat for the British government. Their house overflowed with treasures from around the world, and the bedroom I slept in they called 'the Chinese room'. Although some of the dragon-decorated furnishings were a bit scary, I felt as though I was in an exotic palace.

Again, I enjoyed exposure to a different way of life. Both places that I was fortunate enough to stay at, away from home, taught me many things to which poor Cockney families were unaccustomed. I learned manners, etiquette and appreciation of the finer things in life. I learned about different cultures, art and music, and even a little about gardening. The Vanstones were avid gardeners and had an award-winning collection of roses. But there was one item in their home that I especially admired.

At the Ideal Home Show in London, they had bought an indoor fountain. It was the first I had ever seen and, in my mind, it remains the most beautiful. It consisted of a large clear crystal bowl on a stand, with a raised black glass pedestal fountain in the centre. They kept it on a low Oriental table in front of french windows that led out to the terrace and rose garden. Glistening with droplets from the fountain, the heads of roses floated on the water, lending a delicate fragrance and beauty to the room. I was mesmerized by its magic, and by its elegance.

When the Vanstones' nephew, Chris, was visiting, we'd usually sit down for meals together in the dining room. Sometimes, though, weather permitting, a table would be set up in the garden. Mrs Vanstone called it a picnic, but to me it was far too elegant for that. It was as though I was living inside the illustration of a book; it had a dream-like quality.

At mealtimes, Mrs V., as I called her, kept a little stick next to her plate. It looked like a chopstick, and it had a name. She called it Ticky Toby, and we always knew when our table manners were in question. 'Ticky Toby, Ticky Toby', she'd say, in a singsong, mildly threatening voice.

If the behaviour continued, Ticky Toby would rap the back of the offender's hand. It never happened to me, but Chris often had his knuckles rapped. He was a year younger than I was, and a boy, so he wasn't as good at remembering his manners.

'I'm going over to play mah jong with Mr V.,' I'd tell Mum.

'Mah jong? What the 'eck's that?'

'Oh, you wouldn't understand, Mum. It's ever so complicated.'

Mum would just shake her head, and off I'd go. 'Don't make a nuisance of yourself,' she'd shout after me.

Mr Vanstone had taught me the ancient Chinese game, and we would play for hours. He told me that all Chinese workers, whom he called 'coolies', carried the game, wrapped in cloth, wherever they went. Any time they took a break from work, to rest or eat, out came the game.

I loved the feel and look of the ivory pieces. Called 'tiles', they bore designs of dragons, bamboo and flowers, and as we played, he'd tell me stories of his life in China and about Chinese customs. He also showed me photograph albums; we'd sit at the table together for hours, as he explained each picture.

The first time he showed me pictures he was sitting next to the fire in his big armchair. Mrs V. was sitting across from him in her special chair.

'Would you like to sit on my lap and look?' he asked.

'No, thanks,' I said. 'Can we just sit at the table, please?'

Except for Dad, I didn't like older men to get too close to me. I especially didn't like their hands to touch me, perhaps because of the experiences that haunted me.

Mr Vanstone called Mrs V. 'Kathleen'. His first name was Jim, but she always called him 'darling', which at first embarrassed me. I was unaccustomed to hearing such intimate terms of endearment, but soon got used to it.

'Why don't you call Dad "darling"?' I asked Mum one day.

I thought she was going to spit her false teeth out. 'You must be jokin',' she spluttered. 'You've been readin' too many of them magazines. Your father'd think he'd come in the wrong house if I called him that.'

At the Vanstones', we had to be quiet most of the time. Mrs V., although a lot younger than her husband, had, I'd been told, a heart condition; she had to have lots of rest. I didn't mind: there were plenty of quiet things to do. With lots of books and games, someone to play the games with, and the garden and woods beyond to explore, I was happy.

The Vanstones were kind to me, and thoughtful. I recall how surprised and happy I was to find that Mrs V. had made me a costume to wear to a fancy-dress parade and contest. I'd never had a costume before. I was to go as Little Bo Peep, and the dress she held up was beautiful.

She had made it from one of her old evening gowns. It was pink taffeta, overlaid with black lace and pulled up with ribbons around the hem. She had used one of her straw hats to make me a bonnet. It had pink ribbons hanging from it. Mr V. made me a shepherd's crook from a length of bamboo. I was sure I would win the competition, but I didn't. I came second, and was very proud. I'd put my costume on at home and flounce around the house in it.

'Ooh, la-di-dah! Ain't you the lucky one,' said Mum, when she saw my Bo Peep dress. 'No wonder you don't spend much time around 'ere no more. Don't you be gettin' too 'igh and mighty, though, young lady, with all your posh new ideas.'

'Very nice too,' Dad said. Then, turning to Mum, he added, 'They're nice people, Kit. They're just glad to 'ave a kid around to put some life into that place. If Iris can get something out of it, good luck to 'er.'

I got a lump in my throat and thought I was going to cry when Dad said that. It felt nice to have someone on my side for a change.

I used to hate leaving Auntie Iris's house and the Vanstones' when it was time for me to go home. I didn't like going back to my own messy house, where I was sure no one cared about me. Mum and Dad didn't seem to know I existed most of the time, and they never used napkins at the dinner table.

24

New School, New Desk
and Tyrone Power

I stood and stared at the outside of our new school. The summer holidays of 1950 had ended and, as promised, Hampden Secondary Modern School was ready. I felt a flutter of excitement in my stomach as I prepared to enter the modern concrete-and-steel two-storey building. How different it was from all the dreary schools of the past.

On the front, next to the name, there was a contemporary metal sculpture of two running horses. It made me grin. What a change it was from the stony face of Queen Victoria, which peered down from most other public buildings.

Hampden School was only five minutes from home and I relished the thought of more sleep in the mornings. I also thought how good it would feel to belong. Built for us, this school was ours. No longer would anyone consider us undesirable intruders from the council estate at South Oxhey.

The morning bell roused me from my daydreams and I marched across the playground to follow the excited gaggle of children through the glass double-doors.

Once inside, we were ushered into the assembly hall. There, holding up signs with classroom numbers, nervous-looking teachers awaited their new broods.

We had been told by post which class we were in; now we all scrambled to line up in front of the appropriate sign.

After a short welcoming speech, which I was too excited to listen to, our bobbing lines of youthful energy followed the teachers to the light-filled classrooms.

Wall-to-wall windows looked out over the school's playing

fields, and on to the farmlands beyond. I wondered if I would ever be able to concentrate on the work at hand, especially if it happened to be maths.

The days that followed were filled with discovery as we moved from classroom to classroom. On the second floor of the school's main building there was a large, well-stocked library, with a balcony outside where one could sit and read, weather permitting. The assembly hall had a large stage, complete with professional lighting and curtains. The dining hall's windows overlooked a courtyard garden.

The gymnasium, complete with locker rooms, showers and every conceivable piece of sports equipment, was housed in a separate building. With the body and agility of a spider monkey, I was considered one of the best gymnasts in the school, but the thing I did best was climbing the ropes; it was also the exercise I enjoyed most, for it was at the top of that rope, on my very first climb, that I experienced something wonderful. Giddy with excitement at making it to the top, there was a sudden exquisite throbbing down below. It was my first orgasm and I wished it would last for ever. Then a voice floated up to me.

'Come on down, Jones. Let someone else have a turn.'

Reluctantly, I slid back down the rope, already looking forward to my next trip to paradise.

I hated using the showers, I suppose because of inherent modesty and an aversion to showing off any of what Mum called my 'naughty bits'. I carried many 'Please excuse Iris from the showers' notes to school; the gym instructor must have thought it odd that a girl could have her period as often as I did, but one could be reasonably sure that proof would not be required.

Another building contained classrooms for art, domestic science – now called home economics – and needlework; plus wood and metal workshops for the boys, all equipped with the latest machinery.

Gardens ran along one side of the school building, separating it from the low-lying railway tracks. This was where we'd learn about soil composition, composting, potting and everything else we'd need to know to become self-respecting British homemakers.

As I mentally absorbed Hampden's amenities, I couldn't help thinking it was more like a holiday camp than a school. I realized, too, how far we had come from the bomb-damaged landscape of London. In all, I thought I had landed in Heaven and that an exciting new phase of my life was about to begin.

One thing hadn't changed, though: I was still hungry. At lunch-times, I often hovered around the cloakroom and the kids who brought their own lunch. If someone happened to have an apple, I would always ask if I could have the core. To this day, I can still eat an apple down to the pips.

The new school smelt of fresh-off-the-press books and floor polish. Sparkling clean, light and bright, it felt cheery. Attending school became a pleasure. It was both an inspiration and an invitation to be a good student, which I was. Well, for the most part I was. However, I was soon to prove, not once but twice, the old theory of history repeating itself. The history of what I had done on receiving my first big-girl bed at the age of seven, when I had carved my name into the headboard, and then the great bicycle caper of the previous year.

Lifting the lid of my desk, I took out the new pencil box. I slid back its roll-top, revealing the requisite tools for a fresh school year. There were pencils with sharp points and unused erasers, a pen with two new nibs, a non-ink-stained ruler, a shiny protractor and compasses. The British government never assumed that the families of Britain's working-class poor could afford to buy their own school supplies.

I closed the desk and arranged my books and supplies on its top. The teacher was speaking to us – she must have been: I could see her lips moving. Mysteriously, although it was not the first time it had happened to me, I had gone stone-deaf. My eyes and mind had drifted to the view outside the window. I took a deep breath, then let out a sigh of contentment. I hadn't a clue what was going on in the conscious world. It must have been at that moment that an evil spirit took possession of my mind and made me do things that Iris Jones would never have done.

Using my still-stiff compasses, I proceeded to scratch 'I LOVE T.P.' into the desk's varnished surface. Surely, it was what psychics call automatic writing. Yes, I was crazy about the film star Tyrone Power, but how could I have known that my adoration of him would creep into my mind at such an inopportune time? Where had that idea come from? What was I thinking? Should I get up and run? Should I just kill myself, here and now, using the compasses?

It was all over for me. Suddenly my life had taken a serious turn for the worse. Unless I was not caught. Sitting at the back of the classroom had proved to be a good idea. I slithered across the aisle and sat behind a different desk.

Unlike years earlier, when I had initialled my new bed, this writing exercise was to land me in serious trouble. When the teacher discovered the message, the perpetrator of the dastardly deed remained unknown – for a short while at any rate. Anyone could have scratched the declaration of love, couldn't they? My anonymity was short-lived.

'Who is responsible for this shameful act of vandalism?' demanded our form teacher.

The look on her face might have stopped an oncoming train. There was an eerie silence in the room. No one came forward. She repeated the question. And again, all eyes gazed at the floor. No one spoke up. Then, the look on her face changed, and so did her tone of voice.

'Well, we'll just see about this. Since the culprit appears to be too cowardly to own up, the entire class will be punished.' A chorus of groans rippled through our midst. Actually, it was more like a tidal wave. 'I will let the person who did it have time to think about the consequences for their classmates,' she said. Then she dismissed us, temporarily.

I hung around outside the classroom door. How could I live with the guilt? How could I let the entire class suffer for my stupidity? What if the kids found out and labelled me a coward and a liar? I slunk back into the classroom.

'It was me, Miss. I'm the one who scratched the desk,' I said. I was trembling and could no longer hold back the tears. 'I don't know why I did it, Miss. I was just daydreaming. Please don't punish everyone, just punish me, Miss, but please don't kick me out of school.'

I could feel her disgust as she squinted at me through eyes that I knew did not want to see me. I was unsure if what I saw held sadness and disappointment, or if it was just plain loathing. Either way, it was not the first time such a look had destroyed me.

'We shall see,' she said. I hated it when adults said that. You never knew what the outcome would be. The suspense was a killer. 'Now go and wait in the corridor while I speak to the headmaster.'

Oh, God, please help me, I thought.

I stood outside the classroom, waiting for what I knew would be bad news. I felt as though everyone who passed by was staring at me; it was as though they knew I was doomed. It reminded me of a film I had seen, in which a mob of ragged, toothless people crowded into a town square, waiting to see someone hanged or beheaded. Why is it that people seem to enjoy seeing others suffer?

After what seemed years, a red-faced caretaker in dirty overalls approached. He was pushing a squeaky four-wheeled cart. Balanced on top of the cart was a desk. As he pushed his load past me and into the classroom, I could smell the sweat that was trickling down his face and neck. He did not look happy as he replaced the desecrated desk with the new one. He beckoned me to follow him and, like a small funeral procession, we accompanied the offending desk to a corner behind the assembly-hall stage.

'Wait there,' said the caretaker, as he mopped his brow with a filthy handkerchief. 'He'll be with you in a minute.'

'Who?' I asked, but too late. He was gone. Alone in the semi-darkness, I squinted at the telltale scratchings, praying that I wouldn't have to tell anyone who T.P. was. I'd rather have died.

I jumped when a door banged behind me. Turning towards the sound, I saw the headmaster emerge from the shadows. He strode towards me. I had never seen him up close before. My stomach churned and I thought I was going to faint or throw up.

Mr Westaway, the headmaster, was above average height, and when he stood directly in front of me, it was like looking up at a tall building. I noticed that when he looked down at me from way up there, his jowls and the bags under his eyes hung down. Then, in the sombre voice of a preacher, he spoke.

'You should be ashamed of yourself, Iris. *I* am ashamed of you. What were you thinking? Have you no respect for your school's property, for the property of others?' His voice rose and fell. Had it been the sea, I would have been sick.

'I wasn't thinking what I was doing, sir. I do have respect for school property, sir. I love it. I am ashamed and sorry,' I whined.

He paced back and forth and didn't speak for a while. Then he stopped and ran his hand over the surface of the desk before looking down on me again.

'I've thought long and hard about an appropriate punishment for you, young lady, something that would give you time to think about what you have done.'

'Yes, sir,' I said, stifling a sob.

'You will forfeit all breaks, including lunch time. You are to come straight here to work on refinishing the desktop. You can eat your lunch, of course, but no dilly-dallying with your friends. Mr Gardiner, the caretaker, will supply the necessary materials and show you how to do it. Is that clear?'

'Oh, yes, sir, very clear.' My mind wandered. Part of the punishment was familiar. It wasn't very long since I had had to forfeit breaks and lunch times at Victoria Girls' School, following my infamous bike ride.

'I want to see that desk looking as it was, brand new. Understood?'

'Yes, sir, you will, sir, I do understand, sir.'

'Right.' Tapping a pencil on a pad of paper, he turned on his heel and strode off, leaving me sighing great sighs of relief, and Mr Gardiner rolling his eyes and tutting.

'Just what I needed, another job,' he muttered.

I wasn't all that keen on break anyway, so although I was contrite, I was happy to stay inside to sand away those telltale initials and, hopefully, redeem myself. The sanding took for ever, but when it was finished, Mr Gardiner helped me stain and re-varnish the desktop to its original unmarked condition.

Mr Westaway was satisfied with the result; Mr Gardiner was glad *his* punishment was over; my teacher stopped glaring at me and I was, at long last, redeemed.

'You smell of turps,' Mum said, one day after school.

'Oh, do I?' I said. 'We had art today. It must be from cleaning the paintbrushes.' Little white lies seemed to roll off my tongue with ease.

'You smelt of turps yesterday as well,' she said.

'Yeah, well, I helped clean up some spilled paint. I volunteered for the job.'

'I wish you'd volunteer to do something around here,' she mumbled. If she had known the truth, she would have disowned me.

My friends all thought the incident funny and eventually I joined in the laughter, but I was disgusted with myself for having done such a mindless thing.

Later, I did wonder what Tyrone Power would have thought of my crime. I suspect he would have been proud. I also wonder what he might have thought now, if he could have known I still have all my pin-up pictures of him. He really was gorgeous.

25

High School High Jinks

Each morning, before classes, students and teachers trooped into the assembly hall, except for the Catholics who, although few, went off to a different room. I hadn't a clue what a Catholic was, or what made them different. Morning assembly began with announcements and ended with prayers and a hymn.

Other than the regular 'slow but sure' comments from maths teachers, my reports were usually good. That is, until I started hanging around with 'the wrong crowd', when 'easily led by others' was added to the comment column. My marks slipped, not seriously, but I did start getting into mischief. We were young teens and, I suppose, testing the system.

Polly Randall, our tweedy old-maid biology teacher, took us on nature-study walks. We'd trudge in pairs up Little Oxhey Lane and into the adjacent fields and I would hang back with a friend, letting the rest of the class get ahead of us. Then the two of us would sneak off to visit Mum's friends, Nellie and Jim Leedell, who lived in a caravan in one of the fields. Those dear old folks seemed to enjoy being in on the subterfuge. They'd give us a quick cup of tea, and then, fearing detection, we'd hurry back to rejoin our class.

Nellie and Jim's caravan had no running water or electricity and stood in a field that was part of Brazier's Farm. One of the farmer's retired carthorses also occupied the field. His name was Dick. How our filthy little minds went to work the day dear, naïve Nellie explained how you measured a horse's height. She told us that horses were measured in hands, not in feet and inches, and how many hands high Mr Brazier's Dick was. That, of course, sent us into gales of laughter. She hadn't a clue what we found so funny.

I'll never know how we escaped detection on those little for-ays, but we did. I did wonder if dear old Polly Randall knew that we were gone and was simply glad to be rid of a few of us for a while. We revelled in teasing her. She was somewhat of an eccen-tric in her mode of dress, which usually included unmatched stockings and gravy-stained ties. She was another woman who always wore a tie with her tweeds.

'Ooh, you do look nice today, Miss,' we'd say.

'Oh, thank you very much, dears. How nice of you.' She was one of those marvellous stereotypical British characters.

Ironically, I, too, was teased about my clothes. I never seemed to have anything decent to wear. One day in desperation I decided to wear Mum's twin-set, a matching sweater and cardi-gan. At that age I weighed, at the very most, around five and a half stone, while Mum was more than twice that. The twin-set was huge but I rolled up the sleeves and wore it anyway. As the hot summer day progressed, I began to perspire, and the more I perspired, the larger the twin-set grew. My embarrassment and discomfort grew in equal measure.

'Look at her. It looks like her mum gets her clothes out of the dustbin,' said my old friend Sheila, who was not my friend at the time. I couldn't believe she would say such a thing in front of everyone.

'Oh, yeah? Well, your mum must 'ave put 'em there,' was my pathetic response. Then, Sheila dealt a crueller blow.

'Eeew! Her mum's pregnant,' she mewed. I was mortified. How could she say something so disgusting about Mum? Preg-nancy was not a subject for discussion in those days – at least, not in our house.

As it happened, it was true: my mum was pregnant. No one had told me, and I certainly hadn't noticed. It was difficult to tell if a woman was pregnant because of the smocks they wore around the house, especially during pregnancy. However, I had the last laugh. I discovered that Sheila's mother was pregnant too. We were both embarrassed, knowing what our ancient parents had been doing, and that everyone else knew too. Eventually, Sheila and I became friends again in spite of, or because of, our sex-crazed parents.

Speaking of sex-crazed, there was a new pastime going on at that time of our lives and it was called 'titting up'. Titting up was when boys groped girls' breasts. Well, of course, you had to have breasts to warrant a groping, and since I had none, I was in no danger. I was a bit jealous of the popularity of girls whose breasts were explored, even if it wasn't considered nice. I contemplated stuffing my undershirt with socks, but then realized that if a boy did tit me up, he'd discover the lie and I'd become the laughing stock of the school! I also considered what might happen if one of the socks slipped, resulting in lopsided breasts or, worse yet, if one fell out completely, leaving me with only one breast and the telltale sock lying on the floor. I decided it wasn't worth the risk until I had a brassiere to hold them in place.

I saw a bra I liked in Marks & Spencer and asked Mum if she'd buy it for me for Christmas.

She laughed. 'You don't need a bra for them sparrow's knee-caps. I've seen fried eggs bigger than what you've got. All you need is a couple of sticky plasters.'

Her comments and laughter hurt and embarrassed me. I ran to my room in tears. She must have felt guilty, though, because for Christmas she and Dad gave me the exact bra I had described. It was pale blue, trimmed with beige lace. I was thrilled, and although the smallest size was baggy on me, I would never have told Mum.

We had another old-maid teacher called Miss Chater, whom

we also enjoyed teasing and playing tricks on. She taught English, library studies and, of all things, gardening. The worst thing I ever did in school, and the most severely punished, involved Miss Chater and her gardening class.

It was a beautiful day and we were happy to be outside working in the school's teaching gardens. The first thing our trio of incorrigibles did that day was to lock Miss Chater in the tool shed. She banged on the door from inside. 'Yoo-hoo, girls, could someone please unlatch the door?' she called.

'Oh, there you are, Miss. We were all wonderin' where you'd gone,' said Myra Austin, as she 'innocently' opened the shed door.

If that wasn't enough, that same afternoon we 'accidentally' pushed the poor woman into the compost heap by hitting the back of her knees with a wheelbarrow. The temptation was too great to resist as she bent over, displaying a wide expanse of bottom. Since we had sneaked up from behind, we'd hoped she hadn't recognized us but, alas, she knew her attackers.

At that point, poor Miss Chater had had enough. Her face was bright red, as she brushed compost from her knees and skirt. There were tears in her eyes.

'I will not have this. I just will not have it,' she said, in a quivering voice. Then she surprised us. She sent the three of us off to report ourselves to the girls' headmistress, Miss Lehr. Everyone was scared of Miss Lehr. Known as the Witch, she was one-who-should-not-be-toyed-with. In addition, she was known to mete out major punishments.

We three girls got halfway to Miss Lehr's office.

'Wait a minute,' said Sheila. 'I wonder if Miss Chater would know if we didn't go.'

'What do you mean?' I asked, before realizing that a plot was hatching.

After a brief meeting in the girls' toilets, we decided we were not going the rest of the way: it would be suicide to proceed with confession of our sins – if we could avoid it.

We reported back to Miss Chater, with Sheila as our spokesperson.

'Did you tell Miss Lehr exactly what you did?' asked Miss Chater.

'Yes, Miss.'

'And her response?'

'She was very angry, Miss. She shouted at us and warned us that if we're ever sent to her again we'd get a jolly good caning.' Sheila McDonald was a good actor. She almost had me convinced she was telling the truth. I was sure we had fooled Miss Chater as she nodded in acknowledgement, then dismissed us.

'Phew, that was a close one,' said Myra.

'I knew she'd believe me,' said Sheila, and we all laughed, enjoying the fact that we'd got one over on another teacher.

However, we had seriously underestimated Miss Chater. We couldn't believe she had checked the validity of our story, but she had. We soon found ourselves summoned to her classroom, wondering whatever she could want with us now.

The sizeable Miss Chater sat behind her desk looking very smug indeed. She rubbed her hands together, reminding me of the Wicked Witch of the West, from *The Wizard of Oz*. She almost cackled at us.

'Well, girls, since you were clever enough to concoct such a story today, and even to prescribe your own punishment if ever sent to Miss Lehr again, I am now sending you again. This time, because of your blatant lies, I'm sure Miss Lehr will be delighted to double your punishment.'

Three sets of lungs inhaled audibly. We'd been caught, again. We were dead.

'Now go. You disgust me,' she shouted, pointing her finger at the door.

'But, Miss –'

'Go,' she ordered. There was nothing to do but obey, and off we went. Miss Lehr awaited our arrival. There was no escaping this time.

The three of us lined up outside Miss Lehr's office, awaiting our turn to enter the torture chamber. Victoria Girls' School might have stopped caning girls, but things were different here. After a stern lecture, we each received ten lashes with the cane, as we bent over and touched our toes, skirts raised over our heads. The normal punishment was five lashes. We had brought this on ourselves.

It was a painful experience, and none of us could hold back the tears. The cane left throbbing welts on our behinds for days and, as a cruel reminder, it hurt like hell to sit down. I might add that, not surprisingly, none of us told our parents about that shameful incident of crime and punishment. In those days, only the parents of repeat offenders received notification of misbehaviour.

A day or two after the caning incident, I was summoned to the headmaster's office. As mentioned earlier, Mr Westaway was a tall, distinguished-looking man, and had a disproportionately large head. He was someone we all feared or respected in the way one might fear God. I couldn't imagine why I had been summoned but, considering recent events, I was more than a little nervous.

I sat across the desk from him, and he, shaking his head from side to side and looking over the top of his thick glasses, spoke to me quietly.

'I am worried about you, Iris. You have been one of Hampden's brightest stars, and a number of your teachers had high hopes for you, but I see that you have been getting into trouble lately and your work is slipping. I would like you to think about whom you are spending your time with and reconsider who your friends really are. I would very much like to see you get back to being the special girl that we all know you to be.'

I sat there blinking back tears, at first not knowing what to say. I was dumbfounded. Not only had he seemed to forget about the desk incident, he actually seemed to care about me. Mum and Dad never asked how school was going or what I was doing. I had reached the point where I didn't think it mattered to anyone. I hung my head in shame.

'I'm sorry, sir. I don't want to be bad. I just wanted the other girls to like me.'

He smiled knowingly. 'I know all about that, Iris, but I want to remind you that your future is important to me and I don't want to see you spoil it.' He came around from behind his desk, put his hand on my shoulder and told me that this little meeting was just between him and me, and he wished me luck. 'If you ever need to talk to someone about any problems, please come and see me.' I wanted to hug him but instead I thanked him, and off I went, smiling as though I knew the biggest secret in the world.

After that, Mr Westaway was my special hero. I worked harder than ever, my marks improved and I never got into trouble again – at least, not at Hampden School.

26

Another Brother and Watford Tech

'We're going to need your help here, Iris. You won't be able to go away this Christmas,' Dad announced, and the way he said it told me I had better not protest.

'Okay, Dad. It's all right,' I replied, biting my lip to stop myself saying something I might regret.

Christmas of 1950 was approaching when I received official word that Mum was about to have baby number four, and that she would give birth at home. I would be lying if I said I was excited about it. I was far too disappointed about missing the holiday festivities with my favourite aunt and uncle. This baby had certainly put a dampener on my Christmas.

Late on 22 December, Mum began having contractions.

'Your mother's in labour,' Dad told me.

I wasn't sure what that meant but I guessed that the baby was coming. 'What do you want me to do, Dad?' I asked.

'Nothing,' he said. 'Just take care of Robert and make your mum a cup of tea. I'll be back soon.' And out he went, slamming the door behind him.

Since we had no telephone, Dad had hurried off, on foot, to fetch the midwife. It was freezing cold, and snowing, a rare occurrence in England.

I made Mum's tea and brought it to her. She was lying on the bed.

'Are you all right, Mum?' I asked.

'Yeah. I've just got a bellyache,' she replied. Then her face scrunched up. 'Ooh, here comes another,' she mumbled.

'Another what, Mum?'

'Never mind. Now, go and look after your brother and leave me alone. Don't forget to shut the door after you.' She didn't look well, and I was worried.

An hour or two passed before the midwife arrived, pushing her bicycle through the snow with Dad trailing behind her; he was carrying her equipment, which included an oxygen tank. As soon as they arrived, there was a great flurry of activity, with orders issued left and right, and then, at last, she disappeared up the stairs to take care of Mum. My job was to make tea for everyone.

Some time later, perhaps even the next day, a second nurse joined the midwife. For countless hours, we listened and could hear them walking Mum back and forth. Then we heard them filling the bathtub; they were putting her into a hot bath. Then there was more walking up and down. Her moans became screams and came closer and closer together.

Robert, who was four, and I sat huddled together on the sofa. I was afraid Mum was dying and wished I knew what was going on. Robert looked frightened and I wished he didn't have to hear Mum screaming. To comfort him, I told him that Mum had a bad bellyache and promised him she would soon feel better. When she did, I said, she'd have a big surprise for him. That seemed to please him.

'Will it be my Christmas present?' he asked.

'It's a present for all of us,' I said, secretly thinking what a lousy present it was, especially for me. I tried to block out the sounds by thinking of what might be going on at Auntie Iris's house; I was still wishing I was there.

Dad, between smoking dozens of cigarettes, was boiling gallons of water and, from what I could tell, most of it ended up as pots of tea.

After what seemed an eternity, there was a deathly silence, which was as scary as the screaming had been. Oh, no, I thought, is Mum dead? If she were, it would be my fault for hating the new baby because it had ruined my Christmas. I knew I'd go straight to Hell.

At last, the sound of the nurse clomping down the stairs broke the silence. Still wiping her hands on a towel, she poked her head around the front-room door and made the announcement.

'It took a long time but you have a healthy baby brother, and just in time for Christmas too.' Mum had been in labour for forty-eight hours, tomorrow would be Christmas Day and, hooray, I wouldn't be going to Hell after all!

It was almost midnight on Christmas Eve when we finally saw Mum and the baby. The room smelt like a hospital but that little baby boy, with his red crinkly face, smelt heavenly. We all gave Mum a cuddle and stood around grinning like idiots.

The family agreed that since it was Christmas, the baby's name should be Christopher.

'Well, 'e's 'avin' me dad's name, Thomas, for his middle name. I've already decided,' announced Mum.

'Right,' said Dad. 'You won't get no argument from me cos that was my dad's name too.'

'Oh, yeah. I forgot about that,' Mum replied, looking very pleased with herself.

'Iris, how did I get my name? Who was I named after?' asked a sleepy Robert, as I tucked him into bed that night.

'Well, there ain't no one in the family called Robert or Clive, so you was named after Robert Clive of India, whoever he is. I've seen his name in books at school, so he must be famous.'

'Oh, that's good,' said Robert, beaming as he snuggled down to sleep. Then, lifting his head again, he added, 'I'm glad Mum didn't die, Iris. I didn't want you to be me mum.'

'Well, I wouldn't want to be your mum either, so there. I would have been a good one, though, but I'd still rather be your big sister any day.'

Christmas Day dawned, and Dad and I cooked, or tried to cook, Christmas dinner. We roasted the chicken we'd raised from a chick, acquired from the ragman in exchange for old rags. We had kept the little yellow bird warm on top of the stove and fed it by hand. Eventually it had grown into an enormous cockerel, and Mum hated him.

Squawking wildly, wings flapping, he would chase her up and down the garden. She'd fend him off with the clothes-prop as she attempted to hang out the laundry. We tried to keep him in a coop, but somehow he always managed to break out.

'That bird's evil. He's got the evil eye,' she'd say, and she was elated when, a few days before Christmas, old Mrs Pierce from next door came over to wring that evil-eyed chicken's neck.

It was awful, looking at those dead chicken eyes as we plucked the feathers. Later, when Mum cut the legs off, I entertained Robert by pulling on the ligaments to make the chicken's foot wave bye-bye.

'Do it again, Iris,' he kept saying.

'Here, do you want to have a go?' I asked.

'No, thanks,' he said. 'It's 'orrible.' He'd thought it funny but he wasn't about to touch it.

We ate Christmas dinner upstairs in the bedroom with Mum and Christopher Thomas, who had his dinner under Mum's nightie. Yes, by then I knew exactly what was under Mum's nightie and why she kept sticking the baby's head there. I thought it was disgusting.

I remember nothing more of that Christmas except doing endless laundry and having wet nappies hanging everywhere. It was before the days of disposable nappies, and keeping up with the laundry was a nightmare.

'Think yourself lucky you don't have that crazy chicken after you, Iris. You'd really have something to complain about then,' said Mum.

We no longer had the old copper for boiling laundry; consequently, there were pots of steaming water on the stove all the time. Mum always insisted on boiling the whites. She might not have been the best housekeeper but hers were always the whitest whites in the neighbourhood.

The doctor ordered Mum not to come downstairs for about a week. I overheard the midwife saying Mum had torn badly down below, giving birth to Christopher. I didn't understand what that meant, but didn't want to know anyway. It sounded awful and conjured revolting images.

About six months after Christopher's birth, Mum was again going through some kind of a nervous breakdown, perhaps post-natal depression, but there was no name for it in those days. Somehow Dad arranged for her and the baby to convalesce in the country; they would be staying with the daughter of their friends the Manningses.

Dad, of course, was out at work all day. Peter, aged sixteen, was working as an apprentice compositor at Sun Printers in Watford and attending night school so we didn't see much of him. That left me to take care of Robert and to keep house while Mum was away. I was twelve, had all the responsibilities of an adult and loved it, for the most part.

Dad must have kept me out of school for a while because I don't recall attending classes during that period. I took my job very seriously, and brother Robert still teases me about how strict I was with him, and how he almost kicked the bedroom door down one day when I locked him in for being disobedient.

After doing the laundry, cooking and shopping, I even took

over Mum's role of visiting her friend, Mrs Mannings, for tea. She must have laughed at me: there I was, a twelve-year-old, having afternoon tea and a natter, but I had a job to do and meant to do it well.

I believe I was trying to prove subconsciously that I could do it as well, if not better than, Mum, wanting and needing appreciation. I ironed everything in the ironing cupboard, which was always jammed to capacity. I cleaned up all the clutter, rearranged all the shelves and cupboards, and washed and waxed all the floors. Then, as a surprise for Dad, I turned the collar on one of his work shirts – that was what they did to make shirts last longer. Next, I made short-sleeved shirts from his old, frayed-at-the-elbow long-sleeved ones; it was something I'd heard him ask Mum to do numerous times. He was pleased with my efforts and gave me two shillings, and even Peter gave me sixpence for ironing his shirts. I was rich.

I hated having a messy house and hoped things would stay neat when Mum came home and saw how nice everything looked, but after her return, the house soon became cluttered again. Obviously, she had other priorities. She always had people popping in for cups of tea; the kettle was always on at our house. Mum even made tea for delivery men. You never knew who you'd find sitting in our kitchen having a cuppa. It might be the coalman, the insurance man or the rent man. No matter who it was, according to Mum, they all deserved a sit-down and a nice cuppa. Everyone thought the world of her, messy house or not.

Mum, who cooked dinners out of almost nothing but rarely baked, made the world's best rice pudding. Almost every week she'd make one for her neighbour, Alan Baylis. He loved rice pudding but his wife Rene, lovely in every other way, refused to make it for him. Like me, I suppose, Mum needed to feel appreciated, and seeing the expression on Alan's face when she delivered his 'pud' must have made her feel good.

Rene Baylis and Mum were close friends, as well as neighbours, and I think my favourite story about them is that they shared a cat. They both loved cats but neither could afford to keep one of her own. I've had great fun over the years telling people how my mum and her friend shared a 'pussy', which was what they called it.

'Wow,' commented an American friend. 'That's what I call real togetherness.'

After Mum had returned from her convalescence, life went back to normal. I continued at school until the time arrived for me to take the exams, in my first year, that would determine whether I was a candidate for continuing my education at a technical school or leaving, as soon as I could, to get a job.

To everyone's amazement, including my own, I passed the exams with high marks. The next step was to attend a personal interview. Knowing how important it was that I made a good impression, I put a great deal of thought into what I should wear to the interview.

I settled on a smart second-hand grey pinstriped suit, given to me by a family friend. Under that, I wore a white lace dickey, because I couldn't afford to buy a whole blouse. Over my arm, I carried a stiff and cracked navy-blue plastic handbag, purchased at a church jumble sale. In my hand I clutched one brown glove, which was all I owned. Last, but not least, I had on my pride and joy, a pair of red Cuban-heeled shoes, which, although second-hand, had been worn, I was assured, only once before.

The image of me in that outfit, with my skinny legs and long plaits, still makes me cringe, and I shudder to imagine what the interviewers must have thought of the pathetic waif standing before them.

On the day of the interview, I climbed the wide stone steps of the ancient building, and entered Watford Technical School.

'Are you here for an interview?' a woman asked me, as she eyed me up and down.

'Yes, Miss,' I managed to squeak.

She ushered me through tall double-doors into an enormous room and closed the doors behind me. I stood blinking. It took a while for my eyes to adjust to the dim light. Then I saw them, eight stuffy people hunkered behind a long oak table; they were like vultures, waiting to devour me.

Standing in front of them, knees knocking, I felt like a prisoner in an interrogation room; the only thing missing was a lone bare light bulb shining in my eyes. To make matters worse I was shaking so hard that the stupid glove I was clutching kept catching my eye; it looked as though it was trying to wave at them, and for the life of me, I couldn't hold it still.

A pipe-sucking old geezer peered over the top of his thick glasses.

'Can you explain to us why you think you want to further your education, m'dear?' he asked, as though it was the strangest idea he'd ever heard.

'Well, sir, I want to better myself, and some day have a job that involves travel. I'd like to see the world, sir,' I replied.

An old cow of a woman in an ugly hat laughed – well, it was more of a snort than a laugh. 'My dear child, most people who work do travel, but usually only back and forth to work, not around the world,' she said, with a tone of sarcasm. Everyone at the table snickered.

Swine, I thought. I remember nothing more of the interview, but I do remember hating them all and wishing the ground would open up and swallow them, or me.

Several weeks later, to my surprise, we received official notification: I was to attend Watford Technical School, having been awarded a scholarship. Mum and Dad seemed pleased but made it abundantly clear what a hardship it would be for them.

'They sent a list of all the things you're gonna need and it ain't just the uniform. I don't know where the money's supposed to come from,' moaned Mum.

'We'll have to buy it on the never-never, from Alf Mannings. It's the only way,' said Dad. Alf, their friend, worked for a department store that sold things on credit.

Allowing me to attend school for an extra two or three years meant I'd be bringing no money home: they would have to continue supporting me for that much longer. If all that wasn't enough to worry about, another problem presented itself.

Because of the strengths I had demonstrated in a number of areas in my schoolwork, I had the choice of studying art at a school in London, or commerce at Watford Technical School. I desperately wanted to do art and announced this to Mum and Dad.

'What?' said Dad, almost choking on the word. 'Are you mad? Don't be bloody stupid, Iris.'

'You'd end up starving to death in an attic somewhere,' chimed in Mum. 'And we'd still be payin' for it.'

'There's no future in art. I've never heard anything so bloody stupid in my life,' Dad continued. 'You're throwin' away your only chance to make something of yourself, and I ain't goin' in debt for no art school, and that's final.'

Their comments made me feel foolish and selfish. Bitterly disappointed, I reluctantly agreed to study commerce. It was a decision that backfired, and one I regret to this day.

Watford Technical School was a dingy old building in the centre of town. It had no grounds, just a small courtyard to sit in at break time, and we had to walk about two miles to Cassiobury Park for sport and games. I hated going to the park to play hockey, especially since we had to play in navy blue knickers. They had a pocket down by the elasticated leg-hole to put your handkerchief in; they were practical in an ugly sort of way. I was never fond of competitive sports, and running around in my underwear in public was embarrassing. I did everything possible to get out of playing, usually feigning illness.

Once again, I felt inferior: the majority of students at Watford Tech were from families who owned their own homes and cars, and talked posh. They looked down on me, excluding me from their little cliques, mostly because of how I talked and where I came from. I never felt as though I belonged and the loneliness of exclusion was painful.

In my head and heart, I knew the decision to attend Watford Technical School had been wrong. I despised all of my classes, except English. At home, locked in my room, I cried and tried to think of a way to escape the misery; I even considered suicide. I had no understanding of advanced mathematics and could get no extra help at school or home. At last, unable to do my homework, feeling hopeless and defeated, I stopped trying. You might say that I went on strike. By that time, I felt ill, I had constant stomach pains and no appetite. I stopped eating, not caring if I died; in fact, I would have welcomed death at that low point in my life.

Mum and Dad thought I was simply being dramatic, and nagged endlessly about the money they had spent on my uniform and supplies. They tried to shame me into trying harder, but I threatened to run away or kill myself if I had to stay at that snobbish school where I wasn't studying anything I was even vaguely interested in, except English.

One day, in brazen defiance of the strict uniform dress code, I went to school wearing a pair of sheer nylon stockings with thick black seams and black-outlined heels. Just as I had hoped, they sent me home immediately, and dispatched a letter to my parents. Mum and Dad were ashamed.

'How could you, Iris?' said Dad.

'What are people going to think?' said Mum. I often thought that was all she cared about, that and Dad.

'I don't care,' I cried. 'Please don't make me go back there. I'd rather be dead.' I'll never forget the disappointment, perhaps even disgust, on their faces. I had often thought they were not particularly fond of me, but now I was sure that they hated me.

Finally, after what seemed a thousand eternities, Dad arranged a meeting with school officials. They were to decide what they could, or should, do with me, and after much deliberation, they allowed me to return to my old school. I believe they thought I would be embarrassed to go back to Hampden, but I most certainly was not. I was as happy as the proverbial lark to be there, and worked hard until I left school the following spring.

Many years later, I learned that Watford Technical School had burned down, and thought, Good riddance. The hole I had wished would swallow me on the day of that infamous interview had finally swallowed the school.

27

Mum's Friends, Boyfriends and a Lonely Stage Debut

In many ways, our mum was shy. She never felt she was good enough. As a result, besides taking pity on and serving endless cups of tea to 'those poor delivery men', she usually made friends with people others shunned.

She had taken under her wing two couples who lived in caravans on the edge of a field owned by Brazier's Farm. They were not gypsies, just people who could not afford to live anywhere else, or who chose to live there for one reason or another.

One couple, the Leedells, whom I mentioned earlier, was saving to buy a house. With no children of their own, they had soon become Auntie Nellie and Uncle Jim to us, and although we thought them odd, we came to adore them, remaining close friends until they died some fifty years later. Nellie and Jim eventually bought a house after years of saving and hard work, he as a postman and she as a domestic. It was something our mum and dad were never able to do.

The other caravan dwellers Mum befriended were a young family named Bachelor. They consisted of a handsome ex-serviceman who was something of a ne'er-do-well, his voluptuous blonde German wife, who, according to Mum, had 'the biggest knockers on the block', and their three children. Mum felt sorry for them and did everything she could to help them. They lived a poverty-stricken existence in a space that measured no more than about nine by twelve feet. With no running water, they had to haul water in buckets from a tap at the edge of the field. Candles, or a gas lamp, provided their only light, and a small Primus stove was their only means of cooking and heating water. The local authorities eventually stepped in and moved them to a council house, but not until there were five children. Nellie and Jim, who did voluntary work for the Red Cross, provided most of the used clothing the Bachelors wore; much of my own came from the same source.

Another of Mum's friends was Mrs Gradley, who lived down the next street. She had a son named Dick, who was the same age as our Peter. The two boys went into the army together, to do their two years' national service.

Mrs Gradley had every reason to be proud of her son, who had become a champion gymnast for the British Army, but we collapsed into giggles, of course, when she called in to report the latest news about him: 'Hello, Mrs Jones. Did you see my Dick on the telly last night?' or, one of our favourites, 'My Dick just won a medal, Mrs Jones, might even go in the Olympiads.' Needless to say, the visuals induced by her comments were colourful.

Mrs Gradley also had three daughters, two of whom married American servicemen and left Britain.

'I bet Mrs Gradley was glad her Dick didn't go off to America,' I said to Mum.

'Don't be filthy, Iris,' replied Mum, who then proceeded to laugh until tears rolled down her cheeks.

The Gradleys' middle daughter, June, was two years older than I was but we became good friends. I was in my last year at school when she was working in Harrow, at Her Majesty's Stationery Office (HMSO), which printed all government documents and forms.

HMSO had a social club for their employees, and every Monday night was dance night. With June's help, I learned to dance and began going to the club with her. On Monday nights, we danced to records, but on one Saturday each month, we danced to a live band, and that was when we had the most fun.

We met dozens of young men, and fell in and out of love regularly. Harrow station was a few stops down the railway line from Carpenders Park, and it was always a mad dash to catch the last train home. We missed it once and it took us three hours to walk home. We never made that mistake again.

I spent a lot of time with one of the boys I'd met at the club. We did a lot of kissing and cuddling in a church graveyard at Harrow-on-the-Hill, which is famous for the school that Winston Churchill attended; it is also the highest point in the county and from there you can see for miles around. We would sit on top of a tombstone, gaze up at the stars and out at the twinkling lights all around. It was romantic, like a scene in a movie. The boy's name was Roy Garland and he was my first real love.

'Ain't it lovely?' I'd say.

'Yeah,' he'd reply, between sloppy kisses and clumsy attempts to grope my 'gnat bites', as Mum was now calling them. I felt warm and tingly all over, except for my bum, which was always freezing cold from sitting on that icy slab of stone. We never gave a thought to the poor dead bugger we were sitting on.

I suppose it was during that last school year that I became, according to Mum, too interested in boys.

'Boys,' she'd say, with disgust. 'That's all you ever think of, Iris.' It became her constant refrain. I called it nagging.

My first infatuation had actually been with someone I knew for just a few hours. Our class had gone on an outing to Windsor and, thank God, it wasn't raining. As we sat on the Thames riverbank, eating our lunch, a group of French students arrived and began talking to us.

I sat with a handsome young man named André Buisson. We shared our lunches and personal information. This charming foreigner fascinated me. Everything he said sounded romantic; if he'd said 'sausages', I'm sure I would have swooned. Before parting, we exchanged addresses, promising to write to each other, and to meet again some day. We wrote letters back and forth for a while and declared undying love for one another. Eventually, after I'd met Roy Garland, I lost interest, but I'd loved that romantic French accent: it had seemed refined compared to the coarse Cockney accent I was accustomed to hearing.

I kept some of André's letters; they never failed to amuse and charm with their attempts at English, especially his apology for being unable to express himself well in 'your luggage'. He always signed off 'with many kisses of a French that always love you'. My friends made lewd remarks about me receiving 'French letters' in the post.

I often wondered what happened to my girlhood sweethearts and which paths their lives took.

It was also during that last year at Hampden that I made my stage debut. The school staged a musical production of *Cinderella*, complete with orchestra and hired costumes. I only played a small part but attended every rehearsal and knew every word of every part. Playing one of three housemaids, I wore a French-maid's costume and sang one song.

As we made our curtain calls at the end of each performance, I scanned the audience, looking for Mum, Dad or both, knowing in my heart that they were not there. Then I'd feel it coming, that same old silent scream, to choke me as I experienced the crushing disappointment of having no one there for me. My stomach felt like a clenched fist, an angrily clenched fist, and as long as I kept it clenched, I knew I wouldn't cry. I told myself I didn't care, that it didn't matter, but of course it did.

Why didn't they come? Our house was only one street from the school. Why did they care more about everyone else? Why couldn't they give me the same attention they gave their friends and neighbours, or even delivery men? How and when had I become invisible to them?

Sometimes when I came home from school and Mum wasn't in the kitchen, I would let out a bloodcurdling scream, then wail, 'Oh, my God, oh, my God.' in loud sobbing sounds. Mum would come running from wherever she was and go mad at me for frightening her. She said I was wicked for doing that, but at least I got her attention.

Mum and Dad seemed to have forgotten that Peter and I were their children too. Ever since we'd come home from being evacuated, and ever since they'd had the two other children, it had felt as though our family had split, right down the middle, into two separate families, and that we no longer fitted in. I tried to be happy, but it was difficult.

I could not, and would not, ask them all the questions that swam about in my head and hurt my heart. At fourteen, I was already too proud, too independent.

28

Neighbour Ladies and Mysterious Bubbles

It was in my early teens that I recognized a growing hunger for 'woman-talk'. I had no sister to discuss things with and little hope of getting Mum to talk about them. I asked her a question about sex once, and she blushed. 'I thought you learned about that at school,' was all she said, and that was the end of that. Mum either could not or would not talk to me about such things. I decided I needed a sort of surrogate mother, someone I could confide in, and ask questions of, but who would she be?

Occasionally, I chatted at the garden gate with neighbours, and later, began visiting them. Two women in particular always seemed ready to sit down for a natter and a laugh; I loved sipping tea and chatting with them. It made me feel like a grown-up and, I suppose, valued. They seemed interested in what I had to say and soon I was getting some much-needed sex education. They also told me bawdy jokes.

Living in a small cul-de-sac of ten houses, we all knew one another, except for the old couple at number one whose name I never learned. Next to them were the Harts, then the Wrights, the Bankses, the Harrises, the Lanes, the Banyards, the Harmsworths, the Trings and us, the Joneses. Two of those women were directly responsible for my sex education – among other things.

I began going out regularly with one of them, I'll call her Mrs B., and our outings were always under the pretence of visiting her mother. We would take the train to Harrow and Wealdstone and go to a pub called The Case is Altered. Sometimes, not often, we did meet her mother there.

I usually had non-alcoholic drinks, but occasionally, if

someone bought it for me, I'd have a shandy or a Babycham. However, I felt extremely guilty one night when a Salvation Army group came into the pub. I tried to hide but they zeroed in on me and proceeded to lecture me about the evils of drink. They invited me to march and sing with them the following Sunday. I declined on the pretence of being a visitor to the area, then had visions of myself burning in Hell. Oh, my God, I thought, if you only knew the truth.

On one occasion, another of the neighbours, Mrs H., decided to join us on our evening out. When the three of us arrived at the pub, I was surprised to see that yet another of our neighbours, Mr W., was waiting for us. I had no idea what was going on at first, but I soon discovered that Mr W. was having an affair with Mrs H. What a shocker.

Later in the evening, Mrs B. connected with a gorgeous man, who bought us all drinks. We had a great time singing around the pub's piano until it closed. Mrs B.'s friend said he would drive us home and, of course, we accepted, our only stipulation being that he dropped us off a respectable distance from home. God forbid a nosy neighbour should see us.

The drive home was quite an experience for me. It was not a very comfortable one, what with all the heavy breathing, giggling and other mysterious sounds coming from the back seat. After a while, the driver pulled off the road and stopped the car next to a park. The adults piled out and headed for the bushes, leaving me behind to stand guard.

I sat in the dark, waiting patiently while the four of them 'relieved themselves'. I had never heard such groaning or thrashing about from anyone who was simply having a pee. A grin replaced my quizzical frown when I realized the truth. They were not peeing at all. Why, those dirty old ladies, I thought, and wondered what Mum would have said had she known where I was and what I'd been privy to.

Eventually they returned to the car, looking a little sheepish and a lot dishevelled, and then, except for an occasional giggle, no one said a word for the remainder of the ride home. I couldn't believe they had let me in on their secret lives and it was days before I could wipe the grin off my face.

Later, I realized that my new older friends, Mrs B. and Mrs H., had been using me as their alibi when we went out together. I didn't mind: I had such a good time with them, and where else could I have learned so much in such a short time?

Mum and Dad never questioned me about my activities. I decided that either they trusted me, or they didn't much care. The only thing I remember from either of them was Mum admonishing me not to bring any trouble home. I interpreted that to mean, 'Don't come home pregnant.'

Mrs B.'s husband was a policeman and his working hours were irregular. He was often gone at night and weekends, and if she wasn't going out, I would keep her company. She was an attractive woman, had lived an interesting life and had plenty of stories to tell.

One night, when she was telling me about some of her pre- and extra-marital adventures, I had to ask: 'Ain't you ever afraid of getting pregnant, all the carrying on you do with different blokes?'

She laughed. 'Nah,' she said. 'If they don't bring a raincoat with 'em, I've got me own way of killing them tadpoles.'

'Raincoat?' I said. 'What's a raincoat got to do with anything? And who said anything about tadpoles? I want to know how you stop yourself getting pregnant, not how you kill tadpoles.'

'I'm sorry,' she said, after she'd stopped laughing and wiped the tears from her eyes on the tea-towel. 'I keep forgetting how young you are. I thought you'd know all that stuff by now.'

'Fat chance,' I replied. 'Not from my mum.'

My ignorance in such important matters was a little embarrassing; after all, I was fourteen. I should have known what she was talking about, but I hadn't a clue.

'Well,' she began, '"raincoat" is just my silly name for a prophylactic.'

'What's that?'

'Oh, blimey,' she said, rolling her eyes heavenwards. 'Some people call 'em French letters or johnnies and some just call 'em rubbers because it's a rubber thing, sort of like a balloon, that the man puts over his willy so that when he comes you don't get any inside you. "Tadpoles" is just what I call sperm, and that's the stuff what makes you pregnant.'

'Oh,' I said. 'Now I know what you mean. Why didn't you say that to start with? And what about your secret way of killing the tadpoles, Mrs B., if the bloke don't have a rubber thingy? You forgot to tell me that bit.'

'Oh, yeah,' she said. 'But you've got to promise you'll never tell a soul what I'm telling you. It's very secret. I've never told anyone else.'

'Cross me heart,' I promised, making the sign on my chest.

'After you get finished doing it, you get up straight away, go in the bathroom and cut a lump off a bar of soap. Then you lie down and shove the bit of soap as far up your fanny as you can and you leave it there. The next day it'll come out in your knickers or in the loo, and Bob's your uncle. You ain't pregnant. The soap kills all them little buggers.'

'Blimey, don't it 'urt, Mrs B.?'

'Well, sometimes me fanny gets a bit sore. I think it has something to do with what kind of soap you use. But it's worth it.'

'What if it don't come out the next day, then what?'

'Well, I only had that happen once,' she said, a big grin spreading across her face. 'I can laugh about it now, but I don't mind telling you, I was scared stiff at the time.'

She went on: 'It was after one of me nights out when me

'usband was working the night shift. I 'ad a bit o' slap 'n' tickle with that bloke you met at the pub, and when I got home, I quickly put the soap up you-know-where, to be on the safe side, and off I go to bed. Well, when Larry comes home from work the next morning, 'e's got a 'ard-on as big as a bloody broomstick. So we have a go, and when he's finished, he pulls out his old John Thomas, and it's got blimmin' bubbles all over it. We both looks at it, and all 'e says is, "Crikey, you must have got some soap up your 'ole in the bathtub, mate." Then 'e rolls over and goes to sleep. I didn't know whether to laugh or cry, I can tell you. But I did promise meself I'd be more careful next time.'

She gave me this fake-innocent look then started singing, 'I'm forever blowing bubbles,' and we both dissolved into gales of laughter. Tears streamed down my face as I tried to visualize our very proper policeman neighbour with bubbles all over his John Thomas.

Shortly afterwards, I celebrated my fifteenth birthday. I'd been enjoying my informal education, but now my formal education was about to end.

There was no big fuss made at school, no ceremony, just a final assembly, with a farewell-and-good-luck speech made by the headmaster. We simply cleared out our desks and headed home as usual. It was time to find a job and face an adult world, and I was ready.

29

First Jobs, Knocking Up and Not Getting Knocked Up

With school behind me, it was time to buy some decent clothes for work. The problem was, I had no money, and neither did my parents. They arranged for me to buy what I needed from the department store where their friend Alf Mannings was sales manager. He set up a credit account for me and I went shopping.

Most of my clothes in the past had been second-hand, except for school uniform and the one dress Mum had bought me for our last summer holiday. Buying my own new clothes was satisfying, especially since it was in preparation for the next phase of my life.

I bought two pairs of shoes, a black gabardine skirt, a white blouse, and a coat that Uncle Alf tried his utmost to dissuade me from buying. It was grey gabardine and, I thought, very smart.

'It's too big for you, Iris. That coat would fit your mum,' he said, and we both knew what that meant. She was more than twice my size. 'You really should try on some others.'

'I've tried all the others, Uncle Alf, and this is the only one I like.'

'Your mum and dad will be cross if I let you buy that coat. They'll think we're both mad.' He left me alone and returned to the stock room, hoping, I'm sure, to find another coat for me to try on.

While he was gone, I turned the coat's collar up around my face, cinched the belt in tight, and plunged my hands into the deep side pockets. Checking my reflection from all angles in the full-length mirror, I thought it made me look like a fashion model, or even a film star. I had to have it. Uncle Alf returned, this time with an awful tweed thing draped over his arm. He looked hopeful.

'I don't mean to be disrespectful, Uncle Alf, but this is the one I want. I love it. When I pull the belt tight, it looks nice.'

'But it comes down to your ankles, Iris – your mum'll do her nut if I let you buy it. Please, Iris.'

'No, she won't,' I shot back. 'Not if I'm paying for it she won't.' How could I tell him that one of the reasons I liked the coat was its length? It hid my skinny legs.

Poor Uncle Alf looked exhausted as he wrapped up my purchases and sent me on my way, and, of course, he had been right. Mum did do her nut when she saw the coat. She said everything he had predicted she would say, and more, but I didn't care: I had made up my mind.

The rest of my 'career' wardrobe was supposed to include my old navy-blue school-uniform skirt, even though it was shiny at the seat. That idea was flawed, though, as I discovered the next time I wore it when I went to the HMSO dance club in Harrow.

A tarty girl came up to me in the Ladies. 'Could you turn around, please?' she said.

'What for?' I asked.

'So's I can use your behind for a mirror,' she replied, and laughed in my face.

Everyone else laughed too, but I just wanted to die. I ran outside and rubbed the seat of my skirt back and forth on the brick wall, trying to dull the shine. Later, at home, I used a wire suede-brush, trying to raise the nap of the fabric, but nothing worked; I could never wear that skirt again. I'd have to manage with my one new gabardine skirt, and be careful not to let its seat become shiny, even if it meant standing all the time.

A neighbour gave me a blouse and cardigan that no longer fitted her; they were like new. So now, in spite of everything,

I was all set. I had only one skirt, but with two tops, I could manage. In those days, two outfits were considered sufficient for a working-class girl.

I was hurt and angry to learn that Mum and Dad had had an annuity insurance policy for Peter. It had given him money to get started with, when he left school. Why had they not done the same for me? I concluded that it was more important for him to be well turned-out for the business world than it was for me. It was just another example of the kind of thing that made me feel insignificant.

My first job was as a junior shop assistant at Jax Stores, a women's wear shop on Watford High Street, and, hallelujah, the job came with an unexpected bonus. The company provided its sales assistants with uniforms, laying to rest my worries at having such a limited wardrobe. I could save my lovely new gabardine skirt for best and not be concerned about its seat turning into a mirror. Although we had to work six days a week, I found the job enjoyable. The older shop assistants treated me well, always including me in their conversations, even though I was a lowly 'junior'.

The shop's manageress, Miss Minchin, was a tall, fearsome-looking woman, with enormous feet; her shoes looked like small rowing boats. My grandmother would have said that they were more like the boxes they came in.

Miss Minchin managed several branch stores in the London area, and when she was not at ours, we had fun. We even dared to call each other by our first names, which was against the rules. The business world was formal then, and I found it amusing to be addressed as Miss Jones – even by the older women. Over tea in the staff room, I learned more each day about life, love and heartbreak. However, I never learned anything quite as colourful as I had from Mrs B.

As Jax employees, we received a discount on in-store purchases but I was never able to buy anything. I had no extra money to spend. For my six-day week, I earned three pounds five shillings. I gave one pound to Mum for housekeeping, one pound to Uncle Alf, to pay for my new clothes, and a pound a week went on train fares to Watford. That left me with five shillings to spend on myself, which bought me one ticket to the cinema, plus a coffee afterwards. It's no wonder we girls were anxious to find a boyfriend who could afford to take us out!

I had been working at Jax for about six months when Dad came home one evening looking very pleased with himself.

'I've got good news for you, Iris,' he announced. 'I can get you a job at Odhams, in the bookbindery. You'd be in the printer's union like me, and you'd make lots more money than you do now.'

'But I like my job, Dad. I don't want to work in a factory.'

'You'd be mad not to take this one, Iris. Why work six days a week for bloody peanuts when you've got the chance to work five days a week for four times the money? There's loads of people who'd give their eye teeth to get in the union and work in the print,' he said, now red in the face and almost shouting.

'Leave her alone, Ted,' chimed in Mum, to my surprise. 'She ain't interested.'

'She's bloody daft,' he mumbled. 'She'll never make anything of herself workin' as a shop-girl. First, she gives up college, now she wants to give up the chance to earn some real money. I can't bloody believe it.'

Why was he suddenly taking an interest in what I was doing? Was it just about the money? I couldn't believe Dad would want me to work in a factory. After all, I had heard him complain about it enough times. What did he have for all his years of working in a factory? The answer was, nothing.

A large percentage of Watford's population worked in the printing industry, and they were well paid. However, I was reluctant to exchange my quiet, cosy little job, where I felt like somebody, for a noisy assembly line in one of England's largest printing plants. I promised Dad I'd think about it. He had come home excited about the good news and I knew my response was not what he'd expected. I could see and feel his disappointment. It hurt me to know that I had hurt him. I struggled with the guilt of letting him down, and my own perceived selfishness.

I desperately wanted and needed my parents' approval, and eventually gave in to Dad's challenge to make something of myself. Sadly, I left Jax and entered the world of noisy machines and sweat. At least I could look forward to having extra money, money for myself, I thought, in compensation for my sacrifices. Getting up at six o'clock in the morning was one of the biggest sacrifices of all.

Each day I travelled to work with Dad. We would stop at a café for breakfast with his workmates before going into the factory. He seemed proud to have me at his side. At first, his friends teased him.

'Ooh, Ted, is that the missus, then?'

Dad would grin, and always had a comeback. 'Nah, she's much too old for me, mate.'

I have to laugh when I think of Dad and what a fraud he was. For as long as I could remember he had bragged that he'd never had anything but a cup of tea and a piece of toast for breakfast. Of course, the bottom dropped out of that story when I began going to work with him and discovered that he had a full cooked breakfast with his mates. He was what Mum called 'a holy friar', Cockney rhyming slang for 'liar'. In other words, our dad told 'porky pies'. We often wondered what he did with his money. He always seemed to have plenty in his pocket but was very stingy with what he gave Mum for housekeeping. So, now I knew – well, I knew part of it.

After breakfast, we would walk to Odhams together. Then, at

the gate, he would go off in one direction to the maintenance department, and I would trudge to the dreaded bookbindery. It was a huge building, filled with monstrous machines, conveyor-belts and deafening noise. There were dozens of laughing, chattering girls and women. Most of them appeared to enjoy their work, but I felt lost among them.

The work was hard and fast, fast being something I had never been famous for, and if someone slowed the line, everyone else glared at the offender. They were on 'piecework': their wages and bonuses were calculated on the volume of work produced. Most of the women were helpful and patient with me and at first assigned me such simple jobs as stacking the unbound books, called 'knocking up'. Then I would mark the front pages with an X, which made sure they were fed into the sewing machine the correct way up. Those jobs gave new meaning to the word 'monotonous'. The days felt like weeks and I wanted to scream each time I looked at the clock and saw how slowly time was passing. Later, I worked on the sewing machine. That job, called 'cutting off', involved cutting the books apart as they came off the machine all sewn together. Another boring job, but at least time seemed to pass a little faster.

On a visit to the Ladies one afternoon, I noticed a young girl lying on a bench. She had a sanitary pad, soaked in water, draped across her forehead.

'Are you all right?' I asked.

'I think I've hurt meself,' she replied. 'I found blood on me knickers and I've got a terrible stomach ache and headache. I told the foreman I wasn't feelin' well and he sent me to see the nurse.'

I sat on the bench beside her, and she continued, between sniffs: 'So I went to the nurse and told her I was bleedin' down below, and about the terrible pains and headache. She made me take some aspirin, and then she gave me this cloth thing and told me to go to the Ladies and put it on and then to lie down till I felt better. I'm scared, though. I don't know what's wrong with me and I don't know what to do.'

'Oh, no,' I said, trying to stifle a giggle. 'You weren't supposed to put that thing on your head . . .' I proceeded to explain some of what she needed to know. She was having her first menstrual period and hadn't a clue what was happening to her; many girls didn't, in those days of little or no sex education. I later learned she was the only child of an elderly couple, who were undoubtedly even more embarrassed to talk of such private matters than my mum had been.

I hadn't known about periods either, until I got my first when I was eleven or twelve. When I saw the blood, it frightened me half to death. Mum almost died, too, of embarrassment at having to deal with it. It wasn't until a year or so later that our so-called 'progressive school' decided it was time to educate the girls about feminine hygiene, menstruation and pregnancy.

Another unforgettable experience happened during the time I worked at Odhams; it began with the development of a toothache, and it was traumatic.

Knowing that if I went to the dentist I would have to have the tooth extracted, I tried everything I could think of to avoid going. At first, stuffing an aspirin into the cavity eased the pain, but not for long. Finally, in desperation, I made the appointment. I scheduled a half-day off from work and went straight to the dental surgery after lunch.

I had arranged to have 'gas' for the extraction and because of that, the dentist instructed me to have someone accompany me. Mum arranged for Maureen Tring, the girl next door, to meet me and escort me home afterwards. Maureen was just fourteen and still at school but she met me as planned and sat in the waiting room while I went into the surgery.

Apparently, the extraction was a difficult one, and I began to wake up before the dentist had finished. He had his knee between my legs, braced on the seat of the chair for added traction; he was still trying to remove the tooth's root. Then I saw the blood; it was everywhere. A bowl appeared in front of my face just in time to catch the vomit. A little later, I realized that the screaming I had heard and thought to be a dream had emanated from me.

When I had fully recovered, the nurse cleaned me up as best she could and I staggered from the surgery, into the waiting room. I looked around for Maureen, but she was gone, scared away by my screaming, I guessed. She's probably waiting for me outside, I thought. Then, steadying myself on the handrail, I descended the long dark stairway, pushed open the door and stepped outside. At first the bright daylight blinded me, but then, shading my eyes with one hand, I looked up and down the street. Maureen was nowhere in sight.

With a wadded bandage packed into my mouth to control the bleeding, and a blood-soaked towel held to my face, I managed to get to the station, and eventually home. I remembered little of the journey; I felt as though I was in a dream or, more accurately, a nightmare. As soon as I walked into the house and saw Mum, I began shaking uncontrollably, and broke down in body-racking sobs.

'Where's Maureen?' Mum asked. All I could do was shake my head. 'Come and sit down and I'll make you a cup of tea.'

What I wanted her to do was to take me in her arms to comfort me, but instead I walked into the living room and curled up on the couch, still crying and shaking. Mum stayed in the kitchen, making tea.

The trauma of that experience almost paralysed me; I was unable to return to work for several days, and lay in bed with the covers pulled over my head. Inside I was hurt and angry that Mum had not gone with me. I was just fifteen and, although

I was now a working girl, I knew then, and continue to believe, that no matter what her age, there are times when a girl needs her mother.

I don't remember how long I stayed at Odhams, but it wasn't long. I couldn't stand the noise and never did feel like one of the girls. I also detested having to clean the machines with stinking turpentine every Friday evening when the presses closed down for the weekend. We were responsible for cleaning and re-oiling our machines, ready for the following week. It was filthy, smelly work. The money was good, though, and after I left, I continued to receive bonuses from the piecework for several more weeks. Dad thought I was crazy to go, but I just couldn't tolerate the invasion of my senses or the frantic pace.

I managed to get my old job back temporarily at Jax. They didn't need help but were kind enough to hire me until something else came along.

My next job was at Standen's Newsagents and Confectioners in Market Street where I worked in the confectionery department. I enjoyed arranging all the sweets and boxes of chocolates on the counter and in the window displays, and loved the interaction with customers; I also enjoyed eating all the sweets I wanted; it was one of the benefits.

The counter that sold cigarettes, magazines and newspapers was opposite mine. It was behind that one that I learned about nudist camps. I would take sneaky peeks at the bare bums and breasts in the *Naturist*, and was amazed that people actually liked strolling around with no clothes on. It was even more shocking to see them playing such games as tennis. How could they possibly leap about with all those bits flopping around?

During those early working days, I went out with various young men and sometimes double-dated with friends. Usually we met boys at the Black and White Milk Bar after going to the cinema, or while walking up and down the high street. My friend Sheila McDonald seemed to know all the boys in town; she worked in one of the high-street cafés and was pretty and popular. I remember one night going with her to an old pub in Watford to meet some friends of hers, the Tamplin brothers. I almost died when I saw them. They were the best-looking young men I had ever seen outside the movies. However, the pub itself was dreadful. Tucked away between Benskins Brewery and Watford High Street station, you might never have noticed it. It was one of the oldest pubs in town, tiny, dark, crowded and filthy. The air was thick with the smell of beer, cigarettes and sweat, and the walls brown with nicotine. Cobwebs hung from the ceiling, and the floor was a sticky mess. If it hadn't been for the sight of those handsome Irish lads, I might not have stayed.

The Tamplin boys, with their blue-black curly hair and big blue eyes, were charmers – they even sang to us, beautiful Irish love songs. Completely smitten by the younger brother, Terry, I allowed him to introduce me to a drink that they called Black Velvet, a mixture of Guinness and port wine. The first taste was questionable, but after that, I understood how it had come by its name: it went down 'as smooth as velvet', and looked almost black in the glass. I had no idea how potent the drink was until I tried to stand up. Oh, God, there I was, under age and tiddly. If that wasn't bad enough, I had missed the last train home and would have to walk. Terry said he'd walk with me, and as I had no idea where Sheila had disappeared to, I accepted his offer.

To get back to South Oxhey we had to walk through Bushey Park, where he tried to seduce me. We did a lot of kissing, but then he wanted to go 'all the way'. Well, I may have been a bit tiddly, but I was having none of that. In those days it just wasn't done – at least, not by me.

'Just let me put it between your legs. It'll do ye no harm,' he said. It was the first time, but by no means the last, that I'd hear that request.

'Oh, all right, then, but no funny business,' I told him. I felt guilty afterwards, but I was not confident enough to say an emphatic 'No'. Like many girls, I thought it was the only way that boys like Terry would be interested in me. I went out with lots of boys but I never did go 'all the way'.

The pressure was always on to have a boyfriend. How could you gain the respect of your girlfriends, or yourself, if you didn't have one? I had always liked the company of boys and the idea of being in love. I enjoyed having an arm around me, or just holding hands at the cinema or on a walk. Kissing and cuddling were wonderful, but I did not enjoy having to ward off attempts to go further all the time. The eternal romantic, I lived in a dream world, and was deeply disappointed to discover that Mum had been right about what men wanted. Surely someone could love me without me having to fight him off all the time and without him deriding my 'precious virginity' and me.

30

Yanks' Meat

The US Army and Air Force had bases and airfields all around Watford, in nearby Bovingdon, Ruislip and Bushey. As it was the closest town of any size, Watford was a magnet for American servicemen, especially at weekends, with its half-dozen cinemas, the theatre, numerous eating and drinking establishments and good shopping. There were always large numbers of 'Yanks' in town and their presence, if nothing else, was a boon to the local economy.

It became a standing joke that Americans were easy to identify from behind because of the size of their rear ends. They were bigger than British bums, or so we claimed.

'It's their big fat wallets,' Dad would say.

Uninterested in the size of their bums, or their wallets, I did like their smell: they always smelt clean, as though they had just stepped out of the bath. You could smell their shampoo and exotic spicy aftershave lotions. I would take a big sniff as they walked by.

'Mmm, lovely,' I'd say. My friends thought me strange, but I had always been sensitive to smells; they evoked many memories for me, good and bad. This was definitely a good one.

The local lads were resentful of the Americans. They referred to girls who went out with them as 'Yanks' meat'. It conjured an unpleasant image of raw beef on a butcher's slab. I never wanted a label like that. Some British girls dated black Americans, which was not the social taboo in England that it was then in America. The locals had a name for the black servicemen: they called them 'night fighters'.

'Why are they called night fighters?' I asked my friend Sheila.

'Because they're hard to see at night with their dark skin,' she said.

Sheila was dating an American 'flyboy', and she was anxious for me to meet him. 'Come on, Iris, go with me. It'll be fun. All the boys are nice, not like these poxy English blokes. They'll buy us drinks. They just want the company,' she said.

'I'd feel out of place with them, Sheila. They'll know I'm too young to be in a pub. We could all get in trouble.'

'Oh, don't be daft. Come up to my house. I'll lend you something to wear and get you all fixed up. They won't know how old you are any more than they do me.'

'We'll see,' I said, using one of Mum's favourite noncommittal comments. My old friend almost had me convinced but first I wanted to see how good she could make me look.

Closeted in Sheila's bedroom, she dressed me in a stylish short jacket, a hot-pink chiffon scarf tied at a jaunty angle around my neck, and topped 'the look' off with gypsy-style earrings. Then, with hot-pink lipstick applied and hair styled, she stepped back to inspect me.

'*Ooh, là, là, très chic,*' she said, drawing on what we had learned in our French classes with Madame du Brulle. 'You look at least eighteen, Iris, honest. They'll never guess you're fifteen.'

When I saw my reflection in her wardrobe mirror, I had to agree. I did look older, much older. In a way it was frightening. I had serious doubts about this new adventure, and wondered what I was getting myself into.

After all Sheila's trouble, I agreed to go with her to the Horns pub, in Watford. I had never been there and would never have dreamed of going there since it was at the posh end of town. It was not the kind of place you were likely to find 'common council-house people'.

When we arrived at the pub, Sheila's date was waiting outside with some friends. One was in uniform, but the others wore what I considered typical American sportswear, the kind I had seen in films. They were in light colours, instead of the black, dark brown and grey tweedy clothes that most British men wore. The exception was Sheila's new friend, who wore a black western-style shirt, black jeans and black cowboy boots. He looked exactly like a cowboy. This 'man-in-black' was introduced as Lash LaRue.

'He's a movie actor,' said one of his friends. I laughed and rolled my eyes in disbelief. 'Show your ID, Lash, go on, show her,' said the friend, nudging him with his elbow. Lash reached into a back pocket, extracted his wallet and produced an identification card. He held it out for me to read. There it was, in black and white. 'Name: Lash LaRue, Profession: Actor.' By then, I was too embarrassed to say anything sensible.

'Oh, you live in Los Angeles. Is that anywhere near Hollywood?' I asked. They all laughed and I felt myself blush.

'Your friend here is quite a kidder,' Lash said, to Sheila.

'Yeah, she's full of jokes,' she replied. Well, how was I supposed to know Hollywood was in Los Angeles?

Lash LaRue, who was indeed a movie star, although I didn't know it at the time, was positively gorgeous. I knew immediately why Sheila was anxious to show him off. I'd have done the same thing.

It was a fun evening, chatting and laughing with Sheila and her 'flyboys', but I still couldn't believe I was socializing, in public, with Yanks. I felt self-conscious, uncomfortable and worried that someone I knew might see me. What am I doing here? I asked myself. I was not interested in going out with Americans, and still cringed at the thought of being labelled 'Yanks' meat'.

To tell the truth, I had nothing to worry about. None of them showed any interest in me. I'm sure I wasn't nearly glamorous or sophisticated enough for those swaggering, worldly types, and

I certainly didn't have big enough tits. But I had only just turned fifteen and was far too young to take such risks. Sheila was the same age but had always appeared older, and she was far more experienced. Having worked as a waitress in a café, she was used to handling men and their banter. She was also much more attractive than I was, with her blonde hair and shapely figure. Next to Sheila, I felt like Popeye's Olive Oyl, with my toothpick legs and flat chest. Some people have all the luck and some have none at all.

Sheila didn't invite me to go with her again. I consoled myself with the fact that Americans were reputed to be more sex-mad than British men, that they were always 'randy' or 'horny'. I thought it ironic that they made the Horns pub their headquarters in town.

I remember hearing on many occasions, mostly from British men, that there were just three things wrong with American GIs: 'They're overpaid, oversexed and over here.'

I believe most resentment stemmed from the fact that GIs had plenty of money to spend. British boys didn't think they stood a chance while the Yanks were around, especially not with the prettier girls. However, the local restaurants and cafés did a roaring trade. Some even made an effort to add American dishes to their menus, instead of the usual egg on toast, beans on toast, mushrooms on toast, grilled tomatoes on toast and any-other-bloody-thing-you-could-think-of on toast. At that time, the average young Englishman could rarely afford to eat out, unless you considered fish and chips out of newspaper on a street corner or park bench eating out.

One Saturday evening, shortly after my visit to the Horns, I was walking down Watford High Street with my friend Joyce Banks. We had been to the cinema and were on our way back to the railway station, window-shopping along the way. As we stood admiring the display in Dolcis Shoes' window, we heard some-one call to us.

'Excuse me, Miss.' We both turned. Two American soldiers were hailing us from across the street. We tried to ignore them and walked away but they persisted. 'Could you give us direc-tions to Bushey Hall? We're kinda lost.' We stopped. The soldiers crossed the road and approached us.

One was almost six feet tall and had blond hair and blue eyes. The other, shorter, had brown hair and eyes. They were not what you would call handsome, but nice-looking. There they stood in their immaculately pressed uniforms, caps clutched in their hands.

'We've only been in the UK a couple of weeks and just got our first passes. One of the guys drove us to town, dropped us off and forgot to tell us how to get back,' said the taller of the two.

Joyce and I looked at one another and shrugged. Was this a line? Could they be telling the truth? They certainly looked inno-cent enough, and although still wary, we decided to give them the benefit of the doubt.

'I don't know where Bushey Hall is but I know where Bushey Station is,' I said. 'You can either try to find a taxi to take you back, but good luck findin' one, or you could take the same train as us and get off at Bushey. That's the station before ours. You can get a taxi from there.'

'Sounds good,' said Short Brown Hair. 'If you don't mind, we'll go with you.' He stuck out his hand. 'My name's Rudy and this here is Bob.' We shook their hands and Joyce introduced us.

'I'm Joyce, and this is Iris. We've just been to the pictures and we're on our way home.'

'Pictures?'

'Yeah, you know, the cinema.'

'Oh. You mean the movies.'

Thus began the first of many such conversations: although we spoke the same language, we had to act as our own interpreters.

We walked the rest of the way to the station, bought our tickets and descended the long flight of stone stairs to the platform below. As we waited for the train, I again worried that someone might see me in the company of Americans.

There were few trains running at that time of night and we must have waited for almost an hour. The four of us talked nonstop, asking and answering questions about each other and our respective countries. Joyce and I were careful not to give them too much personal information, not even our last names.

At last the train arrived. It was one of the rickety old brown ones with individual compartments. I wasn't sure I wanted to be in a separate compartment with these two strangers, but we had no choice.

Neither of the boys had been on our electric trains before. They were laughing and gawking, like kids on a grand adventure.

'Wow, this is cool,' said Rudy.

He had a gap between his two front teeth, just as my friend Joyce had. Bob, whom I thought the cuter of the pair, noticed it too. 'You two could be twins,' he said.

'Think yourself lucky you ain't my twin,' said Joyce. 'You wouldn't want my mum and dad.'

'I'm already glad you're not my twin,' said Rudy. 'I sure as heck wouldn't be out with my sister.'

'Well, you're not exactly out with us, are you?' Joyce added. The train slowed as we approached Bushey station.

'Here we are. This is your station,' I said, and I stood, preparing to open the door and say goodbye. Neither of them moved. They just sat there, grinning.

'Come on, quick. This is where you get off,' said Joyce.

'Why don't we just stay on with you? Then we'll take a train back to Bushey,' said Bob. Both Joyce and I started to protest but it was too late to argue. The train was already moving. Oh, no, I thought. This was getting complicated.

'You'd better hope there's a train to take you back. They don't run all night, you know,' I said.

When we arrived at Carpenders Park, my worst fear was realized: the last train going back the other way had already gone. There were no taxis at our little station – no one on the Oxhey Estate could afford to hire one. The boys would have to walk back, and I was already wondering how to explain their route.

'Well, we may as well walk you home. What the heck's the difference now we've come this far? We don't have to be back until Monday morning so we've got plenty of time to walk back,' said Rudy. We all burst out laughing. Rudy had told us earlier that he was a farm boy from Iowa and that he was used to walking long distances.

'Easy for you to say,' said Bob. 'We sure don't do much walking in Chicago, but I'm game for a little stroll. That is, if the girls don't mind.'

'You can walk us part way,' said Joyce, 'but there won't be any funny business.' I nodded in agreement, thinking how glad I was that she'd said that.

This was definitely a strange turn of events. How in the world had we ended up at Carpenders Park station with two American soldiers?

We walked and talked, then stood under a lamppost and talked some more. When the streetlights suddenly went off, which they did at midnight, Joyce and I said we had to go.

'Anyone have a piece of paper we can draw a map on?' I asked, wondering how we'd be able to see to write in the dark.

Rudy pulled a small address book from his pocket and tore out a sheet. 'Anyone have a pencil?' he asked.

'We can use my eyebrow pencil,' said Joyce.

'Brilliant,' I said. Then, giggling like five-year-olds, we got as close as we dared to a house that still had a light on in its front window. There, in the dim puddle of light, we drew the map that would get them back to Bushey station, where we knew there'd be taxis all night because of its close proximity to the American base.

We shook hands. Yes, we did, we actually shook hands, and bade them goodbye.

'Nice meeting you,' I said.

'Maybe we'll run into you again some time,' Rudy said.

'Yeah, we usually go to the pictures on Saturdays,' chirped Joyce.

'Shush,' I whispered, nudging her in the ribs. 'Don't tell 'em that.'

'So long, Limeys,' we heard, from the darkness behind us.

'What does that mean?' I asked Joyce.

'Buggered if I know,' she replied, and we laughed as we ran off towards home.

It had been fun meeting and chatting with those two nice young men, and Joyce and I later agreed that it was too bad we couldn't meet British men like them.

We had not exchanged addresses and, of course, could not exchange phone numbers since we had none. The only thing we exchanged was first names. We made no dates to see them again because neither of us wanted to get a bad reputation. We also knew our parents would not approve, mine because of my age and Joyce's because they were miserable, abusive tyrants. I must admit, though, I secretly hoped we would run into them again.

The next morning I got the usual lecture about staying out late, and what the neighbours might think. Joyce didn't fare as well: her father gave her a black eye and threw her out of the house. She came to us for a while.

'Stay as long as you like, Joyce,' Mum told her.

'Thanks, Mrs Jones. That's ever so nice of you, but it's too close to home and I don't want to risk running into me dad. I never want to see him or me mum again. I'm gonna look for a room in Watford.'

Joyce was almost eighteen and ready to be out on her own, but I wished she had stayed with us. It would have been like having a sister.

About a week or so after that series of events, I was putting stock away at work when the manageress, Miss Minchin, appeared in front of me – I was back at Jax.

'Miss Jones, there's a telephone call for you in my office.'

'Me, Miss? Are you sure, Miss?'

'Yes, you, and make it snappy.'

Who could be calling me? I had never given anyone the phone number at the shop. How could I? I didn't know it. To tell the truth, I didn't know anyone who owned a telephone, and never thought in terms of phone numbers.

In a state of disbelief, I slipped into the manageress's office, sat down in her swivel chair and picked up the receiver.

'Hello,' I said, hoping I had the phone the right way up. Then, when I heard an American accent on the other end of the line, I almost dropped it. It was him, the American soldier. My head was swimming.

'Hi, is this Iris?'

'Yeah, this is me,' I managed to squeak.

'This is Bob,' he said, only it sounded more like Baahb. 'We met a week or so ago. I was with a guy named Rudy, remember?'

'Yes, I remember.' How could I forget? My heart was racing.

'I've been thinking about you, and wondered if I could take you out some time, maybe to a movie?'

'How did you find me?' I asked. Oh, God, I thought, why does my voice sound so shaky?

'Well, I remembered where you said you worked, so I looked

it up in the phone book and there it was. Sorry, I don't know your last name or I would have called you at home. What is it?'

'Jones,' I replied. 'But we don't have a phone at home.'

'Jones? Oh, right,' he said, with a chuckle, 'and mine's Smith,' which it was not.

'No, it really is Jones. I'm not joking.'

'Oh, sorry, I thought you were pulling my leg.' We both laughed, but then, knowing I had to get off the telephone as quickly as possible, I agreed to meet him after work the following Saturday and said goodbye. I sat there thinking I must be dreaming.

Pushing aside the heavy curtain that hung across the entrance to Miss Minchin's office, I stepped out into the shop, still shaking. She and the other girls were waiting expectantly for an explanation, clearly dying of curiosity, but I said nothing as I returned to my work and tried to keep the grin off my face.

That week dragged by, and with each day, I grew more apprehensive. Eventually I told the girls about the date I had made, and how scared I was, and they teased me unmercifully for the rest of the week.

'Ooh, it's almost Saturday, Jones,' they would say, playfully elbowing me, and the more they teased the more scared I became. I wanted to cancel the date but didn't know how. There was no way I could avoid him either, because he'd be waiting outside the shop door; there was no escape. How had I got myself into such a mess? What would I do if he found out how old I was? What would I do if Mum and Dad found out about him? They'd kill me.

At last Saturday arrived, and when shop hours ended, I dashed upstairs to the staff room to change out of my uniform and to apply fresh makeup. Immediately the girls burst into a chorus of 'Yankee Doodle Dandy'.

'Knock it off, you lot,' I said. 'I'm already nervous enough. Can you see me shaking?'

'No – but is that your knees I hear knocking?'

'Very funny,' I said, as I put on my too-long coat. 'Here I go, wish me luck.'

'Good luck,' they called, as I descended the stairs. Still shaking like the proverbial leaf, I pushed open the shop door, and there he was, all bright and shiny, and smelling of Old Spice. I glanced back and there were my workmates, noses glued to the shop window. They looked like idiots, just standing there, grinning.

'Don't mind them,' I told Bob. 'They're all morons.'

He laughed as he took my arm and steered me off on my first ever date. He had actually come to pick me up. I hadn't had to meet him on a street corner. Suddenly, I wasn't scared any more. He was a real gentleman.

Conversation came easily to us, although we still had problems with language and accent differences. We talked about where we had gone to school, and what Bob did for a living back home. We discussed families and told a little about previous boy- and girlfriends. We shared music preferences, and I learned that he played the accordion, which was interesting since Dad could play the accordion too. We walked, talked and laughed, then stopped to eat, and then we talked and laughed some more. We never did make it to the cinema. By the time we stopped talking, it was too late, but we didn't care.

At last, our evening ended. Neither of us wanted to miss the last train this time, so we walked to the station together.

'When can I see you again?' he asked.

'I don't know,' I replied.

Of course I wanted to see him again but I was frightened. What could I say, without letting on about my age – at twenty, he seemed much older than me – and my fear of derogatory name-calling? I'd gone out with him once and nothing terrible had happened, but . . .

'Can you phone me at work later in the week? I'll see what I can arrange.' There, I'd finally said it.

'Great,' he said, a big smile spreading across his face. 'For a minute there I was afraid you were going to say no. I'll know when I'm on guard duty by then too.' And that was how we left it.

He kissed me goodnight, gently on the lips, and I felt that kiss right down to my toes. Bob was different from anyone I had ever been with before. He had made me feel special. However, that one big problem loomed ahead. If we continued to see one another, how would I ever tell him my age? That, I decided, would have to wait, but in the meantime, I knew I would have to tell Mum and Dad about him, before someone else did.

31

Courtship

'What would you say if I told you I wanted to invite an American soldier home for Sunday tea?' I asked casually, and then continued my pretence of reading the newspaper.

It was the day after my first date with Bob. Was I mad? What was my big hurry? I hadn't meant to say anything to them yet, and I already wished I had kept my big mouth shut.

Cigarettes flew from their mouths. Mum drew in breath, choking on smoke she should have exhaled. Dad spluttered, showering me with a fine mist of tobacco-laced spit. The horror on their faces said it all. Then, after gaining a modicum of composure, Dad spoke.

'How do you know a bloody American soldier?' he asked, and I tried to explain, as nonchalantly as possible, about our accidental meeting.

'Are you barmy?' Mum said. Her voice was strange, sort of strained and high-pitched, the way her eyebrows now looked. 'What would the neighbours think?'

Hmm, I thought, how had I known that would be Mum's biggest concern? She always worried about what the neighbours thought. If she knew what I knew about some of their shenanigans, she'd die of shock, especially if she knew of my involvement in some of their escapades. It would make bringing home an American look like a Sunday school outing.

'Does he know how old you are?' Dad asked, relighting the squashed cigarette that had somehow survived the squall.

'What would he need to know that for? I just want to invite him for tea. I don't want to marry him. He's not interested in me that way,' I lied, glad that I had inherited my father's skill as a 'holy friar'.

For the next hour or so, Mum and Dad took turns to lecture me about my age, bad reputations in general, and what people might think. They must have smoked a packet of cigarettes between them; the air was thick with smoke and verbiage.

I listened patiently while they ranted, and then, when I thought they were finished, I began the case for the defence.

'He's just a young boy away from home for the first time. He misses his family and he's very lonely. I just feel sorry for him, honest, that's all, poor bloke.'

At that time, my brother Peter was doing his national service in Germany with the British Army. I used that as added ammunition in my plea for compassion.

'How would you feel if someone invited Pete home for a meal over there and knew he was lonely? You'd think it was really kind, wouldn't you? You'd be grateful.' I could be very persuasive when I needed to be and I was a good actor too. Mum often referred to me as 'Sara Heartburn', and was forever telling me that the only thing that had kept me off the stage was rotten eggs.

'Are you sure that's all there is to it, Iris?' she asked, her eyes all squinty. She looked suspicious, as though she didn't trust me.

I tutted and closed my eyes in mock disdain at the very thought. 'Don't be daft, Mum. What else could it be? You don't really think he'd be interested in me, do you?' I laughed and put on my innocent face. 'What harm can it do, inviting someone to tea?'

'I dunno,' said Dad, shaking his head. 'I don't like it, Iris.'

Strangely enough, Mum was the first to crack. She visibly softened when I talked about Peter. I knew in the end she'd say yes and that Dad would soon follow, out of curiosity, if nothing else, and I was right. They finally did agree, but reluctantly.

'All right, then. He can come Sunday, but just for a meal, mind you. Don't you think for one minute, my girl, that it can be a regular thing, and don't start thinkin' it's okay for you to go out with him neither,' Dad warned, wagging a finger in my face. The knot in my stomach relaxed. I could hardly wait to tell Bob, if he ever called me again, and he did, the following day.

Sunday seemed to take a month to come round, and my family was just as nervous and excited as I was about having an American home for tea. They still fretted about what people would think, but none of us considered how nervous Bob might be.

I met him at the station, and then, arm in arm, we went home to face the inquisition. As we approached our house, several of the neighbours' curtains twitched. No faces were visible but I waved anyway. I was grinning inside.

'Who ya waving at?' Bob asked.

'Nosy neighbours,' I said. 'This'll give 'em something to talk about.'

He chuckled. 'Yeah, I bet it's not every day you get American soldiers visiting Lundin Walk.'

'You're the first. Are you nervous?'

'What do you think?'

'Don't be. We may be strange, but we're not dangerous.' We were still laughing as Dad opened the front door. They had been watching for us.

After introductions and that first cup of tea, tensions eased and Mum and Dad treated their visitor like an old friend. Conversation was a little strained at first, but my two young brothers, Robert and Christopher, were fascinated, especially by the American accent. Robert, at seven, was full of questions, while Christopher, who was only three, just grinned and hung on to Mum.

'Do you have any medals?' asked Robert.

'They don't give us medals for coming to England. You have to do something brave to get a medal.'

'Maybe you should get one for comin' here today then,' Dad said, and we all laughed.

Robert was not to be distracted, though. 'Do you live near cowboys and Indians?' he asked.

'Well, you don't see many cowboys in Chicago, but there are Indians living not too far away at a place called Wisconsin Dells. Sometimes we go there on vacation.'

'What's a vacation?'

'A vacation? Well, let me see, what do you call it when you go away somewhere? Like in the summer when there's no school.'

'We call it a holiday,' Robert said, looking at Bob as though he was stupid. 'Vacation. That's a funny word for a holiday. What does it mean?'

'Well, I guess it means holiday,' replied a patient Bob.

'Why don't you just call it a holiday, then?'

We'd all been enjoying this intense conversation between Robert and Bob, but now we burst out laughing again. Robert went on with his next question.

'Well, what about all them gangsters? Ain't you afraid of gettin' shot?'

'Nah, the bad guys don't come anywhere near where I live.'

Robert looked disappointed.

Mum and Dad asked Bob lots of questions, mostly about his family. He told them his father drove a bus, his mother was housekeeper for the pastor of their church and his only sister worked in a factory. I'm sure they were relieved to know he came from ordinary working-class people and not from a posh background.

All was going well until Mum asked a simple question that changed the comfort level drastically, at least for a while.

'What's Chicago's weather like in winter then, Bob? Does it get very cold there?'

'Well, ma'am, sometimes it's cold enough to freeze your fanny,' he replied innocently.

I blew tea out of my nose, and Mum and Dad's mouths dropped open. There was an immediate and deathly silence. Poor Bob. How was he to know that in England 'fanny' meant 'vagina'?

While Mum and Dad carried dishes out to the kitchen, I explained the unfortunate linguistic error to him. He was mortified. I then explained the difference to Mum and Dad.

'Oh, my Gawd,' Mum said. 'I thought they spoke the same language as us.'

'They do,' said Dad. 'They just don't speak it proper.'

We often laughed about that incident, and years later Mum confided to me that, at the time, she'd had visions of icicles 'hangin'' off me minge'.

After spending an otherwise enjoyable evening together, Bob returned to his barracks with an invitation from Mum and Dad to come back any time. The only person in the family who was not happy to hear about my friendship with an American soldier was my big brother, Peter. I'm sure he was worried about his little sister and her reputation.

At first, I thought our friendship might be a passing fancy, especially on Bob's part, but he and I became inseparable. We spent every possible minute together, and Mum and Dad accepted it. They never tried to put a stop to it after they'd met him; neither did they lecture me about the possible dangers. I'm not sure if they trusted me, but they appeared to trust him with me. As for my two little brothers, they were crazy about him. Especially after he took them to see Walt Disney's new film, *The Living Desert,* and bought them all the sweets and ice cream they could eat.

When our days off coincided, we did all the things courting couples do. We went sightseeing in London, which I had never done before. We visited such landmarks as Windsor Castle and St Albans Abbey, and took a boat trip down the River Thames, which included a stopover at Southend-on-Sea and dinner on the way back. It was wonderful to share and enjoy new experiences with someone special. I loved holding hands with him and taking leisurely strolls. It seemed that every time I looked up at him, he was looking at me, and each time our eyes met, I felt as though something was tickling me inside.

Soon I began taking Bob to meet my relatives. We visited my grandparents, aunts and uncles, family friends, everyone I could think of. I wanted to show him off and to share my world with him. It soon became apparent that this fancy was not a passing one. We were falling in love.

It was good to be part of what I thought of as the 'grown-up world'. Accepted not only as an adult but also as a woman, I no longer felt like the invisible child. My mother began talking to me about things she never would have mentioned before, and we had many laughs together. I think she was quite smitten with this charming young American too. He was generous to the family, often bringing gifts of food, drink and, best of all, cigarettes, all of which he could purchase on the base inexpensively. Mum and Dad were both heavy smokers, even though Mum claimed that she never inhaled, and cigarettes in England were expensive.

'No wonder they're cheap. They ain't nearly as good as English cigarettes,' commented Dad.

'Beggars can't be choosers, Ted. Besides, who said you had to smoke 'em? I'll have your share,' said Mum.

An amusing story involved one of Bob's gifts, a bottle of fine cognac. The sight of it almost brought tears to Dad's eyes; it was something the average British worker could never have afforded.

Dad placed that precious bottle, with something akin to reverence, in the back corner of the sideboard. 'That's for visitors,' he announced. 'But only on special occasions.' He then mumbled something about wishing the sideboard had a lock.

When visitors and that special occasion arrived, Dad opened the cabinet door and reached inside. 'What the hell?' he shouted, as he took out the bottle and held it up. 'Who's been havin' a go at this, then?'

'I've had a few little drops, Ted. I couldn't have had all that, though. It was just for medicinal purposes. I've been ever so chesty,' said Mum, with a little cough-cough. She hadn't realized that her 'few little drops' had almost emptied the bottle.

'Chesty, my eye,' Dad spluttered, his face turning bright red. 'You've almost polished off the bloody lot. Do you have any idea how much that stuff costs? Why didn't you just get some bloody cough medicine?'

'All right, all right, stop naggin', Ted. How was I to know you'd begrudge me a drop of whisky?'

'It was brandy, Kit. Not medicine. Not whisky. It was bloody beautiful cognac brandy,' he said, shaking the bottle at her. I thought he was going to cry.

He had forgotten the visitors who sat there on the sofa, trying to be invisible and probably wishing they'd never accepted the offer of a drink.

Mum was embarrassed and defensive and, oh, how we teased her about her 'tippling'. She certainly wasn't a drinker, but as many older people believed, and I'm sure still do, a little 'nip' was good for whatever might ail you. The problem was the abundance of Mum's ailments: she had tablets and potions for everything and was always happy to share them. Perhaps that was why she was surprised at Dad's reluctance to share his 'medicine'.

Now, I mentioned older people, but Mum and Dad were only about forty; it seemed old to me, when I was just fifteen.

One of the first 'special events' I attended with Bob was Thanksgiving Day dinner at the army base. The amount of food was unbelievable; I was astonished. We queued, holding large divided trays, and were served by servicemen. Some of the foods I could not identify.

'What's that?'

'Candied yams.'

'Candied yams? What's yams? And what's that there?'

'That's carrot and pineapple Jell-O.'

'Are they for dessert?'

'No, it's a side dish, like a salad. They'll bring desserts out later.'

'You eat sweet stuff on the same plate with meat and veg?'

'Yeah. Don't you?'

'Of course not. Sweet stuff is for afters – I mean dessert. I couldn't eat jelly, I mean Jell-O, with my dinner.'

And that was how I began to learn the weird eating habits of Americans. No wonder they said English food was terrible. They must have been bored with our everyday diet of meat, potatoes and vegetables.

When we had been dating for about six months, Bob said he wanted to ask me an important question. Oh, no, I thought. He wants me to have sex with him.

'Go on, then,' I said. 'But don't be surprised if the answer's no.' I was ready, or so I thought. He took both of my hands in his.

'I love you, Iris. Will you marry me?'

His words were like an electric shock: they stunned me. My knees turned to rubber. My mouth was so dry I could neither speak nor swallow. I felt myself sway and was sure I was about to faint.

'You don't have to answer right away,' he said. 'Take your time, but please say yes.' He put his arms around me and held me close to him. Laying my head on his chest, I could hear and feel the pounding of his heart against my face. 'Please,' he said again.

Oh, God, no, I thought. This was something I had dreamed of; it was also something I had feared. The long-dreaded time had come for me to tell him how old I was. How was it possible that in the six months we'd been together the subject of my age had never arisen?

I ran my tongue around the inside of my mouth, trying to find enough moisture to form the words I needed to say. Pushing myself back from him, I swallowed hard and took a deep breath.

'I can't marry you, Bob.'

'Why not?' he said. 'I thought you loved me.'

'I do love you, Bob, I really do, but I can't get married. I'm only fifteen years old.' There. It was out. My heart was about to explode from my chest and my head was throbbing as the tears began to fall and I shook uncontrollably.

'Oh, my God,' was all he said. Now it was his turn to be stunned. Then, after what seemed minutes, he spoke again. 'You're joking, right?'

'No, I'm not joking. I've wanted to tell you, but I just couldn't. I knew it would ruin everything. It never seemed important before. I never thought you'd want to marry me. I never thought anyone would ever want to marry me.'

When he realized I was telling the truth, he blanched. He covered his face with his hands and at first just stood there, rocking back and forth.

'Why the hell didn't you tell me?' he said, through clenched teeth.

I had never heard him use language like that before and I was afraid he might hit me, but instead, he just turned and walked away without another word. I leaned against the doorframe, sobbing, as I watched him disappear from sight.

We didn't see each other or communicate for a while. I was miserable and felt that my heart would break, but what could I do? The answer was simple. Nothing. I didn't tell Mum and Dad what had happened; I did not want to hear, 'I told you so.' They obviously knew something was wrong, but they, too, remained silent, leaving me, once again, in solitary despair.

At last, when I had almost given up hope, he came to the house. I had heard a knock on the front door but thought nothing of it, but then Mum came into the living room and turned off the radio.

'There's someone here to see you, Iris,' she said. 'He has something he wants to say to you.'

I looked up, and when I saw him standing there, my heart did flip-flops inside my chest. Poor Bob, he looked as awful as I felt.

'I don't care about your age. I'll wait for you as long as I have to,' he said, and we collapsed into one another's arms and wept.

Later that evening, we had a long talk with Mum and Dad. It was Dad's turn to cry next, but Mum didn't say a word. She just sat, stony-faced. I don't think either of them was surprised by what we had to say.

They finally agreed that we could become engaged on my sixteenth birthday, which was only a few months away, but added that we would have to wait a lot longer than that before thinking of marriage. The understanding was that he would go back to the States when the time came, and that he would send for me later.

When Mum and Dad were sure that we understood the conditions, and had agreed to their terms, Bob and I went to London and chose the most beautiful engagement ring I had ever seen. On my sixteenth birthday, 5 July 1954, he slipped it onto my finger. I had never been happier in my life. I loved that blond-haired, blue-eyed 'Yank', who always smelt of Old Spice aftershave, and for the first time in my life, I felt truly loved too.

32

Marriage

So there I was, engaged. Plain, skinny, nobody: Iris Jones was engaged.

I'd look at myself in the mirror, and hold up my left hand. It reflected back so it must be true, yet it seemed like a dream.

At work the following Monday, I said nothing of my engagement. I simply went about my business, making exaggerated hand movements as I flitted around the shop. At last, the flash of diamonds caught someone's eye and, like ants at a picnic, the girls soon surrounded me, their eyes boggling in disbelief.

'You're engaged? You can't be.'

'Your mum and dad let you get engaged?'

'When are you gettin' married?'

Questions flew, and I waited for a lull before attempting to answer them.

'Yeah, I'm engaged, but we won't get married till I'm at least eighteen,' I told them.

'When does he go back to the States, then?'

'I don't know for sure but he'll have to go without me. I'll go later.'

'Blimey, I'd hate that.'

'Me too.' I groaned.

They oohed and aahed over my beautiful ring; like me, they'd never seen anything like it. It was American-styled, the kind with a matching wedding band. Everyone said how happy they were for me and we jabbered on until customers came into the shop. I don't know how I got any work done that day; it was difficult to concentrate three feet above the ground.

That ring on my finger was in many ways a talisman, a magic key. It held all my hopes and dreams. It was my passport away from memories of a miserable childhood, from the oppression of British social class and from the family I had never felt a part of since the war had ended.

In subsequent years, people hinted or suggested that I had married an American just to get to the United States, but that was not so. The idea had never entered my mind. My engagement ring as a 'passport out of the oppression of British social class' meant only one thing: if the fates had not been kind to me in bringing me my American soldier – whom I loved with all my being – I would have eventually married someone of 'my own station', of 'my own class'. I would have remained mired down in what felt at the time like the hopelessness of Britain's poor working class. Bob himself was the true magic, and the ring its symbol. I loved him and I knew he loved me. All I had ever wanted was to find someone gentle, refined, kind and sober, someone who would value me. That, and that alone, is why I married my American soldier. I would have travelled to the ends of the earth with him. I would also have stayed in England, if that had been his choice.

By then, Bob's family knew of his plan to marry an English girl, but he had failed to mention one or two small details: he had not told them my age or that he'd have to leave me behind until I was eighteen. I learned later that his mother had cried for weeks at the prospect of her only son bringing home a foreign bride. His family was convinced that he was marrying out of loneliness, and that someone was taking advantage of him. At the time, I knew nothing of the letters in which they tried to dissuade him. Had I known, I would have been devastated. It would have plunged me back into the abyss of the unwanted, the undesirable, but he protected me with his silence.

'You never show me letters from your family any more,' I remarked one day.

'Oh, sorry, I keep forgetting,' he replied. 'Anyway, they're all the same, just about what they had for Sunday supper and the price of steaks. If you've read one, you've read them all.' I took him at his word, having seen some of the evidence. Each of their letters had been a duplicate of the last, always containing a complete rundown of meals eaten, and bargains found at one grocery store or another. Those Americans, I had thought, they're obsessed with food.

After our engagement, it soon became obvious that Bob and I could never be happy living apart. How could we tolerate thousands of miles separating us for two years? We conspired and began our campaign to be married before he shipped out.

By then, we were engaging in a lot of heavy petting, mostly on the couch after Mum and Dad had gone to bed, and often came close to 'going all the way'. I have no idea how we managed to control ourselves, but we did. Had the situation gone on for much longer, we might have made a serious mistake. I might have 'brought trouble home', and that was something neither of us wanted.

First, Mum and Dad had to be convinced that marriage was our best option. I'm sure they already knew I'd be miserable and impossible to live with if Bob left without me. Mum had already made it abundantly clear that she found me difficult to live with; I felt certain she would be easy to convince.

'You're never satisfied,' she'd say. 'What do you want from me?'

'A little attention would be nice, and a few kind words,' I'd told her, on many occasions.

'Grow up,' she'd tell me. 'Don't be a big baby.'

'I'm not a baby, Mum. It's just that you don't seem to know

I'm here most of the time.' I'd always end up in tears, and she would throw up her hands and walk away. Those conversations had been going on for years. I was sure Mum disliked me and just as sure that she wouldn't miss me. Dad might be a different matter, though.

Bob and I had long discussions with them.

'Are you sure you know what you're doing?'

'What if you discover you've made a big mistake?'

'What if you're unhappy in America? You wouldn't be able to run home, Iris.'

Most of the questions came from Dad. Mum just listened, her lips pursed. We covered all the what-ifs numerous times. I cried, Bob cried and Dad cried. Later, I asked Mum why she never cried.

'I don't have no tears left,' she said. 'Nobody knows the tears I've shed. I've cried bucketfuls.' She wouldn't elaborate on what she meant. It was many years before Mum made me privy to her secrets. It came as no surprise that all of her tears had been over Dad.

When Mum and Dad finally caved in, we faced the next hurdle, which was to convince the United States Army that I was sufficiently mature to take the giant plunge into marriage and subsequently into leaving family, home and country. Once again, I was a nervous wreck. What would we do if they denied our request? What would I do if they sent Bob home without me? What if his family talked him out of waiting for me? It was another set of what-ifs. All I could do was concentrate on looking confident and mature, and I began the mental rehearsal of walking tall and using a strong voice. Time would tell if my act of confidence would work under pressure.

A white-collared army chaplain and one of Bob's brass-bedecked commanding officers interviewed each of us separately, then together. Their questions were much the same as Mum and Dad's had been.

'Help me understand. Tell me in your own words why you think you're ready to marry and leave home so young,' said the chaplain.

'Convince me,' said the officer, and I tried to explain.

'I was separated from my family for two years during the war, when I was evacuated. The war made us grow up fast. I took care of the whole family when I was twelve and my mother had a nervous breakdown. I've been making my own living for some time now. I think I've already proved I can make adult decisions and live in an adult world,' I answered, with confidence.

There were other questions and answers, but that one seemed to make the most impact. After that, the interviews became a blur.

I maintained my act of confidence, keeping eye contact with my 'interrogators' while the rest of the room disappeared in blackness around me. I was aware of mouths moving and heads nodding; it was the only indication that we were still speaking.

Suddenly, we were on our feet, shaking hands and exchanging thanks. Then we were outside, and my lungs were working normally again, having apparently been put on hold.

'I don't remember what I said, Bob,' I told him. 'I think I did okay, though.'

'You can stop shaking now, Iris. It's too late to worry about it now. We'll just have to keep our fingers and everything else crossed.'

'What did they ask you?'

'Oh, the same old stuff,' he said. Later I learned that they had tried to dissuade him from doing something he might regret. They had also advised him, if they granted our request, not to start a family too soon – in case things didn't work out, I suppose.

After the same military officials had met my parents, we were not kept waiting long for their decision. They granted us permission to marry.

The next step was for Mum and Dad to retain a solicitor. Legal papers had to be prepared and signed, giving me, as a minor, permission to marry before the age of twenty-one. Our meeting with the solicitor turned out to be the worst experience of all. His disapproval of what we were doing was obvious. He treated us with outright disdain. His mouth curved down at the edges, around a spider-veined chin, as though he'd just tasted something disgusting and couldn't wait to spit it out.

'Bloody toffee nose. I wanted to wipe that sneer off his face,' Dad growled, as we descended the stairs from the lofty chambers that matched the lawyer's arrogance.

'Yeah, I know what cockroaches feel like now,' I mumbled.

'I wonder what he thought of us, Ted, letting Iris get married so young,' said Mum.

'You mean you couldn't tell?' I shot back, thinking, there she goes again, worrying about what people might think, and not about how we'd been treated. Poor Mum, she just didn't get it.

At last, with the red tape out of the way, we could begin the happier business of planning our wedding. Bob had received his orders and knew he would be returning to the States the following February. It was now August: we had less than six months to organize a wedding and complete the long immigration process.

We chose 16 October for our wedding, then booked the church, the reception hall and a week's honeymoon at a seaside hotel in Falmouth, Cornwall, then filed my immigration application. There was much to do, but we were on our way.

As his wedding gift to me, Bob paid for my dress. My friend Joyce, who had been with me when I met Bob, was to be my only bridesmaid, and my brother Peter, home on leave from the army, would be Bob's best man. I bought a dusty pink suit as my going-away outfit – which was almost as important as the wedding gown. The local newspaper always described in detail both the wedding gown and the honeymoon-travelling outfit. In fact, after our wedding, the newspaper story covered an unusually large spread, complete with pictures, details of my age, the Cinderella aspect of our romance, about Bob's mother and her journey to attend the wedding, and our own forthcoming voyage to America.

'It looks like we'll have to cancel our honeymoon,' Bob had announced one evening.

'What? Why?' I asked. He waved a letter at me, and then handed it to me to read, but I didn't get far. 'Your mother's coming to the wedding. Oh, my God. Why's she only staying four days?'

'Read the rest of the letter,' he said.

'I can't. I'm too nervous. Read it to me.' Laughing, he took it and began. My head whirled, but I heard the important parts.

'Can only stay in England for four days . . . Afraid to fly . . . Coming by ship . . . Sailing on the *Queen Mary* . . . Travel time for that alone adds up to ten days . . . Roberta [Bob's older sister] expecting her first baby the beginning of November . . . Must be home for that . . . Can only be away from home for two weeks . . . Can't wait to see you and to meet Iris and her family.'

We cancelled our trip to Cornwall and instead planned a two-night stay in London. That would give us time to get back to see her before she sailed away again.

I dreaded meeting my future mother-in-law, but Bob, whom she called 'Robert', assured me that she was not an ogre. Before her arrival, I had dreams about her, and in the dreams, she always said the same thing, that I was much prettier than my pictures. Perhaps it was dreaming, but the truth is, they actually were the first words out of her mouth.

'Oh, Raahbuurrt, she's even prettier than her pictures.' I was flabbergasted. In private, I tried saying the words 'Robert' and 'prettier' the way she did, in what I learned was a Midwest accent, 'Raahbuurrt', 'priddeeyer', all the while thinking how strange it sounded. Getting used to the American language and its different expressions was one thing, but I had yet to learn of America's many geographically and racially influenced accents. There were no comparable racially influenced accents in Britain at the time, and it was difficult for me to understand Bob's surprise upon hearing a black British-born person speak with a British accent.

Although very sweet, Mrs Irvine was a bit of a shock to us Brits. First, she was loud. I'm not sure if it was due to nervousness or if all Americans tended to speak louder than the British did, but I suspect it was a little of each. Her coat was also on the 'loud' side. It was bright electric-blue bouclé, nice, but next to all the English grey, navy and black, it stood out like the proverbial sore thumb. The second shock was that not only did she wear ankle socks, she wore them with skirts and high heels. We had never seen that before and thought it most peculiar. Thank God she didn't wear them on the day of the wedding.

The poor woman almost froze to death while staying at our house; its lack of central heating would have been a shock to anyone coming from America for the first time. With hot-water bottles and a blazing fire in the fireplace, Mum and Dad did their best to keep her warm, but it was not enough. By the time she departed British shores, her American Midwest accent sounded like that of a strangled duck. She had a terrible cold that confined her to her cabin for the entire voyage home.

At last the big day arrived, and after Joyce and I had finished dressing, everyone except Dad and me left for the church. Then, after checking my makeup for the hundredth time, with the veil draped over one arm, and my gown lifted clear of the stairs, I descended the narrow flight. At the bottom, my father stood waiting. He took one look at me, pulled out a large, new-for-the-occasion white handkerchief and began bawling. 'You look like an angel,' he sobbed.

'Thanks, Dad, but I'm so scared I think I'm going to be sick.'

'Just a minute, love,' he said, blowing his nose loudly. 'I'll get you something to settle your stomach.' He disappeared into the kitchen for a few minutes, and when he returned, he had something milky in a glass. Insistently, he shoved it towards me.

'What is it, Dad?'

'Never mind, just drink it down. It'll do wonders for you.' I took the glass from his hands and gulped its contents.

'Okay, now tell me what it was,' I insisted.

'A couple of raw eggs, milk and a drop of whisky,' he replied. 'I bet you feel better already, don't you?'

'Raw eggs?' I spluttered. 'No wonder it slid down easy. Did you have some?'

'Nah,' he said. 'Just the whisky.'

I was sure it wouldn't work, but he was right, my stomach did feel better. I took a deep breath and held out my hand to him.

'Well, Dad. This is it. It's time for us to go.'

'It's not too late to change your mind, Iris. Are you sure you want to do this?'

'Yes, Dad. I really do.'

His lips quivered. Then they relaxed and melted into a broad grin. I hooked my arm through his and we walked out of the front door to where a crowd of neighbours stood watching for us. We waved at them.

'Good luck, Iris,' they called, as we climbed into the hired, ribbon-bedecked Rolls-Royce limousine that stood waiting, like Cinderella's coach, to whisk us off to the church.

At the time, the only consecrated church in South Oxhey was

the lovely old Blackwell family chapel at Oxhey Manor. At our wedding in that ancient chapel, I felt honoured to be in the presence of the spirits that had once occupied the gracious home, the spirits of people now interred in its walls and graveyard.

A new church, built next to the old chapel, was not yet consecrated; hence, marriages performed there would not have been legal in the eyes of the Church.

After the pronouncement that we were now 'man and wife', the entire wedding entourage trooped outside, across the graveyard and into the ultra-modern new church for the rest of the service.

For me, the unusual procedure had special beauty and significance: we had passed from the old to the new, both physically and spiritually.

After the ceremony, when we were safely outside the sanctuary, Bob and I dissolved into fits of laughter.

The vicar who had married us had, without a doubt, the foulest breath on earth; it had almost knocked us over. Unfortunately, one of the hymns we had chosen was 'Holy Holy Holy', and each time he exhaled the 'H' of 'Holy', my eyes crossed and I sang, extra loudly, 'Lord God Almighty'. I suppose it would have been even worse had we chosen 'Breathe on me, Breath of God'!

'I've heard of people fainting at the altar, but never because of the vicar's bad breath!' laughed Bob.

'What were you two laughing at up there?' Mum asked, as she joined us.

When we told her, she gave her usual comment: 'Take big sniffs. It'll soon be gone.'

'Blimey, if we'd done that, Mum, we'd have both turned blue.'

'Poor bloke,' she said. 'He probably needs a dose of opening medicine.' I had to laugh. I did love Mum's sayings and cure-all remedies.

The ceremony and official picture-taking finished, everyone made their way to the reception at Oxhey Golf Club, a beautiful old English country house. We had most of the food catered, but Mum and other volunteers still ended up in the kitchen, making mountains of sandwiches. Many people had come, not only because it was my wedding but also because they saw it as a farewell party for me. It was possibly the last time some of them would ever see me, but I tried not to think of that.

A dance band played, and besides all the familiar waltzes, fox-trots and polkas, we had fun teaching the Americans some of the traditional English party dances, like 'Knees Up Mother Brown' and 'The Lambeth Walk'. I laughed until tears dripped off my chin as I watched the Americans trying to make sense of, and participate in, 'Knees Up Mother Brown' while the British belted out the song.

'You English sure have some strange customs,' said one of the 'Yanks'.

They might have thought us odd, but they seemed to have a great time, especially since many of them had contributed generously to the bar supplies.

As I watched everyone having fun, it occurred to me there was no one there from Dad's side of the family. I asked him about it.

'Your mum thought they might embarrass you with their drinking and carrying on,' he said. 'So we thought it best not to invite them.'

'They couldn't have been any worse than this lot, Dad.'

'Try telling that to your mum.'

When I asked Mum about it, she seemed shocked. 'It was your dad that didn't want them. He was afraid they would embarrass him!'

Now it was my turn to be shocked. Bob and I had provided a list of friends to invite; we had left the family list up to Mum and

Dad. If only I had known. That revelation was the only sad note to an otherwise perfect wedding.

When it came time for us newlyweds to go back to the house to change our clothes and get ready to leave on our little honeymoon, Dad took Bob aside. He was drunk and, not surprisingly, in tears.

'Promise me you'll try not to hurt her, mate,' he blubbed. I don't know who was more embarrassed, Bob or me.

'Don't worry, Mr Jones – er, Dad. I'll take good care of her.' We dashed off then, leaving poor old Dad at the door, mopping his eyes.

We travelled by train to London, where we had booked two nights at the Strand Palace Hotel. It was my first time to stay in a hotel. I was nervous and self-conscious but I grinned when I heard Bob register us as Mr and Mrs Robert Irvine. It sounded wonderful.

When the porter showed us to our room, I held my head high and tried to look as though I had done this hundreds of times. Then I caught a glimpse of myself in the lift mirror and was mortified. I still had confetti stuck all over my hair. We had travelled on the train like that too. Everyone must have known we were honeymooners. No wonder they had been smiling, or smirking, at us.

Our room was not en suite; they rarely were in those days. All we had was a tiny washbasin in the corner. The bathroom was down the landing. We didn't leap into bed straight away, as one might expect. In a most civilized manner, we took turns going to the bathroom to change into our nightclothes. After all, I had to make use of my first-night negligee, didn't I? I was grateful that I had received a dressing gown as a gift, another first for me; it would have been embarrassing trotting down the landing in a see-through nightie.

The truth of the matter was that we were both virgins. Neither of us had ever had actual intercourse before, and it did hurt at first.

We whispered our passion and giggled under the sheets, afraid someone might hear us. Then, not wanting the chambermaids to see the bloody mess we had made on the sheets, I tried to sponge the evidence away.

'Don't worry about it, Iris. These people will never see us again,' Bob assured me. 'I'll leave them a nice big tip.'

We were only there for two nights but by the time we returned home, I could hardly walk. My sweet husband wasn't too comfortable, either, but it was a very nice discomfort. In those early days of marriage, I seemed insatiable. Poor Bob sometimes had a hard time keeping up with me, especially if he had been on guard duty all night.

'Mercy!' he'd say.

And so my love and I began our married life. So far, it had been all I had hoped for, and more. Now the next phase was about to begin. It was time to prepare for another big step, the step towards leaving the nest and starting out on another journey – a journey into the unknown.

33

Preparing to Leave England and Wales

Returning from our brief honeymoon, and following my mother-in-law's departure, we found that Mum and Dad had given us their bedroom to use until we, too, left England. Touched by their generosity, we were also a little embarrassed.

'You didn't have to do that,' I protested.

'Well, it's only for a little while,' Mum said. 'We don't want your marriage to get off to a bad start, do we?'

'You don't have to worry about that, Mum. I think we could sleep on the sofa if we had to.'

'Yes, I suppose you've had some practice at that,' she said, with a knowing grin.

On that first night at home, we discovered that Mum and Dad had played a few tricks on us. They had 'short-sheeted' the bed so we could get just halfway in, sewn the bottoms of Bob's pyjama legs shut, and put two water-filled condoms between our sheets. The condoms were a surprise: I hadn't thought Mum knew about such things. In fact, I'd never seen one myself until then. I later wondered if they bore an unspoken message, but if they did, we missed it and simply joined in the fun. Carefully, we removed the 'water-balloons' from our bed and put them in Mum and Dad's bed, where the unsuspecting victims burst them and had to sleep on wet sheets.

'You buggers,' we heard from the next room, followed by laughter on both sides of our bedroom's adjoining wall. We didn't discover Bob's sewn-together pyjama legs until several days later. At that point, who was wearing nightclothes?

The following few months whizzed by in a flurry of preparations for my journey to America, and one of the more unpleasant things I had to do, in accordance with army and immigration regulations, was have a series of inoculations. One or two made me feel ill, but by far the worst was the small-pox vaccination. Unvaccinated as a child, I now had a terrible reaction.

'Here, put this over it,' Mum said, producing a small wire cage-like apparatus to place over the site. It had strings to tie it in place.

'What the heck's that?' I asked.

'They gave it to me when the boys were babies and had their vaccinations. It's to stop the scab getting knocked off.'

'I wish I'd had mine when I was a baby. Why didn't I, Mum?'

'Dunno, Iree. It might have been because you had pneumonia when it was time to have it. We must have forgot it after that, what with the war and all.' Mum tied the cage in place on my arm.

'I'm not wearing this thing,' I protested. I had put my cardigan on over it and it looked as though I had one giant muscle.

Mum burst out laughing. 'Oh, I see what you mean,' she gasped. 'Do you want me to see if I can get you another one for the other arm so your muscles match?'

'Ha ha ha,' I said. 'Very funny, Mum. Maybe I could use them in me bra after that.'

Later, when my arm became swollen, inflamed and extremely painful, I did use it. That little cage thing proved invaluable. I would have gone through the ceiling had anyone accidentally touched my vaccination site.

Next on the agenda was the acquisition of a passport and visa. The visa required a trip to the American Embassy in London where, among other procedures, I had to undergo a complete physical examination. The worst part was having a doctor look down my knickers with a flashlight to make sure

I was showing no sign of venereal disease. I'd never been so humiliated.

'I've been interfered with by a stranger, Mum,' I told her, when I got home.

'What?' Mum looked alarmed.

'Yeah. Some old geezer looked down me knickers with a torch, and you know what I said to 'im?'

'No, what?'

''Ad yer eyeful, George?'

'You never did.'

'No, but I wanted to.' We had a giggle about that. It was nice to be able to laugh about such intimate matters with my mother. It seemed funny that she and I were actually bonding over such matters when she had always seemed so naïve and bashful in the past. She was to surprise me even more with things she said in later years.

Finally, all my papers were in order. I had my passport and visa. Now, all I needed was a ticket to travel. The US Army gave me the choice of sailing to America on the *Queen Mary* at the cost of about two hundred dollars, which was a lot of money, or going with Bob on a troop ship for twelve dollars. It was an easy decision to make. I wanted to be with my husband, and the price was right.

While we waited for our official army 'shipping-out orders', military personnel came to the house to crate up our personal belongings, and that was when I realized I was really going. When I saw my meagre possessions packed into a box with an American address on it, the reality of what I was doing sank in. There would be nothing left of me in this house – in this country. It was the first time I had felt anything like fear, and as I watched the army vehicle drive off with our belongings, I had a little cry, but did not let anyone see my tears.

Shortly before we left, my family surprised us with a farewell party. Again, friends and family came to say their goodbyes. Although many tears were shed, one incident in particular caused a veritable cloudburst. It was when my beloved Auntie Iris presented me with a vial of British soil to take with me. 'Keep this with you, Iris,' she said. 'You'll always know that you never truly left English soil.' Handkerchiefs appeared all around. I could hear Dad sobbing as I embraced and thanked my aunt. It seemed that all I'd done lately was cry. Mum disappeared into the kitchen – to wash dishes, of course.

At home, we didn't talk much about me leaving; it seemed easier that way.

'I'm just going to tell meself you're going away on holiday,' was all Mum said – repeatedly. I knew she was preparing me for her lack of tears. She simply could not cry. Dad didn't say anything, but I could see the sadness in his eyes.

Then the news arrived. We would be starting our journey on Valentine's Day. Of all days, I thought. I would never be able to forget the date I had left home.

It was now mid-January of 1955, and I'd developed a nagging desire to visit my wartime Welsh family before I left Britain. I tried to push the thought aside, but it began to keep me awake at night. I couldn't get it out of my mind.

One night, when Bob was on duty at the base and everyone had just gone to bed, I called to my father.

'What's wrong, Iris?' he called back.

'Could you come here for a minute, please? I want to talk to you about something.' In seconds, he was there. I patted the bed beside me, signalling him to sit down.

'What's up, mate?' he asked, as he laid his hand on mine.

'Oh, Dad, I don't know what to do. I know I've only got a few weeks left here with you but something keeps telling me to go and visit the Coopers in Wales. Would it be really selfish of me to do that?' I felt my lips quiver and realized what an emotional issue this had become.

'Selfish? That ain't selfish, Iris. You must go if it's that important to you. If you can, you should always follow your heart. If you don't, you'll live with regrets all your life. Believe me, I know.' And he proceeded to tell me about his own dreams and of how he had sacrificed them. 'Me brother and me wanted to emigrate to Australia years ago. We wanted to start a building business over there. We could have made a fortune, but your mum wouldn't go. We could've 'ad a good life, and I've always regretted that. You go to Wales, Iris. Don't you go makin' the mistakes I did.'

I threw my arms around his neck and we both cried. I felt sorry for Dad: I had always sensed some kind of resentment between him and my mother and now I knew, well, part of it anyway. 'Thanks, Dad. I knew you'd tell me the right thing to do. I'll talk to Bob when he gets home and see if he wants to go with me.'

When I explained to Bob what I wanted and needed to do, he supported me one hundred per cent. He understood. 'Of course I want to go with you,' he said. 'I've heard so much about Wales and your other family. I sure do want to meet them. Let me see when I can get a couple of days off and we'll go.'

The following day, he told me that if we went it would have to be within the next few days, the only time he could schedule any leave. We had three days to prepare. There was no time to write to the Coopers and, of course, they, like us, had no telephone. We had to trust our luck.

'Do you know how to get there?' Bob asked.

'No, I haven't the foggiest, but we'll figure it out, don't worry.'

'You still ain't bought yourself a warm coat, Iris,' Mum reminded me. 'It'll be freezin' in Wales. They might even have snow. Anyway, you're gonna need one for them cold winters in Chicago. You don't wanna freeze your fanny, do you?'

'Mum!'

I spent the following day in Watford, looking for the perfect warm winter coat. My final choice was of fake fur. It was made of the same material they use to make teddy bears. In fact, in it, I looked exactly like a teddy bear, except for my now permed hair and my skinny legs.

'Blimey,' said Mum. 'You could go to the North Pole in that thing.'

'I know, Mum. Ain't it lovely?'

'What's them strings hangin' off the bottom?' she asked.

I looked down.

'Ha ha ha.' She laughed. 'Oh, sorry, it ain't strings, it's yer legs.'

'Bloody cheek,' I said. 'You've really 'urt me feelin's now, Mum.' Then I joined in with her laughter. I'd heard so many jokes about my skinny legs that I was immune to them. It had been only a few days since little brother Robert had made me feel 'so special'.

I had been standing with my back to the fireplace, warming my behind.

'Iris,' Robert said.

'What, Rob?'

'Do you know what your legs look like?'

'No. What?'

'Sausages,' he replied. 'They look just like sausages.'

Mum, who was in the kitchen, heard our conversation. She exploded into laughter and came into the living room, wiping her eyes on a tea towel.

'Thanks a lot, you two,' I said, feigning hurt feelings. 'You really know how to make a person feel good.'

Some years later, on hearing the story of my 'sausage legs', a friend, who was a cartoonist, drew a caricature of me, with strings of sausages for legs.

Three days after we'd been discussing a visit to Wales, we were on our way. We found that with two changes of train, we could get as far as Ferndale, just one town before Maerdy. We learned that Maerdy's station, where I had arrived eleven years earlier as an evacuee, was now out of service. 'We'll get a taxi or a bus to go the rest of the way,' I assured a slightly worried Bob.

When the rickety old train trundled into Ferndale station, it was dark. As we stepped down onto the platform, a light snow was falling. It twinkled like millions of diamonds within the circles of light under the lampposts. It had been years since I'd seen snow, and for a moment I stood and stared. Memories crashed in, but I forced myself back into the present.

It looked as though it had been snowing for some time, but the path to the station building had been cleared. As we approached, the station master appeared. 'Can I be of help?' he asked, in his melodic Welsh accent.

'We're trying to get to Maerdy,' I told him.

'Hmmm,' he mused. 'You'll not be gettin' to Maerdy tonight. It's too late for a bus and our taxi went 'ome, what with the weather and all. We don't get too many visitors this time of the night, specially in the snow.'

'Is there a hotel here?' asked Bob.

'Yes and no,' he replied. 'We do 'ave one but I'm sorry to tell you it's closed this time of the year.'

'Oh, no! Now what do we do? Can you suggest anything?' I pleaded. The man removed his cap and scratched his head.

'Well, now, there is a woman, Mrs Evans, up the road who do sometimes take in travellers. She'd be the only one I know of, *bach*.' I remembered that *bach* meant 'friend', or something like that. He took out a small notepad and wrote down directions for us. 'Tell her Ewan Davies sent you.'

Following directions, we headed up a steep hill. The inky black shapes of the mountains were barely visible against the snowflake-speckled night sky, but the pull on back and leg muscles told us we were climbing. All sound was muffled by the hills around us, and by the heavy blanket of snow that covered them. We talked in whispers to each other so as not to disturb the fragile atmosphere, but then I heard something that literally stopped me in my tracks. Adding to this magical night, I could hear singing, and I remembered: it was Sunday. The music was coming from a nearby church.

There are no words to describe the sound of a Welsh choir. The sound penetrates to the core of your being. Not only does it register in your ears, it resonates throughout your body and soul. I put down my bag and stood there, inhaling the beauty of the moment. My heart was full, tears blurred my vision, and in that instant, I knew I was meant to be there, on that special night.

'We'd better get going,' Bob said, and I had to force my mind to the task of finding a place to sleep for the night.

'Do you hear that?' I said. 'Isn't it beautiful?'

'Reminds me of Negro spirituals,' he replied.

At last, gasping for breath, we reached the top of the hill and found ourselves outside the house we were looking for. There were no lights in any of the windows. My heart sank.

'Uh-oh, it doesn't look as though anyone's home.' Bob groaned.

We walked up the short path and rang the doorbell anyway.

'Maybe she's already in bed,' I said. I heard Bob say, 'Shit,' under his breath.

In seconds, a light came on in the hall and the door flew open.

'Helloo, helloo, and what might I be doin' for you?' said a plump elderly woman.

'Ewan Davies sent us. He thought you might be able to put us up for the night,' I told her. 'I'm sorry to disturb you so late.' I hurried to explain our dilemma.

'No need to be sorry, girlie, come in, come in. Of course I'll be puttin' you up for the night,' she said, as she ushered us inside. It was actually more like herding, the way she flapped her arms all around us.

'We didn't see any lights,' said Bob.

'Ah, that's because we're in the back room, see. My friend is here [she pronounced it 'yer'], and we're havin' a cup of tea and bit o' supper. Come and sit with us and I'll make you a fresh cup.'

As much as we needed that cup of tea, we both had a hard time choking it down. It smelt like rotten eggs. The water must have come from a well.

After a second cup of stinky tea and lots of conversation, Mrs Evans's friend finally saved us.

'Your guests look very tired, Mrs Evans,' she said.

'Oh, indeed to goodness, what was I thinkin'? There I was, blabberin' on and on, and you so tired after a long day of travellin'. Come on now, I'll show you where you'll be sleepin'.'

We struggled up the narrow staircase and into a bedroom that looked like a diorama in a museum. The bed was on a platform, and piled high with feather bedding.

'Up out of the draught,' she explained. 'There's a stool if you need it to climb into bed and a chamber pot underneath. You'll not be wantin' to go down the garden in the night. I'll bring you tea in the mornin' and a jug of hot water for you to have a wash, and then you can have a lovely cooked breakfast before you go on to Maerdy.'

'Thank you so much,' we chorused.

'Goodnight to you, then, and God bless you,' she said, as she backed out of the room and closed the door behind her.

We buried our faces in the feather bed to stifle our laughter.

'Don't say I never take you anywhere nice,' I said, to my bewildered husband.

The room was freezing and our teeth were chattering, but once we had climbed up onto that mountain of featherbed, we soon warmed up. We must have sunk into it at least twelve inches – we could hardly see each other.

'I feel like the princess and the pea,' I told Bob.

'I just hope I don't have to pee,' he said. 'I'm not sure I'd be able to figure out how to get out of this mess.'

Exhausted, we were soon asleep. We couldn't cuddle in all that bedding: it was like wallowing in a bowl of jelly, and difficult to get a grip.

The next morning, as promised, there was a knock on the bedroom door. A still-smiling Mrs Evans entered, with a lovely pot of stinky tea and a large jug of stinky water for washing.

'*Bore da*,' she said, then corrected herself, 'I mean, good morning, good morning. I trust you slept well.' I noticed her glance at the chamber pot. 'I see you didn't have to use the pot then. You must be about to burst. Come down when you like. I'll have breakfast ready and you can go on out to the toilet too.' So much for modesty, I thought.

A little later we went downstairs. 'Holy cow,' Bob said, when he saw the breakfast spread. There was enough food on the table to feed half a dozen people.

'I was thinkin' you probably didn't have any dinner last night, and as how you must be starvin' by now. I hope it's to your likin', and don't be afraid to say if you want more.' More! I thought. She must be joking.

We dug in, and when Mrs Evans wasn't looking, we held our

noses to drink the tea. When we could eat no more, we thanked our hostess and told her we needed to get going.

'What do we owe you?' Bob asked.

'Would two pounds be all right?'

'Two pounds!' he exclaimed.

'Ooh,' said Mrs Evans, misunderstanding his response. 'I was afraid that was too much. How about thirty shillin's, then?'

'No, no, no. I meant two pounds wasn't enough.' Bob laughed, as he thrust four pound notes into her hand and gave her a hug. 'Now, if you'll just tell us how to get to Maerdy.'

As we headed back down the hill, dear Mrs Evans waved from her doorstep until we could no longer see her. It was like leaving an old friend.

'Amazing,' said Bob, shaking his head in disbelief.

At the bottom of the hill, we turned onto the main street and soon found ourselves back at the railway station. We hadn't noticed it the night before, but the bus stop was in front of the ticket office. We set our bags down and hoped it would not be a long wait. The sun was shining, but the air was frigid.

'There you are, then, and it looks like you've had a good rest.' It was the station master, Mr Davies, from the previous night. 'Did you tell Mrs Evans I sent you? There's a lovely woman for you, boyo. I knew she'd be takin' you in out of the cold. That woman's got a heart of gold she does. Such a tragic life she's had, mm-mm, terrible, just terrible.' He would have gone on but, thankfully, the bus arrived.

We shook hands with him, thanked him, and climbed aboard the shabby vehicle.

'Americans, is it?' the driver said.

'Well, just one of us,' I said, realizing that all eyes were on Bob and his uniform. 'I was evacuated to Maerdy during the war,' I added. 'I've come back to visit my mam.'

'There's lovely,' said a woman, who was sitting behind the

driver. Then she swivelled in her seat to face the back of the bus. 'Evacuee she is. Come back to see her wartime mam,' she told the rest of the occupants.

'There's lovely,' echoed throughout the bus, and all heads nodded in approval.

We hardly had time to sit down before the driver called out that Maerdy Road was just ahead and asked us which end of the street we wanted to get off.

'I don't remember,' I told him. 'It's been so long. I'm looking for number sixteen.' He slowed the bus until it was barely moving. Everyone on board peered out of the windows, looking for the address.

'There it is,' someone called. 'There's number sixteen.' The bus lurched to a stop. We thanked everyone and clambered down the steps. As the bus pulled away, we could see that everyone had moved to one side of the bus and was waving to us.

'Amazing,' Bob said, for the second time that day. We stood there for a moment and I looked all around, taking in the scene. Nothing seemed to have changed. In spite of the snow, everything looked, smelt and sounded the same.

'Do you hear that?' I said.

'What?'

'The sheep.' The familiar sound of their bleating drifted down into the valley from the hillsides. 'I love that sound,' I told my city-boy husband.

'Are you excited?' Bob asked.

'I'm scared to death. What if they don't remember me?'

'Well, let's find out,' he said, pushing me towards number sixteen.

I drew a deep breath, pushed the doorbell and then cringed when the bell chimed, loudly, the sound of Big Ben.

'Blimey,' I said. 'That's enough to wake the dead.'

Through the pebbled glass panel of the door, I could see the vague shape of someone approaching. My mouth was dry. I was trembling.

The door opened slowly and a tiny woman, whom at first I didn't recognize, stood there.

'Hello,' she said, with a puzzled look on her face.

'Auntie Nell? Do you remember me?' Her hands flew in the air.

'Dilwyn, Dilwyn, come quick and see who's here. It's our evacuee! It's Iris!' She put her arms out to me and we hugged each other. 'Oh, my God, I never thought I'd ever see your lovely face again,' she said. By then, Uncle Dil had appeared and, with a huge grin, he joined in the hugging and hand-shaking.

I stepped back and looked at them. They were so short I laughed.

'Didn't you used to be much taller?' I said.

'No, boyo, it's you that used to be much shorter,' laughed Uncle Dil.

'Who's this with you, then?' asked Nell.

'This is my husband, Bob. I'm going back to America with him soon and I wanted you to meet him before we went.'

'There's lovely,' said Nell, dabbing at her eyes with the corner of her apron.

We spent two wonderful days with the Coopers. I was surprised, and amused, to find that there was now an indoor toilet; it had been installed in the old larder.

'You 'ave to go into the larder to do a wee now, girlie,' chuckled Uncle Dil.

'We still take the pot up to bed with us, though. I don't fancy comin' down them blimmin' stairs at night,' added Nell. They insisted we take a pot up to bed with us too.

There was so much to talk about, and dear Auntie Nell provided endless meals. She even baked my old favourite, whimberry tart. We had picked the tiny dark berries on the mountainside many times while I lived there.

Bob had a hard time understanding the lilting Welsh dialect, while I slipped back into it easily. In turn, they had difficulty with Bob's Chicago-ese, but we managed to communicate – with a little translation here and there.

Somehow, word of our visit had leaked out into the village. Neighbours called with little presents and, I'm sure, to have a look at us. I don't know what they were more excited about, the fact that an evacuee had returned 'home', or the sight of an American soldier. Whatever the reason, Nell and Dil seemed proud to share us, and to tell everyone how far we had travelled to see them.

In spite of the snow, we took walks to old familiar places, accompanied by Uncle Dil. We showed Bob the old railway station, the Maerdy coal mine, the school and chapel I had attended, and we walked as far as we dared in the snow and ice up the mountainside, to where I used to hide and play.

Too soon, it was time for us to leave.

'I couldn't leave without seeing you,' I told them. 'I had to come.'

They walked with us to the bus stop, where we shed a few more tears.

'Thank you for thinkin' of us,' they said.

'How could I ever forget?' I replied.

From the back window of the bus we waved until we could no longer see them.

Then we settled back in our seats, each with a deep sigh of satisfaction, and began the long journey back to South Oxhey.

'Wonderful people,' commented Bob.

'The best,' I said, before retreating into my thoughts of the next set of farewells – farewells I feared more with each passing day.

34

Leaving Home for America

At home again with Mum and Dad, I wondered where the last few weeks had gone. Suddenly it was 13 February, the last night I would sleep in my parents' home. Panic rose in my chest as I willed myself into sleep; tomorrow would come soon enough.

Awakened by the jangling alarm clock, I reached out and punched it into silence.

Dawn and its grey light had yet to penetrate the winter darkness, to illuminate this familiar room, this house, my home. With eyes wide open, I stared blindly at the ceiling, a blank screen of the unknown. I shivered, not only from the cold damp air but also from the gnawing awareness that this was the day I would leave my family and all that was familiar to travel to a new life. A life that awaited me, thousands of miles away, in the storybook, movie-set country called America.

'It's time to get up, Bob,' I whispered, as I shook his shoulder and kissed his neck.

'Jeez, it seems like I only just fell asleep.' He turned and put his arms around me. 'Are you okay?'

'Yeah. I was so nervous I didn't think I'd ever get to sleep last night. I'm scared about today, you know, about Mum and Dad and all.'

For a few minutes, we clung to one another.

'We'd better get up. I can hear Mum downstairs – sounds like she's already got the kettle on. She won't want us to leave without having breakfast, but I don't think I can eat anything.'

I thought back to my wedding day. I had felt the same grinding nausea then, when Dad had made me drink that mixture of raw eggs and milk to settle my stomach. Perhaps that's what I need this morning, I thought, but all I wanted was the comfort of a cup of tea.

'Okay, honey. Up and at 'em, then,' Bob said, cheerful as always. Swinging his legs out of bed, he turned and whipped back the covers.

'Dirty rat! It's bloody freezing,' I shouted, as I crawled out of bed and swatted him with my pillow. It would have been easier to play, but it was not the time for games: I had to face the dreaded business of the day.

We took turns in the bathroom and dressed in near silence, both tense and jittery, Bob with excitement and me with nervous apprehension. He was going home after eighteen months in England; I was leaving home, perhaps for ever. Every once in a while the reality of it all pierced me, sending shock waves of fear through me. I tried to make sense of my thoughts and feelings; there was something strangely familiar about it all. The sensations were those of mental and emotional paralysis within a tornado of events and activity.

Then, for a moment, I was back on a railway-station platform, alone and frightened, leaving my mother, going who knew where. It was evacuation time again, but now I was sending myself away. This time it was by my own choice, and all I could hope was that I had made the right one. I shook away those thoughts and memories to re-enter the unstoppable whirlwind of events.

Bob and I descended the stairs and entered the kitchen, where Mum and Dad sat in silence, at the oilcloth-covered table. The radio was not on; they were not listening to the BBC morning news as they always did each morning. The stillness seemed strange, almost eerie.

In the middle of the table, on a stained cork mat, sat our old aluminium teapot, kept warm by its green and white hand-knitted tea-cosy. Hot tea awaited us, ready to calm nerves and soothe emotions. Pouring it would provide punctuation for the fumbling conversation that would follow.

'Would you like a nice cooked breakfast, Bob?' Mum broke the silence.

'No thanks, Mum. Just some toast would be great.'

'You sure?'

'Sure,' he replied. 'With marmalade, please.'

'What about you, Iree?'

'I'm not hungry, Mum. Just tea for me, thanks.'

'Sorry to make you get up early, Pete,' I said to my brother, as he stumbled into the kitchen, yawning.

'It's okay. I couldn't let you leave without saying cheerio, could I?' He sat next to me. Mum poured his tea. 'I'll have some toast, Mum,' he said, before she had a chance to ask him. I didn't know how they could eat. I wanted to vomit.

'Do you want me to get the boys up now, Kit?' Dad asked.

'No, don't, Dad. We'll go up and say goodbye. There's no point getting them out of bed,' I said.

'You sure, Iris?' Mum said.

'Yeah.'

We sat then, the near silence broken only by the self-conscious crackle of toast and slurped tea. How long we remained lost in those moments, I do not know, seconds, minutes or hours, caught up in a state of suspended animation.

Clutching my stomach with one hand and holding my cup in the other, I was jarred back to consciousness by the blare of a car horn. The taxi was waiting.

We pushed back our chairs and stood up, like soldiers called to attention. We looked at one another. Faint smiles disguised true feelings. My eyes stung, my head and heart pounded; there was an ache in my jaws and throat. I have to be strong, I thought. I must not break down or everyone else will cry too, and then what shall I do? A vision flashed across my mind, of me, crumpled on the floor, just inside the front door, like a wet rag. No, I must not cry. If I did, I would lose the courage to leave.

Bob and I went upstairs to the boys' bedroom. I leaned over and kissed my still sleeping little brothers.

'Ta-tah, Rob. Ta-tah, Chris,' I whispered.

''Bye, kids. Be good boys,' said Bob.

They each mumbled in response, then turned over and went back to sleep.

Robert was eight, and Christopher just four. They haven't a clue what's going on, I thought, as I wiped away tears and realized that soon they might not even remember me.

Downstairs again, we scurried to finish getting ready. Bob, Dad and Peter carried our luggage out to the taxi. Then, it was time to say our last goodbyes.

Peter was first. He didn't say a word, just looked into my eyes and gave me a peck on the cheek. Many years later, he told he couldn't believe what was happening as he watched me leave. He said he was thinking, she's only sixteen. How can she be married and going off to America? How could Mum and Dad have allowed it to happen?

Mum, expressionless, gave me a quick, distant hug, and then kissed Bob on the cheek. 'I'm not going to cry,' she said. 'I'll just pretend you're going on holiday.'

How many times had I heard that? If only she had shown some emotion. My heart ached for her to hold me, to let me know she felt something – anything. I knew she wouldn't cry – at least, not for me.

'Take care of her, Bob. Good luck, mate,' Dad said, as they shook hands and pounded each other on the shoulder.

'Don't worry,' said Bob.

Dad turned to me. Tears brimmed over from red-rimmed eyes. He drew me into his arms and sobbed, his body heaving against mine. I buried my head in the warm smell of his neck and felt the familiar stubble of his unshaved chin. He hadn't always been the best father, but he had been good for me in many other ways. I wanted to curl up in his arms and stay there. There was a comforting strength in those sinewy, scarred limbs. He was crushing my ribs, but it was my heart that was breaking.

Gently, Bob took my arm and eased me out of Dad's embrace. 'We have to go,' he whispered.

'I know,' I said, and my voice snagged on a sob as I blew my nose for the hundredth time into a sodden wad of handkerchief.

We tore ourselves away, leaving three forlorn people huddled together on the step – a family portrait.

Bob helped me into the back of the taxi. The door slammed behind me, shutting me off from my old life, and as the taxi pulled away from the kerb, I turned and looked through its dirty back window. I gazed at my family, and at the place where I had never truly fitted in since my return to them after the war. Suddenly I felt old, as though my life was behind me, and in a way, I suppose it was – at least, that life was. I stared through a misted veil until it had disappeared from view. For all I knew it could be the last time I'd ever see them. I was gone now and they were still there, and I wondered if they would go back inside the house, have another cup of tea and carry on as usual. How could life simply go on? But I knew it would, they without me and me without them. Tears spilled down my face and Bob drew me into his arms.

'Everything's going to be all right,' he said, as he rocked and patted me.

I had to believe him as we started out on our new life's journey together. Perhaps in America I would find the place where I felt I belonged.

*

A guard eyed us, saw Bob's uniform, touched his gloved hand to his cap, then waved the old London cab on, through the gate of Bushey Hall Army Base. Our driver seemed to know where he was going, and I wondered how many times he had made this trip. We followed the curving road that wound through the barracks buildings to where two buses stood idling in front of base headquarters. American flags flapped and snapped in a brisk wind, and as we climbed from the taxi to join the assembling group of GIs and their wives, it seemed as though we had already landed in a foreign country.

People shifted from foot to foot, slapping arms against bodies to keep warm. I stayed cosy in my teddy-bear fur coat, glad of its warmth and the comfort of Bob's arm wrapped protectively around my shoulders. Scattered laughter and excited chatter filled the air, cutting through the tension of the moment. Looking around at the other women, I noticed how at ease they appeared with themselves and the situation. I envied their animated conversation, their touching of one another's arms, their familiarity and agreeable nods. Then I saw myself, standing among them in my fake-fur coat, with my freshly permed hair. I felt like a fraud, and one of my mother's old sayings ran through my mind: 'Look at her, mutton dressed up as lamb.' It was a remark she often made of older women who dressed in a manner deemed too young for them. At that moment, I felt the exact opposite: I felt that I was 'lamb dressed up as mutton'. I wondered if people could see through my disguise, if they could tell I was just a girl, dressed up as a woman. Then, catching a glimpse of my own distorted reflection in the side of the bus, I decided I did look older than my sixteen years, and clung to the hope that they would accept me as one of them.

'Should be getting on the bus soon,' Bob said, glancing at his watch.

'Hope the darned thing has heat,' someone nearby said. 'You never know with these English.' Some of the men chuckled.

'Can I have your attention, please?' An officer addressed the group from his position atop a low whitewashed wall that encircled a small flowerbed and the flagpoles. 'After I make sure everyone's here who's supposed to be, and no one's here who shouldn't be, we'll be ready to roll.' Laughter rippled the crowd. 'Please step on to the bus after I call your name.'

The boarding process did not take long. Eager to escape the cold, damp air, everyone responded quickly upon hearing their names. Thankfully, the idling buses had their heaters running full blast and it was toasty-warm inside. Good, I thought. That's one thing they can't complain about or blame the English for.

Apparently, everyone on the passenger list was present and accounted for, and no stowaways found. Then, with coats shed and hand luggage stowed in the overhead compartment, we sat and waited. The same officer bounded up into the bus, turned to face us, wished us all '*Bon voyage*', saluted, and then, as quickly as he had appeared, was gone. Our bus driver closed the door, meshed the gears into action and the crowded vehicle eased forward. At last, we were on our way.

I remember little of the journey that day. At first, I gazed out of the window, taking in the passing scene, trying to imprint it on my mind, not knowing how much I was to miss even the smallest things. Eventually, resting my head on Bob's shoulder, I drifted into the sanctuary of sleep and the fragmented dreams that awaited me there.

The sound of changing gears and squeaking brakes roused me.

'We're here, sleepyhead,' said Bob, shaking my arm.

'Where?' I asked, straightening from a backbreaking slump.

'Next stop,' he replied. He was grinning. 'Let's go, kiddo.'

We gathered our belongings and shuffled behind the line of our fellow passengers. Slowly, we moved down the aisle and out into the fresh air where everyone stretched stiff limbs and began searching for toilets.

'I'm dying for a cup of tea, Bob,' I said.

'Good luck,' he offered. 'You may have to settle for coffee.'

'Toilets that way,' a voice shouted. 'Gather back at this point in ten minutes.'

Our group scattered.

We had arrived at Tidworth Army Base, near Salisbury, Willshire. It was almost identical to the base we had just left; for all I knew, we could have driven around in a circle and ended up where we started. The journey seemed to have taken for ever but there was no fast way to get anywhere in those days. This was where we would have our papers processed. From here, buses would take us to the port of Southampton, where a ship would be waiting to transport us across the Atlantic.

After our ten-minute comfort break, the group reassembled at the designated meeting point. There, we received our next directions, barked at us in typical military style.

'Men and dependants will please follow me to the reception centre. You will have your papers checked and you will receive room assignments. Dependants will be housed separately from enlisted men. You will be permitted to dine together in the mess hall. Mealtimes are posted in rooms and the reception centre. Any questions?' There was none. Our 'tour guide' turned on his heel and headed down the path. We followed, like a flock of sheep, and again the experience reminded me of the day of my evacuation during the war. It was exactly the same kind of herding, except this time I sort of knew where I was going.

We stayed at Tidworth for two nights. The men slept in barracks, the women in small dormitory-style rooms, furnished with army-green government-issue metal bunks and lockers. With no one else assigned to my room, the loneliness was excruciating.

That evening, Bob and I ate together in a mess hall decorated with large shiny red hearts and Cupids. At each table setting, on the trestle-style dining tables, a cellophane bag filled with heart-shaped sweets reminded us it was Valentine's Day.

After dinner, during scheduled free time, couples and friends exchanged animated conversation before they had to return to their respective quarters. That night, I curled up on the hard creaky lower bunk, pulled the khaki army blanket over my head and cried myself to sleep.

The next day, between paperwork, mess-hall meals and a brief organized tour of Salisbury Cathedral, time passed quickly, but in the evening, besides separation from my husband, I was to feel still more anguish. It seemed that all, or most of, the other British girls were standing in line outside the reception hall at a bank of public telephones. They all appeared to be calling home. With my fuzzy coat collar turned up around my neck, I sat on a nearby bench and listened for a while to 'Hello, Mum, hello, Dad, I'll ring you again tomorrow', unable to phone home myself, since Mum and Dad had no telephone. Envying them the comfort of their family connections, I was anxious for the day to be over and the next to arrive, when perhaps I could bury my loneliness and immediate fear in another flurry of activity.

February 16 dawned bitterly cold but bathed in misty sunlight. Thank God, I thought. Another day without rain.

After breakfast, it was again time to regroup. We stood in line, two by two, reminding me of the passengers on Noah's Ark, as we waited to have our names checked against yet another list before climbing aboard the buses that would take us to the port of Southampton and our ship.

Physically and mentally exhausted, but kept awake by the buzz of excitement and my own apprehension, the journey passed quickly. It was almost impossible to watch and take in the passing scene of rural England, its villages and towns. The cold early-morning temperature battled against that of a busload of warm bodies and conversation. Steam obscured the view, and finger-wiped peepholes soon disappeared into trickles of condensation that only served to remind me of the tears I knew I had yet to shed.

When we arrived at the docks, our small convoy of vehicles came to a stop in an adjacent parking area. Several other buses were already there, and two or three more pulled in behind ours. Soldiers and their families emerged through the buses' narrow doors, clattering down metal steps. Men assisted wives and carried luggage; women carried babies and held children's hands. A military policeman gave hand signals, ushering everyone towards the 'Embarkation Area'. We followed the crowd, by now anxious to see our ship.

I don't know what I had expected, but it was not the USS *General Callan*, a converted battleship, painted, of course, battleship grey. I suppose I had imagined something more like the *Queen Mary* or some other cruise liner, but although this grey monster was something of a shock and a disappointment, it was exciting in an overwhelming way. It was by no means a large ship, but it loomed tall over the pier, its gangway long and steep.

As we gathered in a roped-off area beside the ship, I could see that already a large number of people were on board. Men, women and children lined the railings of the main deck. I learned that the ship's voyage had originated in Bremerhaven, Germany, where GIs and their dependants from several European countries had boarded before it sailed on to pick up the British contingent. From what I could see, the British group would be in the minority.

Bob grabbed my arm for what seemed the hundredth time since we had left home – was it only two days ago? 'Here we go,' he said. Someone had signalled us to begin boarding, and we moved forward.

As we mounted the first step of the gangway, I looked behind me and noticed that a crowd of people had gathered to see their loved ones off. I scanned the crowd — perhaps someone had wanted to surprise me and come to see me off — but there was no one I knew. For the third time in as many days, I was reliving the scene from eleven or twelve years earlier of my evacuation, when I had looked out over the crowds at the railway station, hoping that my granddad was there, looking for me. At that moment I knew I had to choke off all feelings, all emotions. It was a terrible feeling, a sickness in the pit of my stomach, knowing that, again, no one was there for me.

As we inched further up the clanking wood and iron gangway, I looked back, just one more time, at the flag-waving, handkerchief-waving crowds. Suddenly, my heart gave a lurch. I blinked. Was I dreaming? No, I was not. There was Uncle Tom, my mother's younger brother, frantically waving first one and then both arms. At last our eyes met and we smiled. I thought my heart would come crashing out of my chest as we continued to wave at one another. Happiness swelled inside me until I thought I would burst. Someone was there for me. Thank you, God, I said, in a silent prayer, thank you, thank you, thank you.

Apparently, my grandmother had told Tom I would be sailing from Southampton and that no one would be there to see me off. Realizing that he would be working in Winchester, just an hour or two from the docks, he had taken time off and driven down on his motorcycle. Never in my life had I been happier to see someone.

I don't recall how long it was before our ship cast off, but after we had located our cabins, women once more separated from men, we found our way back up onto the deck to wave goodbye. Throughout my life, the image of my uncle on that day has remained printed on my mind. Uncle Tom, standing at the end of the pier in his heavy black overcoat, collar turned up against the cold wind, waving a handkerchief until he was no more than a dot in the distance.

Standing on deck for what must have been hours, I watched first the docks and then the coastline slowly disappear, swallowed by the descending dark of a starless night. I was sailing away from all that I had known, family, home, culture and an entire history. Silent tears spilled down my face. I felt desperately alone and frightened.

Late into the night, I lay on my bunk thinking, not only of the long journey ahead but also of the real and metaphorical journeys of my life and of how far I had already travelled, not in miles but in so many other ways. Somehow, in spite of everything, I had survived world war, poverty, neglect, humiliation and a hundred disappointments, and I knew I had to hang on to my inherent sense of humour and optimism. I had to stop crying over something that perhaps never was. I had to have hope.

Then, as the gentle roll of the ship lulled me into sleep, I had one last mental image. It was of me, the all-American housewife, dressed in a frilly apron, hair in a ponytail, standing in front of a white clapboard house with green shutters, on a lawn surrounded by a white picket fence, in the land of Doris Day movies.

Now, with so many journeys behind me, I had one momentous journey ahead, and this time I planned to get off at the right station.

JEFF PEARCE

A POCKETFUL OF HOLES AND DREAMS

The poor boy who made his fortune . . . not just once but twice.

Little Jeff Pearce grew up in a post-war Liverpool slum. His father lived the life of an affluent gentleman whilst his mother was forced to steal bread to feed her starving children. Life was tough and from the moment Jeff could walk he learned to go door to door, begging rags from the rich, which he sold down the markets. Leaving school at the age of fourteen, he embarked on an extraordinary journey, and found himself, before the age of thirty, a millionaire.

Then, after a cruel twist of fate left him penniless, he, his wife and children were forced out of their beautiful home.

With nothing but holes in his pockets, Jeff had no alternative but to go back down the markets and start all over again. Did he still have what it took? Could he really get back everything he had lost?

A Pocketful of Holes and Dreams is the heartwarming true story of a little boy who had nothing but gained everything and proof that, sometimes, rags can be turned into riches . . .

Christine Marion Fraser

BLUE ABOVE THE CHIMNEYS

The wild childhood of a Glasgow tenement urchin

Born during the Second World War in Glasgow, Christine Fraser was her mother's eighth child. Growing up with her siblings in a tiny flat, learning to avoid her hardworking, hard-drinking one-eyed father, making a menace of herself in the streets along with the other urchins, Christine lived an impoverished life but never once cared. Until she was struck down by a terrible illness.

Suddenly, her wild days of childhood were over. A long spell in hospital completely changed her life. Now she found herself dependent on others for so many of her needs. And on top of that her mother and father died.

Yet Christine was always resourceful and never once looked down. She knew that always there, if you looked hard enough, was some blue up above the chimneys.

MOLLY WEIR

SHOES WERE FOR SUNDAY

'Poverty is a very exacting teacher and I had been taught well'

The post-war urban jungle of the Glasgow tenements was the setting for Molly Weir's childhood. From sharing a pull-out bed in her mother's tiny kitchen to running in terror from the fever van, it was an upbringing that was cemented in hardship. Hunger, cold and sickness was an everyday reality and complaining was not an option.

Despite the crippling poverty, there was a vivacity to the tenements that kept spirits high. Whether Molly was brushing the hair of her wizened neighbour Mrs MacKay, running to Jimmy's chip shop for a ha'penny of crimps or dancing at the annual fair, there wasn't a moment to spare for self-pity. Molly never let it get her down as she and the other urchins knew how to make do with nothing.

And at the centre of her world was her fearsome but loving Grannie, whose tough, independent spirit taught Molly to rise above her pitiful surroundings and achieve her dreams.